PUEBLO NATIONS

Eight Centuries of Pueblo Indian History

JOE S. SANDO

Foreword by Regis Pecos

Clear Light Publishers
Santa Fe, New Mexico

Clear Light Publishers, 823 Don Diego, Santa Fe, N.M. 87501

Library of Congress Catalog Card Number: 91–72483

Library of Congress Cataloging-in-Publication Data

Sando, Joe S., 1923–
    Pueblo nations: eight centuries of Pueblo Indian history / Joe S. Sando; foreword by Regis Pecos.
    p.   cm.
    Includes bibliographical references and appendixes.
    ISBN 0–940666–17–0: $22.95. —ISBN 0–940666–07–3 (pbk.): $14.95.
    1. Pueblo Indians—History.   I. Title.
E99.P9S186, 1991
973'.0497—dc20   91–72483
                                                            CIP

ISBN 0–940666–17–0

Printed in the U.S.A. by R.R. Donnelley & Sons Company
First Edition

Editor, Ann Mason; Photo Research, K.C. Cress.

Typeset in Simoncini Garamond by Rick Heide, Redwood City, CA.

Front Cover: Corn Dance at Santa Clara Pueblo, New Mexico, 1992, copyright © Marcia Keegan.

 recycled paper

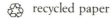 The paper for text and end sheets used in this publication meets the minimum requirements of American National Standard for Information Sciences—Permanence of Paper for Printed Library Materials, ANSI Z39, 48-1984.

reinforced binding

This Book Is
Dedicated to
JUANITO SANDO
(November 13, 1890–April 5, 1973)
My Father

Acknowledgments

I AM DEEPLY grateful to the Ford Foundation for making this book possible through financial assistance for my initial research. My thanks to the Southern Pueblos Agency for allowing me to study the files and records of the former United Pueblos Agency, as well as for the privilege of speaking to some of the "old-timers" of the Bureau of Indian Affairs.

Thanks also to the personnel who helped me at the Archives of New Mexico in Santa Fe, as well as those at the National Archives in Washington, D.C., who assisted me in finding information and pictures.

My gratitude is due to the Indian Historian Press of San Francisco for publishing my first book, *The Pueblo Indians,* which served as the basis for the present, substantially revised and updated edition, *Pueblo Nations.*

Finally, with all my heart, *tsa-ba-no-pah* to the scores and scores of Pueblo Indian people, relatives, friends, and acquaintances of the outstanding personalities described in the biographies.

The Nineteen Indian Pueblos
in New Mexico

Acoma
Cochiti
Isleta
Jemez
Laguna
Nambe
Picuris
Pojoaque
Sandia
San Felipe
San Ildefonso
San Juan
Santa Ana
Santa Clara
Santo Domingo
Taos
Tesuque
Zia
Zuni

Contents

MAPS

ILLUSTRATIONS

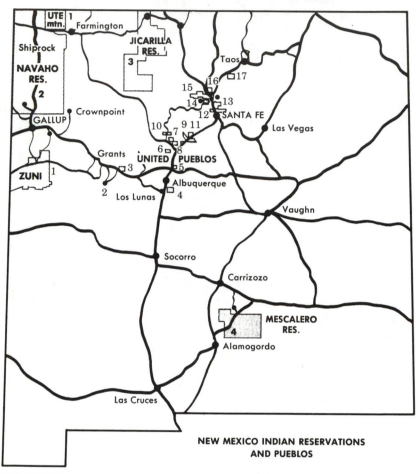

**NEW MEXICO INDIAN RESERVATIONS
AND PUEBLOS**

1 UTE MOUNTAIN
2 NAVAHO
3 JICARILLA APACHE
4 MESCALERO APACHE
1 Zuñi, near point of Coronado's entry.
2 Acoma, the Sky City, with original Mission.
3 Laguna, on highway, with original Mission.
4 Isleta, on main highway, with original Mission.
5 Sandia, on highway just north of Albuquerque.

6 Santa Ana, with original Mission still in use.
7 Zia, with strange original mission, still in use.
8 San Felipe, with interesting rebuilt Mission.
9 Santo Domingo, with unusual rebuilt Mission.
10 Jémez, in the beautiful Jémez Mountain region.
11 Cochiti, between Albuquerque and Santa Fe.
12 Tesuque, with part of original Mission.

13 Nambé, of the Rio Grande group near Santa Fe.
14 San Ildefonso, famous for its black pottery.
15 Santa Clara, ranks with San Ildefonso for pottery.
16 San Juan, named by Oñate in 1598.
17 Picuris, between Taos and Santa Fe.
18 Taos, with the largest communal dwellings.

Foreword

BY REGIS PECOS
Director of Office of Indian Affairs,
State of New Mexico

In the year of the Columbian Quincentenary, it is timely for Pueblo author, historian, and diplomat Mr. Joe Sando to rise to the challenge of writing about our Pueblo history. Of utmost importance is his point of view; as a Jemez Pueblo Indian, he shares with the world a picture of Pueblo life. Considering the fact that most books about Indian peoples are written from a non-Indian perspective, it is commendable of Mr. Sando to accept the call of recording significant events of the Pueblos from the viewpoint of a Pueblo historian. As a historian, Mr. Sando has been at the forefront of expressing that perspective by interweaving his personal experiences with the uniquely rich history, culture, and traditions of the Pueblo people.

As Pueblo Indians, we value our people, traditions, and culture as vital to the continuation of our communities. It is the community that has survived the loss of land and near extinction of portions of our culture. The emphasis on our communities and our ceremonies ensures the continuity of our culture and traditions. Our relationships and dependence on each other provide a positive foundation that allows for the revitalization and the perpetuation of important concepts such as respect. And the concept of respect we learned from our community is found throughout Mr. Sando's work.

The daily ceremonial life of our communities continues in spite of the detrimental federal policies of the United States. The intimacy and spirituality of the Pueblo communities have survived some of the most devastating policies, such as assimilation and termination. The Pueblos have endured numerous shifts in national Indian policies, and have prevailed over the dominant society's need to have Indians disappear into the mass of non-Indian society. Historically, America grew in strength and population, and it became apparent that individuals were encroaching upon Indian lands. This non-Indian aggression had to be justified and stabilized. The answer was to move us to reservations; and the journeys were often made under extreme hardship and suffering. However, this diminished land base laid the groundwork for later protection of tribal sovereignty.

As reflected in Mr. Sando's book, during the late 1800s there was increasing dissatisfaction with the reservation policy. To remedy this situation, the Allotment Act (Dawes Severalty Act of 1887) was used to counter the poor tribal economies under the guise of breaking up the land base by allotting portions of reservation land to individual Indians. The impact of the act was to further the goal of bringing Indians into the non-Indian culture, and to destroy tribal traditions and influence. This devastating piece of legislation resulted in the severe reduction of Indian-held Land—from 138 million acres in 1887 to 48 million acres in 1934. It was fortunate that the Pueblos escaped allotment, and today we continue to hold our land in fee simple for the community. This title is virtually unique and continues the trust relationship with the federal government.

The attempted assimilation policies of the era of the Allotment Act ultimately failed, and the federal government had to respond to the Meriam Report (1928), which documented the failure of Indian policy during the period of the Allotment Act. The report was the impetus for a sweeping change in federal policy. Therefore, the era of Indian reorganization and the preservation of tribes began, with new hope for Pueblo people. The most significant provision of the Indian Reorganization Act (1934) was the ending of the period of the Allotment Act and the constitutionalization of tribal governments. Some of the pueblos chose to implement this plan. However, many of the traditional pueblos choose to keep their original governments intact. Those tribes represent the few remaining traditional forms of self-government that have survived this broad constitutionalization. Today, it is our duty to protect these rare surviving governments that have withstood the test of time, especially our traditional tribal governments and courts, which ensure the protection of our values, culture, and tradition. Even though the Indian Reorganization Act prevented the further rapid erosion of our land base, the encouragement of tribal self-government had a more limited success. The tribal constitutions adopted under the act were suggested by the federal government and modeled after the division of government into the executive, legislative, and judicial branches. This was not suited to traditional tribal needs, nor to the strong influence of our religion on our structure of government.

The most devastating federal policies we had to counter were the "termination" and "relocation" policies of the 1950s. The calculated aim of the federal government was to make the Indians within the United States subject to the same laws and entitled to the same privileges and responsibilities as other citizens of the United States. The result was tragic to many tribes whose lands were sold and whose federal status and benefits were terminated. At the same time, the Bureau of Indian Affairs was encouraging us to leave the reservation under its "relocation" program. We were sent to various metropolitan areas to get an education and join the work force of America. However, the effect was to create a population of unemployed Indians who suffered all the problems of the urban poor compounded with the trauma of dislocation. The Pueblo people were not immune to this devastating policy. Significant to our sovereign status, we were protected from the termination law (Public Law 280), which provided for the state assumption of civil and criminal jurisdiction over Indian country. The civil and criminal jurisdiction over the people within our territory are the basic tenets of sovereignty we still hold; but legislation and Supreme Court cases have further eroded parts of that jurisdiction (such as criminal jurisdiction over non-Indians).

The assimilation and termination policies have had a severe impact on our people, but the policy of self-determination serves to strengthen our tribal governments and has provided the mechanism to assume control and responsibility for our own communities. One of the most important highlights in our history is the contracting of the Albuquerque-Santa Fe Indian Schools under the Indian Self-Determination Act (Public Law 93-638). The Pueblo people recognized the need to effectively educate our children as vital to our future. Education from a Native American perspective is providing the base for reaffirming our values within a strong academic curriculum—a situation that will ensure the success of our children in both Indian and non-Indian worlds. The need for our students to learn and read from material written by our own Pueblo writers, like Mr. Sando, is critical to this process. There has been a recognizable void in this area, and it is essential to provide this opportunity for students of all ages.

We must remember the lessons of the past and accept the challenge of building a promising future. Learning the most difficult lessons of our own history can be the best guide to the present and the future. We live in an unsettling time when the world is forced to pause and rethink negative policies—the frantic pace of modern civilization and the destruction of people and the environment. As Pueblo people, we have a duty to prevent the development of detrimental policies that historically have nearly shattered our Indian way of life. From our past experience, we can share the knowledge and wisdom we have received from our elders. The challenge we face is to demonstrate how the values and culture we cherish can serve to positively impact the many changes we are confronted with on a daily basis. Our traditions have been the foundation of our survival in the midst of a rapidly changing world; and our culture and language, which have withstood the dramatic changes of modern life, are at the heart of that survival.

Our unchanging traditions and culture have survived because we have cherished them and have held steadily to the ways of our Pueblo people. As sovereign nations, we demonstrate to the rest of the world that our fundamental principles of self-government are a living testimony to the ability of a native people to survive within the strongest and most powerful and progressive country in the world, the United States of America. Mr. Sando has emphasized that, as traditional Pueblo people, we can demonstrate compatibility with this most powerful nation as long as we are not willing to compromise our way of life, a way of life that allows us to live in perpetuity.

The reader will encounter many stimulating concepts as he or she reads about Pueblo culture, including numerous bold intellectual and spiritual understandings that have enabled us to survive in the midst of incredible hardships and policies. Our ceremonies and community life are filled with important lessons that we should all consider in our efforts to make the next five hundred years an era in which all people enjoy the freedom and protection of rights guaranteed to us by the Constitution of the United States.

It is a great honor to introduce the work of Mr. Sando. He has served as an educator rising to the challenge of writing about our Pueblo history. As Pueblo people, we are most proud of his determination to share with the world an authentic historical view of our life. Most importantly, we salute his unfathomable faith in his traditions and people, and his courage to leave an everlasting influence on Pueblo and American history—a history that will always live within us.

Introduction

THE PEOPLE OF the Pueblo Nations of New Mexico's nineteen pueblos are the descendants of the original natives of North America's vast southwestern region. The Athabascans, ancestors of today's Apaches and Navajos, came to the Southwest between 1400 and 1525, according to social scientists. Aboriginal occupancy of the Southwest by the Pueblo people is estimated at about ten thousand years before Christ.

There is, however, more historical literature about the "late comers" than is available about the original natives, although a considerable amount of anthropological and archaeological work does exist. In part, such native history as has survived is due to the militancy of the Athabascans, who defended their people and their lands against the European invaders. The story of their struggle is a vital force in North American history, and is one of persistent efforts to maintain a harmonious relationship of man with his neighbors, and of man with his environment. This accommodation is deep in the ancient traditions of the Pueblo people, traditions that even today shape their character and their reactions to issues and events.

A great deal has been written about the Spanish in the Southwest, about both civil and religious aspects. Documented accounts of their entry into the world of the Pueblos have been produced by the Catholic priests who formed the vanguard of Spain's military outposts in the "New World," establishing missions and making Catholic converts, often with ferocious zeal.

The Anglo "roughnecks" of Territorial New Mexico are also well represented in the literature. However, the United States has always laid a heavy hand on the interpretation of historic events. Conquest became "adventure." Land grabbing became "a pioneering effort." The extermination of Indian culture, religion, and economy became a worthy crusade to bring the Indian into "the mainstream of American life."

History following the European invasion has many bitter memories for the Pueblo people. But time has resulted in changes. Today, many Pueblo Indians are descendants of both Spanish and Indian forebears, and the blood of the Anglo has mixed with that of the

Indian. Yet, the Pueblo Indians remain predominantly Indian in culture, spirit, and tradition, the Spanish blood more than any other an enriching element in the life of the people.

This book is an effort to fill a certain vacuum in Pueblo history. I feel also that the traditional Pueblo history should be revealed, as the Pueblo Indians themselves know it. Our traditional history is quite different from the formalized narratives, dominated by European ideology, that are taught in the schools. Religion, as only one example, was not a casual Sunday morning incident. It was life itself.

Traditional Pueblo history is taught among the people even today. To understand its rich literary and spiritual heritage is to take a long step towards understanding the people. Events and issues influencing the course of Pueblo life must be understood as well, and I have attempted to bring some light to such historic events, which can be understood best against the background of Pueblo beliefs and traditions. Since many tribes have begun to call themselves "nations," the title of this book reflects this development.

As an educator, I have been confronted many times by the demands of my students for authentic historical information about the Pueblo Indian people. As a Pueblo man of Jemez, I feel that the Indian people have a duty and a challenge to write their own history.

Thus the task of writing *Pueblo Nations* has been the consequence of impelling forces, as well as a labor of love. Since the Western Hemisphere anticipates, in 1992, the quincentenary of the arrival of Columbus with a myriad of activities, activities reflecting either celebration or ambivalence, a chapter has been included that reviews the effects of Columbus's arrival on the Pueblo Nations.

JOE S. SANDO

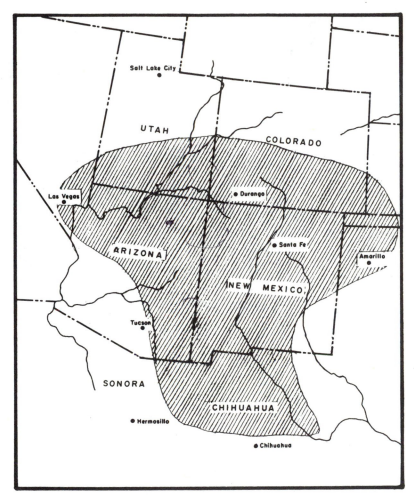

Map showing the extent of Pre-historic Pueblo Indian culture, encompassing the present states of Utah, Colorado, Nevada, Arizona, New Mexico, Texas, and northeast Mexico. (Courtesy The Pueblo Indians of North America by Edward P. Dozier, Holt, Rinehart and Winston, Inc., 1970.)

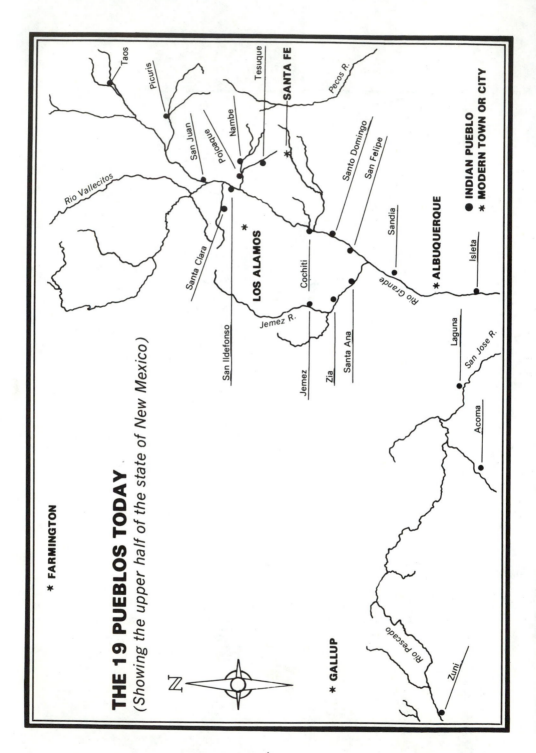

THE 19 PUEBLOS TODAY
(Showing the upper half of the state of New Mexico)

* FARMINGTON

* GALLUP

N

* ALBUQUERQUE

SANTA FE

LOS ALAMOS

● INDIAN PUEBLO
* MODERN TOWN OR CITY

Taos
Picuris
Tesuque
Pecos R.
San Juan
Nambe
Pojoaque
Santo Domingo
San Felipe
Rio Vallecitos
Santa Clara
Sandia
San Ildefonso
Cochiti
Rio Grande
Isleta
Jemez R.
Jemez
Zia
Santa Ana
Laguna
San Jose R.
Rio Grande
Acoma
Rio Pescado
Zuni

4

1

Nations Within a Nation

THE ABORIGINAL PEOPLES of the Western Hemisphere had a unique culture, an economy suited to their needs, and governing bodies ranging from relatively simple social structures to well-established socio-political entities that the Europeans treated as nations. Considerable differences existed, however, among the many peoples of aboriginal America. The Iroquois Nations in the eastern United States differed from the peoples in the Southwest; the Indians of California had different forms of society than the Cherokees of the Southeast; the Eskimos of Alaska differed from all of these in both culture and form of society.

In spite of these differences, all the native peoples had this in common: they had achieved a high order of their society; they had developed various forms of democratic government placing them in history as nations. Their leaders governed, in the deepest meaning of the concept, "by consent of the governed." Today, the United States Government and the Indian tribes, whether the various tribes known as the Iroquois in the East or the Pueblos of the Southwest, have a relationship comparable in many respects to that found in colonial countries dominated by a foreign government. The Indian people know themselves to be nations, and the demand for self-determination and self-government is the articulation of that knowledge.

A fundamental consideration of the differences in government among the native tribes of the Western Hemisphere is the task of a comparative historical study, and is not the purpose of this book. There are, however, certain basic differences that should be borne in mind as the Pueblo Nations are here described. Indian tribes living in other regions of the United States who met non-Spanish Europeans experienced cultural genocide through the loss of their land and forced relocation to other areas. Whole tribes were transplanted to regions with inadequate, and more often extremely poor, natural resources. Their economy and their adaptation to their environment were destroyed. Much of their culture was lost in the process. But the Pueblo people still reside today where the invading Europeans first saw them, although many changes have occurred both in their economy and their relations with the surrounding population. Human society is not static. Changes occur in social relations as conditions change. However, in spite of the changes wrought by time and foreign intrusion, the Pueblos have retained a great part of their culture. In most pueblos the language, religion, and philosophy of the people remain intact.

Pueblo life has made accommodations, developing a unique "mix" of European governing structure, Christian formalities and beliefs, and legal forms imposed upon the people by governmental requirements. Underlying these influences is the enduring foundation of Pueblo traditional leadership and government. Within the space of two hundred years, the Pueblos have lived under and been subjected to the domination of three forms of foreign government: the Spanish, the Mexican, and that of the United States. Living as they have under three flags, their accommodation to the bombardment of foreign cultures is little short of remarkable.

While academic historic exposition takes one chronologically through the various stages of a society's development, leading one from earliest to contemporary eras, it seems more useful to this writer to introduce the Pueblo people as they are today, and move backward in history for a more complete understanding.

Locations and Language

The nineteen pueblos of New Mexico are also referred to as the Rio Grande pueblos. They are located in eight counties of present-day New Mexico. Two Tiwa-speaking pueblos, Taos and Picuris, are located in Taos County in the northern part of the state. Below this county is Rio Arriba County, where there are two Tewa-speaking pueblos: San Juan and Santa Clara, located along the banks of the Rio Grande.

The pueblos of Nambe, Pojoaque, San Ildefonso, and Tesuque are located further east, closer to the Sangre de Cristo mountain range, in Santa Fe County. San Ildefonso also lies along the banks of the Rio Grande, below Santa Clara.

In Sandoval County, further south, are seven pueblos. The Keresan-speaking villages of Cochiti, Santo Domingo, and San Felipe are located along the Rio Grande; and the pueblos of Santa Ana and Zia are situated along the banks of the Jemez River to the west and north. Jemez Pueblo, a Towa-speaking village, is a few miles northwest of Zia.

A Tiwa-speaking pueblo, Sandia, is also located in Sandoval County on the Rio Grande, twelve miles north of the city of Albuquerque. In Bernalillo County, a dozen miles south of Albuquerque on the Rio Grande, is the Tiwa-speaking pueblo of Isleta, which straddles Valencia County as well.

To the west, in Cibola County (formerly called Valencia County), are the Keresan-speaking Laguna and Acoma pueblos with their villages, while further west in McKinley County (bordering the Arizona state line) is the Zuni tribe, the largest Pueblo group in population. For purposes of reference and identification, the nineteen pueblos are listed as follows:

The Northern Pueblos		The Southern Pueblos	
Taos		Jemez	
Picuris	Taos County	Cochiti	
Nambe		Sandia	Sandoval
Pojoaque	Santa Fe	San Felipe	County
San Ildefonso	County	Santa Ana	
Tesuque		Santo Domingo	
		Zia	
San Juan	Rio Arriba		Bernalillo
Santa Clara		Isleta	& Valencia
		Acoma	Counties
Zuni	McKinley	Laguna	Cibola
	County		County

Zuni Pueblo, nineteenth in the list, has its own administration and United States Bureau of Indian Affairs agency structure. Zuni is located in western New Mexico.

Anthropologists have classified the pueblos as "Eastern" and "Western" according to certain considerations of social and cultural differences. Two scholars in this field have divided the pueblos also according to Eastern and Western divisions, with further modifications. Generally, the pueblos of Hopi, Zuni, Laguna, and Acoma have been placed in the Western Pueblo division. The Tanoan pueblos (except Jemez, which is considered "transitional") are designated as Eastern. The Rio Grande (or Eastern) Keresan pueblos are also considered transitional by some scholars. These considerations are important for analyses of cultural traits and social differences, but we will not enter the anthropological fray in this discussion. Suffice it to say that early classifications of the Indians of the Southwest by anthropologists merely divided the people as "Pueblo" and "non-Pueblo." A lack of understanding of the variety in Pueblo culture was responsible for this error in classification. Later studies took note of differences, and the Eastern and Western designations followed. Anthropologists are still discussing what is "Eastern" and what is "Western," and there is discussion also of "transitional" pueblos. Pueblo events and issues today take note of the northern and southern pueblos, and we will use these designations herein for reasons of expediency.

The nineteen pueblos share a common traditional native religion, although rituals and observances may vary; a similar lifestyle and philosophy; and a common economy based on the same geographical region occupied by them for thousands of years. But the pueblos have an independence similar to that of nations; although they are in close proximity to one another, and subject to the same natural forces, each maintains a unique identity. Thus the pueblos have common elements, but are distinctive entities in their own right. The languages spoken vary greatly, even within dialects related to a single stock. That is why the pueblos are considered historically, according to language as well as culture and social relationships.

There are three distinct and different language families with diverse origins. These language families are grouped as Keresan, Tanoan, and Zunian. The Tanoan language is further divided into three dialects: Tewa, Tiwa, and Towa. A view of these divisions will provide further understanding of the distinctive characteristics of the pueblos of New Mexico:

A. The Tanoan language, which includes the three dialects of Tiwa, Tewa, and Towa:
  1. The Tiwa speakers are the Taos, Picuris, Sandia, and Isleta pueblos.
  2. The Tewa speakers are the San Juan, Santa Clara, San Ildefonso, Nambe, Tesuque, and Pojoaque pueblos.
  3. Towa is spoken only by the Jemez.
B. The Keresan language is spoken, with few changes, by the Acoma, Cochiti, Laguna, San Felipe, Santa Ana, Santo Domingo, and Zia pueblos.
C. The Zuni language is spoken only by the Zunis.

Due to these diverse languages and dialects, the Pueblo people were multilingual. In pre-Spanish times, the seven pueblos speaking the Keresan language could converse with the eleven pueblos speaking the Tanoan dialects, as well as with the Zunis and the Hopis

8

in the far West. (Many years ago, the "far West" was Arizona.) In their relations with the Apaches, Navajos, Kiowas, and Comanches, many Pueblo people picked up their languages also. The Spanish language then followed as a means of official communication when the Spaniards arrived in the Southwest. Finally, when the American Territorial Government moved into New Mexico after 1846, they brought the English language along, and the Pueblo people began to speak the new foreign tongue. Today, most Pueblo Indians speak their own tribal language, with English as a second language. The university-educated Pueblos communicate equally well in English and in their native language. The older Pueblo people also speak Spanish, with a sprinkling of other Pueblo dialects. But the younger Pueblos tend to speak less and less Spanish. Since conversation in the English language is predominant, a knowledge of other Pueblo dialects and Spanish is no longer a necessity. Thus the Pueblo people are now becoming more bilingual than multilingual, using both English and their mother tongue. In meetings of the Pueblo tribes, however, it is still necessary to have a translator from English into Indian; in the past, two translators were needed: from English into Spanish and Spanish into Indian, and vice versa.

There has been some borrowing of Spanish and English words in the everyday Pueblo languages. However, in the religious or classic languages, the vocabulary and terminology remain unchanged.

The Hopi Indians, although they are within the Pueblo family, will be discussed only incidentally in this work. Their distance geographically from the other Pueblos, their identification by the United States Government, which places them under a separate federal administrative agency, and their progress in history have tended to individualize their social structure, their issues, and their responses to events. There are other differences that make it necessary to consider the Hopis separately. The heritage of the New Mexico Pueblos today is freely sprinkled with Hispanic traditions. The Hopi tradition is not. The Hopi people are of the Uto-Aztecan language stock, considered by some linguists as having a place in a fourth division of the Pueblo Indian family of languages. Further, a group known as the Tewas of Hano, or First Mesa, are mentioned herein as the Tanos of San Cristobal and Galisteo. These ancestors of the Hano Tewas left New Mexico after the Spaniards returned in 1693.

While there is considerable difference of opinion among scholars as to the aboriginal population of the pueblos of New Mexico, and even as to the population during the Spanish regime, there are figures available for the Pueblo population today. These population figures are given in the Appendixes. However, it is interesting to note that the Pueblo population, as given in the first figures by the Spanish priests, was reported as "60,000 converts," by the Franciscan de Benavides. Such figures are suspect, however. It is most difficult to reconstruct the demography of Native Americans, and in more recent years the approximate figures of the Indian historians have become more acceptable to the anthropologists. The Spanish priests were eager to prove conversion to Catholic faith, and exaggerated the number of native converts. Spanish adventurers, otherwise known as "explorers," were in the habit of overstating the population in order to receive support from the Crown or private entrepreneurs. In the years following both Spanish and American domination, the results of genocide and disease were hidden in population figures that were largely inaccurate. Those taking the census found it useful to falsify demographic records in order to serve their best interests. When the truth is finally known (and this will occur when the Indians themselves are believed), the world will be shocked and dismayed at the massive decrease in Indian population following the entrance of the foreigners into the Pueblo world.

While it is indeed true that the Pueblo Indians sustained less fundamental change than was the lot of most other Indian tribes, there were changes, and these should be considered. The Pueblos, in greater or lesser degree, have been influenced both by their natural environment and their human contacts. To take an example from modern times, the Santa Fe Railroad had a definite impact on the two western Keresan tribes of Laguna and Acoma. Many of the families joined the railroad company as employees and moved to Gallup, New Mexico; to Winslow, Arizona; or to Barstow and Richmond in California. When ceremonial dances or fiestas occurred in their villages, the transplanted Indians either rushed home the night before, or even failed to return to their villages for participation. If they hurried home, they were ill prepared. Hence, store-purchased ribbons began to appear in the attire of the dancers, and are often used today in place of the dignified and traditional fir branches.

The eight northern pueblos were strongly influenced by non-Pueblo tribes. Taos and Picuris had the Jicarilla Apaches as neigh-

Comanche Dance at Taos Pueblo, 1971. (Photograph by Marcia Keegan.)

bors, in the Cimarron region. Consequently, these three tribes share many traditions. The most easily observable traditional event is the footrace performed by all three tribes on their annual feast days.

Other influences came from the Plains tribes and largely affected the northern pueblos. Some of these are the beaded moccasins, vests, and hairstyles of the men. Most Pueblo men wear the traditional *chongo,* the hair tied behind their head. But the northern Pueblo men wear braids like the Plains tribesmen. Many of these influences probably arose in the days of hunting and trading by the Pueblos with the southern Plains Indians. During treks to the Llano Estacado for annual buffalo and antelope hunts, the Pueblos met and traded with the Comanches, Kiowas, and Apaches. At this time the Pueblos also incorporated the Comanche Dance into their social dances. What the Plains people call their "war dances," the Pueblos have named their Comanche Dances. Taos Pueblo appears to have been most highly enamored of the Plains Indian dances. While embracing these elements of Indian life and further enriching their joy in the dance, not merely as entertainment but as an art, an expression of cultural amenity, and a ritual observance, the Pueblos maintain their own religion. Most particularly in their ceremonial observances, the Pueblos have retained the basic nature of their art of expression through the dance.

The pueblos of Sandoval County, on the other hand, have influenced one another, and have generally kept intact their own traditions and dances. These pueblos are Cochiti, Jemez, Sandia, San Felipe, Santa Ana, Santo Domingo, and Zia. Other traditional pueblos are Zuni, San Ildefonso, Tesuque, and Taos. Still other Pueblo villages have some "traditionalists" among them who dance on feast days. Non-dancing Indians enjoy watching the dances, but they are content to let others be the "Indians."

Another factor to be considered in connection with Pueblo mores and traditions is the nature and extent of Spanish influence. Final acceptance, willingly or unwillingly, of Spanish political domination did not result in utter cultural domination by the foreigners, as was the case with many tribes elsewhere. The Pueblos developed a unique accommodation to Spanish rule, which helped them preserve their own distinctive religious life. They retained their traditions and ritual observances, and the important values of the Pueblo way of life.

Government

The Pueblo tribes today operate under a form of government that is at once native and European, the European form of government having been introduced by the Spaniards in colonial times. There are two forms of this Spanish governmental structure. One form was introduced by Oñate in 1598. The other occurred by royal decree in 1620. While each of the nineteen pueblos is autonomous, most of them being governed according to ancient tribal systems, they also operate a coalition system of government under the All Indian Pueblo Council. This permits mutual counsel, and allows for the development of a degree of political power in pueblo relations with the state and federal governments.

The titular head of the traditional pueblo is the cacique, together with his staff, the cacique being the theocratic leader "from the time of the emergence from the underworld," as the people say. A few pueblos no longer have a cacique, nor do they have religious societies. Responsible to the cacique and his staff are the war chief and his assistants. They are the functioning arm of the leadership that enforces the rules, regulations, and ordinances of the theocratic system. All of these are lifetime positions. There are no successions. All persons are selected, and they serve for a lifetime in their designated positions. Occasionally, an assistant may be acting in the temporary absence or the death of a head man, but he does not take a position or a title that was not given to him by the people.

Another branch of government under the war chief includes the positions of war captains and their aides. These positions are filled annually by the cacique, his staff, society leaders, and the war chief. A war captain with five aides is selected from either of the two moieties (divisions of society for ceremonial and social purposes) of the pueblo in alternating years. The lieutenant war captain also has five aides. These men are responsible for policing the pueblo, and for conducting and supervising the traditional social activities of the people who are members of either one of the two moieties. Such moieties are the Turquoise or Squash moieties, the Summer and Winter, the North and South, or the Blackeye and Redeye moieties. The social activities range from ceremonial and social dances to recreational rabbit hunts, competitive footraces, and the hunting of game animals.

The war captain is also responsible for the reservation land, as well as the domestic and wild game animals. When planting season begins, the war captain informs the pueblo governor that domestic animals must be removed from the farmland. Prior to World War II, before the wheat threshing machine came to the pueblos, herds of horses were used to thresh wheat. These horses were gathered up during June, then taken to the mountains to be tended by young men who represented their families, or were paid for the task by the family. The horse herders were responsible to the war captains, who kept a list of the families that were obliged to produce their share of labor in caring for the horses. When the horses were returned to the villages, the wheat was threshed for the people. A corral or enclosure was built, and the wheat was placed in the center. The horses were put into the corral containing the wheat, and were then run round and round until the wheat was thoroughly threshed.

Because the war captains and their staffs are responsible for wild game animals, they are the first to sponsor hunting parties, and the first to go on hunting expeditions. After them, other hunting societies take their turn; they are guided by one or two aides of the war captain. The buffalo and antelope hunting parties of earlier times were handled in this manner.

The office of pueblo governor, an institution introduced by the Spaniards, was incorporated into the Pueblos' own governmental institutions, and shows the unique character of this great people. This office, originally designed for Spanish domination, was converted by the Pueblos into an effective bulwark against intrusion by foreigners. The governor, in effect, protected the spiritual leaders. Thus were their human values preserved. The governor is responsible, under the cacique, for all tribal business of the modern world. He is the liaison with the outside business and economic world and its various activities. In the evolving new age, the complexity of the governor's office constantly increases.

The governor has an official staff composed of a first lieutenant governor and a second lieutenant governor, both of whom act under the governor's jurisdiction. A sheriff is also a member of the official staff. This staff is comprised of five aides who serve as messengers, as well as in various other service capacities. Other members of the governor's staff are the fiscales, or church officers. The fiscale has a lieutenant and five aides. They are responsible for activities involving the Catholic church, such as burials, janitorial duties, and maintenance of church property. In some pueblos there are "ditch bosses," who supervise and coordinate the irrigation systems of the farming pueblos, and those who maintain the systems.

These officials are selected annually by the cacique and his staff. Traditionally, pueblo officials serve without salary and consider the year's service as a duty to their people and their pueblo. Recently, however, in some of the nineteen pueblos, the governor has been salaried.

A typical organization chart, depicting the governmental system operating in most pueblos today, would show the following:

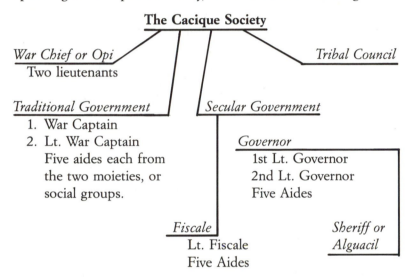

The Cacique Society

War Chief or Opi
Two lieutenants

Tribal Council

Traditional Government
1. War Captain
2. Lt. War Captain
   Five aides each from
   the two moieties, or
   social groups.

Secular Government

Governor
1st Lt. Governor
2nd Lt. Governor
Five Aides

Fiscale
Lt. Fiscale
Five Aides

Sheriff or Alguacil

A pueblo council guides the affairs of the whole people. Except in six pueblos, the council is composed of former village governors. Upon completion of their term of office they become lifetime members of the council, unless old age or a physical handicap makes it impossible for them to continue. "Old age" to the Pueblos is well past the age of eighty. There are six pueblos today that elect their governors and council through the balloting system. These are Isleta, Laguna, Pojoaque, San Ildefonso, Santa Clara, and Zuni. Due to an apparently unsolvable situation arising in the 1890s, Santa Clara Pueblo approved the Wheeler-Howard Act of 1934 (known also as the Indian Reorganization Act). This statute instituted a form of constitutional elective government for many tribes throughout the country under then President Franklin D. Roosevelt and John Collier, Sr., commissioner of Indian affairs. Thus, at the end of 1934, the people of Santa Clara voted for their governor in the European way, and the next year they had a new form of government.

Isleta Pueblo has also chosen to elect its officials; their people cast ballots for governor and councilmen. The candidate for governor who accumulates the largest number of votes becomes governor, while the second largest vote-getter becomes president of the council. The one who receives the third highest number of votes in the election for governor becomes vice-president. These officials then select their lieutenants, councilmen, and judges. The Isletas began using the ballot system in 1947.

The Laguna Pueblo people adopted a constitutional form of government in 1949. They voted for their officers at that time by means of a standing vote of those present in the council hall at a time named for the election. The Lagunas amended their constitution and bylaws on November 10, 1958, permitting absentee voting. Now at Laguna there are many voters who mail in their ballots. According to strict guidelines, the off-reservation Lagunas (called "colonies"), who reside in Albuquerque, Gallup, and elsewhere, have the right to vote by mail. These "colony" Lagunas are employed by the Santa Fe Railroad and in various government agencies as well as by private firms. By 1974, Pojoaque and San Ildefonso were also selecting their officials through the ballot system.

According to tribal legends and oral history, the All Indian Pueblo Council has existed for many centuries, and 1598 is used by the people as its date of origin because that is the recorded meeting date with the Spaniards under Governor Juan de Oñate.

The nineteen governors are official representatives of their pueblos to the All Indian Pueblo Council. They alone may vote in the council. The governors elect a chairman, vice-chairman, secretary, and treasurer, all of whom serve as council officers. According to a modern constitution adopted in 1965, the governors may delegate this authority by proxy in writing to any one of the officials in his village. Thus, with all present at the All Indian Pueblo Council, official business is conducted. Attendance of ten pueblo delegates at any meeting is sufficient for a quorum. An issue is generally discussed until all parties have thoroughly understood it. Then a resolution is drawn up and acted upon by the delegates. A simple majority of those present is sufficient to decide any matter. However, if an issue is of maximum importance, even those present constituting a quorum have been known to refuse to act, demanding a greater number to be present for decision-making purposes. In the old days, meetings were held for several days and often longer, until all the pressing issues were decided. The length of time required to make a decision was due, in part, to the multiplicity of languages and dialects. The official language today is English, and the meetings proceed more quickly, although the older councilmen still require interpreters.

The Pueblo Indians did not have a treaty with any foreign government—Spanish, Mexican, or American. Their relationship with the United States has its origins, and its continuing principles, in laws by which nations are guided internationally, and by the Treaty of Guadalupe Hidalgo. This treaty, which ended the war with Mexico, was ratified by the United States and Mexico on May 10, 1848, and ceded to the United States the states of California, Nevada, most of Arizona, New Mexico west of the Rio Grande and north of the Gadsden Purchase of 1853, Utah, Colorado west of the Rocky Mountains, and southwest Wyoming. The land thus acquired by the United States contained a total of 334,443,520 acres (552,568 square miles). All of this was Indian land, owned by Indian tribes and recognized internationally as Indian land.

A unique relationship exists, and has existed historically, between the United States Government and the Pueblo tribes. Welded into this relationship are the legal and international ramifications of the Pueblo relationships with the Spanish and Mexican governments, and these have weight even today because of various international treaties, land grants, and court decisions.

The full scope and complexity of these relationships will appear more clearly in the following chapters. This overview of the Pueblo people as they are today serves only as a center of reference.

The Pueblos are members of a distinct race, known (for want of a more accurate name) as the Indian race, a name given to them in error by Christopher Columbus, who made the most ludicrous navigational mistake in all history when he thought he had reached India. He had landed on an island off the North American continent. To understand the Pueblo people, it should be noted that the Pueblos are not a single people. They are a group of peoples, related through geographical area, material culture, and political necessity. Despite their varied traditions, languages, and observances, they had managed to live peacefully and in a spirit of greatest cooperation, until the Europeans arrived.

The Pueblo tribes are nations within a nation. The peculiarity and uniqueness of this situation lie at the heart of all the issues and problems with which the Pueblos are faced today. Conversely, this uniqueness lies at the heart of the problems faced today by the United States Government, in its attempt to fulfill the obligations of a federal government that has accepted the role of trustee of Pueblo assets, and is only now attempting to right the wrongs of the past.

Street scene, San Juan Pueblo, ca. 1904. (Photograph by Edward S. Curtis, courtesy Museum of New Mexico, Negative No. 144550.)

Oraibi Mishongovi
Walpi
Awatobi
Shipaulovi
Shongopovi

Teotho
O' Kayng   Welai
Xa' pogeh   Jacona
                          Nambe   Po' joageh
Po' sogeh   Cuyamungeh
La Cienega
Ko' chites   Tetsugeh
                                    ✳
Hemich   Cicuye   SANTA FE
Tsiya   Khewa   San Marcos
Tamaya   San Cristobal
Kuaua   Galisteo
Puaray   Kutscha   San Lazaro
Nafait   ✳
                ALBUQUERQUE
Halona
Hawikuh   Tuei   Chilili
Kechibawa   Akome
                            Tejique

                            Quarai
                            Abo

                            Gran Quivira

Teypana

SOCORRO ✳
Senucu

Rio Grande

ARIZONA   NEW MEXICO

● Indian Pueblo
✳ Modern Village or Town

✳ El Paso

THE PUEBLOS IN THE SIXTEENTH CENTURY

20

❧ 2 ❧
In the Beginning

THE PUEBLOS ARE an ancient people whose history goes back into the farthest reaches of time. Archaeological exploration sufficiently confirms the fact of their occupancy of the Southwest from time immemorial, and this information is best learned from the scholars in that discipline. However, to gain a modern perspective of the Pueblo place in history, one need only remember that at the time of the infamous European Inquisition of 1100–1200, the Pueblos had long been living in peaceful settled communities. They had a well-organized system of self-government, with an efficient system of law and order that protected society as well as the rights of the individual.

When England and France were in the throes of the Hundred Years' War (1337–1453), the Pueblos were raising corn, squash, beans, and many other varieties of foods, in villages where each individual had a role to play in work and worship, and society served the needs of the people.

These people had no written history; theirs was an oral system of maintaining the records of ages. The history of the people had a reverent place in the whole society, and was not tilted to adorn the reputation of one or another newcomer who had pretensions to leadership. Nor was it changed or distorted to supply credibility to the demands of a powerful political structure. Tradition was history; history was tradition. In reverent narration, through the art of ritual dance and mime, the Pueblo people related their traditional history, passing the story down from generation to generation. That the traditional history survives is shown in the many additions made through time, as events have shaped and altered the lives of the people. Thus it is that the Spaniards appear in the ritual narratives of today. It is not beyond expectation that, in their own time, the impact of the Anglos upon Pueblo life will also be incorporated into Pueblo dance and mime, as the people continue persistently to retain their culture and their arts.

The people tell the story of their history, "from the beginning," with all the artistry of the traditional storyteller, complete with age-old mythology and beliefs formalized into narrative, from the Hegira to the invasion by the Europeans. In the mind's eye one sees the elders speak, their eyes alight, their gestures emphasizing or elaborating a point, as they reveal the ancient record of the Pueblo people.

The Traditional History

The people came from the north to their present areas of residence, from the place of origin at Shibapu, where they emerged from the underworld by way of a lake. During their journeys they were led by the war chief. This chief served for life. With his assistants and the annually appointed war captains and their staffs, he constituted a force responsible for clearing the path upon which the people traveled. And with them came the Great Spirit, and He guided the ancient ones through the many arduous tasks of daily life. For unknown ages the ancient people were led from place to place upon this great continent. Many of them finally settled in the Four Corners area, where they developed their civilization and settled for some hundreds of years before moving to their present homeland. As the ancient ones relate, it was in order to preserve the people from total annihilation that the Great Spirit impelled them to migrate. This they did, in groups and in different directions. Thus it is that the people created new dialects.

The country where the ancient ones lived was a vast open land of deserts, plains, and mountains. Here they built their villages and enhanced their lives. But they were filled with longing for perfection in their society, harmony with their environment, and so they moved from time to time to other places with better sources of food and a better environment. The Pueblo people built so well, and their culture worked so harmoniously, that they prospered. Their way of life spread over an area covering vast parts of the Southwest, including Colorado, northwest New Mexico, and west central New Mexico, as well as northeast Arizona and east central Arizona. This was the homeland given to the ancestors of the Pueblo people by a divine being at the beginning of time. (Many places settled by the Pueblo people are now national parks and monuments.)

Over a period of time spanning thousands of years, the people were brought to a land where they were safe from the catastrophes of nature. There would be no tornadoes and no floods. Here in the new land they received their final instructions. The One above reminded them of their past trials and dangers, the sorrows and joys they had known together, and the strength they had demon-

*Cochiti women grinding corn. Each granary had three grades of metate:
fine, medium, and coarse. (Courtesy Indian Pueblo Cultural Center Museum.)*

strated because of their unity. They were told of the necessity to plant and harvest crops for survival. They were shown the indigenous plants that grew wild and abundantly upon the land. The food was plentiful. And so the civilization of the ancient ones developed around the planting of foods, more especially of corn. The systematic raising of corn led to the shaping of Pueblo religion, with rituals and prayers for rain and other conditions favorable to the crops. The need to know the proper time for planting, cultivating, and harvesting led to developments in astronomical observation. They studied the movement of the sun, the moon, clouds, the wind, and the timing of the vernal equinox.

Various dances were held, according to the seasons: prayer dances for rain during the growing season, for snow during the winter season, and thanksgiving dances for a bountiful harvest or a successful hunt. These prayer and thanksgiving dances are the ceremonial dances of today, while the public dances, held for entertainment, are the social dances of today.

The Spirit warned the people to respect and obey the laws of nature, and the orders of their leaders: the chief, the war captains, and the cacique. The cacique was to guide them spiritually. In him was vested the power of authority to legislate laws. The Spirit cautioned that this was the only way for them to live together in peace and to be protected. The Pueblo people had confidence that the cacique and the other leaders had power and wisdom because they were guided by the One above. Under this government the people made religion a part of their daily lives. Since resources of the land were plentiful, warfare was unknown and hospitality was a way of life. As barren as the desert may appear, and as rugged as the mountains may seem, the ancient ones wrested their livelihood from the land. The secret of their success was simple. They came face to face with nature, but did not exploit it. They became a part of the ecological balance instead of abusing and finally destroying it. They accepted the terms of their existence in what may be considered today as a harsh environment, and lived in it for thousands of years until the technological Europeans arrived, bringing in their wake the pollution and rampant misuse of the land that we see today.

The people were also warned that there would be dangers. It was predicted that the dangers would become apparent as more people began to inhabit their homeland. They were advised to build fortress-like communities for protection, and were promised the guardianship of the warrior twin gods, Maseway and Sheoyeway. They were to pray to them for aid in those times of conflict and danger that were to come.

Thus were the divine instructions given to the people. And then the Great One returned to his home beyond the clouds. The people were left under the spiritual leadership of the cacique and his appointed leaders. They policed the communities; they set the rules and regulations agreeable to all, with penalties for offenses well understood by all.

There were guidelines for well-ordered living. What the Pueblos have now as an unwritten "tribal code" was essentially in operation in ancient times, remembered and obeyed as though carved in stone. The code was respected, understood, and taught from generation to generation. The oath taken by the leader in those ancient times, given then as a divine command, is still used today by the pueblo governors.

Crime as we know it and fear it today was nonexistent. If an offense was committed, the individual was given the opportunity to state his case; he had the benefit of witnesses and every chance to clear himself or explain himself before judgment was passed. Since the cacique and the other leaders were responsible for governing, the clowns (*Kushare* in the Keres language, *Kosa* in the Tewa tongue, and *Tabosh* in the Towa language) were that group of society responsible for the entertainment of the people. All these peoples, with their many and varied responsibilities, were under the titular leadership of the cacique and his staff. He was in direct control of the religious programs, and of the societies that functioned for specific purposes. The cacique had received a mandate from the One above to rule in humble dignity, and never to show a sign of force. He was to rule in peace, in harmony with nature. Today as in the past, the cacique is forbidden to kill even the smallest of animals.

Thus paraphrased, is the history of the Pueblos narrated, now as in ancient times.

During their migrations in prehistory, the ancestors of the Pueblo people covered a vast territory in the Southwest. Anthropologists trace the various tribal groups through their ceramics, remnants of an economy long dead. The Pueblo people themselves, however, rely on the songs of the various societies in tracing the places where their ancestors may have been, as these songs mention various

25

deities who were recognized as the "honored" ones, or keepers, of a certain area. For instance, the Hopis have a name for the deity on San Francisco Peak near Flagstaff, Arizona. The Acomas have a deity on Mt. Taylor, north of their pueblo. The other Rio Grande pueblos have references to most of the higher peaks along the Rocky Mountains in New Mexico and Colorado. The society songs also have references to lakes and large bodies of water. The ancient Hopi songs mention the Colorado River flowing through the Grand Canyon, since their ancestors lived as far west as the southern tip of Nevada and the southern half of present-day Utah. The Tewas, who were in the southern Colorado area before they moved to the northern Rio Grande area, refer to the mountain ranges in central Colorado in their songs.

The Towas of Jemez have many references in their songs to Stone Lake on today's Jicarilla Apache Reservation, and to some shrines around Largo Canyon in Rio Arriba County. The area is one from which the Towas migrated to the present Jemez country in the thirteenth century A.D., following the drought which began in 1250 and lasted until 1290. Other references made in songs of the societies are to the Sierra Blanca area near the Mescalero Apache Reservation in Otero County. Jemez legends say that the Arrow Society was evicted from the main Jemez group, and the members journeyed toward the southwest until they settled with the Tampiros who lived in the area at that time. Some of the references in the songs are entirely foreign in the Towa dialect, so the deities described may be Tampiro words and songs. The Arrow Society eventually returned to the Jemez country and established a village on the ridge east of today's Ponderosa, before they were welcomed back into the community of several Jemez villages in the mountains north of Jemez Pueblo.

Areas along the Mogollon Rim of the New Mexico-Arizona border contain many ruins of former Pueblo Indian sites. Many of these sites and the higher mountain ranges have Zuni names, and it is with these Zuni names that other Pueblos refer to the area. In many instances, Pueblo people make songs for their dances and refer to the areas that have gone into non-Indian ownership many long years ago.

It is believed that some native North Americans originated in the Tehuacan Valley in what is today Mexico. According to Richard MacNeish, civilization began in phases (Graham 1981). The first developmental phase, following the hunting and gathering stage, is

Kiva, Nambe Pueblo, ca. 1915. (Photographer unknown, courtesy Museum of New Mexico, Negative No. 3044.)

called the Ajuereado Phase, which ended in 7200 B.C. This was followed by the El Riego Phase, which ended in 5200 B.C. This was the period when avocados and chile began to be consumed by the natives. Following this period was the Coxcatlan Phase, which ended in 3400 B.C. This period is important because corn was domesticated at this time. And because of the nature of corn, civilization took a few steps forward with amazing new developments; corn could be saved and replanted; and it could be stored, prepared in various ways, and taken on journeys. As a result, it is believed that the people began to move and migrate; it is probable that they went north and south.

The Olmec culture developed, followed by the Toltec and Mayan civilizations; each of these compared favorably with the cultures of other leading civilizations on other continents at the time. The future Pueblo Indians probably brought fragments of the cultures of the Mesoamerican civilizations with them, since one sees exhibits and pictures in Mayan museums that show cultural practices similar to those of Pueblo Indians today. Many modern educated Pueblo Indians of New Mexico and Hopis of Arizona have agreed about this phenomenon.

The Tanoans probably arrived first in the Southwest and settled in the Cortez, Colorado, area, according to oral history. This oral history specifies that the Tanoan speakers were a unified people at one time and that southwest Colorado was likely their home. But when they began to leave the area, most probably they stopped at Mesa Verde for a time before moving on. Mesa Verde was occupied at different sites from the sixth to the thirteenth century; there are 3,900 sites and 600 cliff dwellings there.

Meanwhile, the Keresans arrived sometime later than the Tanoans and occupied Chaco Canyon, the Aztec Ruins of today, and the Bloomfield area. Chaco Canyon is known to have been occupied for two hundred years along a ten-mile stretch in which thirteen ruins have been excavated thus far (Frazier 1986). The Keresans brought with them the Bear Cult and the Corn Dance, which the majority of pueblos perform on their annual Christian feast days.

According to their legends, the Hitsatsinom, or ancient Hopis, probably wandered to either or both Chaco Canyon and Mesa Verde, and intermarriages probably took place, since the Sun Clan, especially, exists in most of the pueblos—Keresan, Tanoan, and Hopi.

Also according to oral history, a long drought ensued during the

Mission, Picuris Pueblo, ca. 1911. (Photograph by Jesse L. Nusbaum, courtesy Museum of New Mexico, Negative No. 28703.)

twelfth century, and this has been verified by tree-ring dendro-chronology. The ancient ones said that Mother Earth was splitting apart. Thus they began to vacate the northwest area in favor of the area of the Rio Grande and its tributaries. This was where the Spaniards found them in the sixteenth century.

Religion

The Pueblos have no word that translates as "religion." The knowledge of a spiritual life is part of the person twenty-four hours a day, every day of the year. In describing the beliefs and practices of today, the traditional religion may also be understood. There is little basic change. The tradition of religious belief permeates every aspect of the people's life; it determines man's relation with the natural world and with his fellow man. Its basic concern is continuity of a harmonious relationship with the world in which man lives. To maintain such a relationship between the people and the spiritual world, various societies exist, with particular responsibilities for weather, fertility, curing, hunting, and pleasure or entertainment. Even today, most Pueblo people belong to a religious society, and have an important place in pueblo religious activities. The tradi-tional calendar of religious events is so full that there is no time left for any new or innovative religious practices as is sometimes possible with non-Pueblo Indians who accept, as one example, the Peyote Way. Many tribes that espoused new religions that combined old and new beliefs suffered various defeats, lost their land to white invaders, and lost a great part of their culture as well. Certainly they could not remove their sacred artifacts nor their religious shrines at the point of a bayonet. Thus they had to revive their religion in a new homeland.

But the Pueblos are still living today upon the sites where the Spaniards found them in the sixteenth century. This is the principal reason for their religion being practically intact. The people took their religion underground around 1692, due to harassment by the Spaniards in their attempt to substitute another religion for the native one. This fear still persists, and it generally explains why a non-Indian is not permitted to observe a religious ceremonial dance in the pueblos, and why no cameras or sketching are allowed.

The religious rituals and ceremonials themselves, maintained by the Pueblos today, are the same ones they have practiced since their ancestors lived in pit houses. The oratories, prayers, and songs are

30

[Above] Feast of San Estevan, Acoma Pueblo, 1899. (Photograph by Charles Lummis, courtesy Museum of New Mexico, Negative No. 1926.)
[Below] Corn Dance, San Ildefonso Pueblo, 1950. (Photograph by Tyler Dingee, courtesy Museum of New Mexico, Negative No. 120200.)

31

the same. These observances are not spontaneous outpourings, nor outbursts of the troubled heart. They are carefully memorized prayerful requests for an orderly life, rain, good crops, plentiful game, pleasant days, and protection from the violence and the vicissitudes of nature. To appease or pledge their faith to God, they often went on sacrificial retreats, often doing without food and water as penance or cleansing of body and soul for the benefit of man throughout the world.

In the dominant society of America, religion is largely an exclusive property. Usually a certain set of beliefs and rituals is identified, written into sacred books and religious manuals, and maintained by a certain sect. It is presumed to be the one and only true, if not the first, religion. Belonging to different religions or sects simultaneously is discouraged, but proselytizing is a virtue. Facts such as these lead one to suspect the particular belief system. Pueblo religion does not proselytize. It is not written, but is enshrined in the heart of the individual. Although most Pueblo people have been nominally Roman Catholic for more than three hundred years, the native religion is the basis of their system of belief. The two systems are maintained by a process that Pueblo scholar Alfonso Ortiz once described as "compartmentalization." Each of the two religions is a distinct socio-ceremonial system; each contains patterns or ways of worshipping not present in the other.

Elements of Catholic rituals that have been accepted are: worship on Sundays and receiving the various sacraments, confirmation, baptism, weddings, and the native social dances of the saints' days, Christmas, and Easter. These rituals are now accepted as traditional Pueblo social and cultural patterns. In the end, all people throughout the world look to one personification, though they may address Him in different ways. As a writer from another continent said, "All paths lead to the same summit."

Some observers have said that the Pueblos "dance all the year round." This may be true, and was more the case in the past, since their ceremonial calendar covers the whole year. Through dance and song one can realize a sense of rebirth and rejuvenation. The great summer Corn Dances of the Pueblos have caused many non-Indians to rejoice over the wonderful feeling of spiritual rebirth they have experienced.

The Pueblos believe that the Great One is omnipresent. They

ask for permission to use the physical form of an animal before it is killed. They believe that animals have an inner spiritual component. This is the spiritual life they invoke with a short prayer. It is not a new idea; other natives throughout the Americas have this ritual. In taking branches from the sacred Douglas fir tree, the Pueblo men will inform the Creator that the intent is not to mutilate the tree, but to decorate the human being in the performance of a sacred ritual or dance in His honor. In Pueblo religion, the Douglas fir is used to adorn most dancers, male and female. It is also used to decorate the altar and shrine, where a likeness of a patron saint is kept during the day of the feast. For many years Pueblo families did not have Christmas trees, since the purposes were not native. The dominant society often uses fir trees for Christmas trees. An unsold fir on a sales lot is a sad sight indeed, and is considered sacrilegious. This tree is not used to decorate a front yard either, since tradition has it that one is changing nature when a fir tree is dug up and moved to the yard in a pueblo or a village.

After a fir branch has been used during a dance, ceremonial or social, the branches are taken away and disposed of in the river. Often some are kept in the home until dry. They are then burned in the open fireplace to produce the fresh smell of the fir tree in the room, or taken to the garden or farm where they will decompose and thus serve as fertilizer while returning to Mother Earth.

Among the Christian concepts and observances adopted by the Pueblos are feast days for the patron saints. Every Pueblo village has a Catholic church named after a patron saint. On their patron saint's name day the "fiesta" is held annually. This day generally begins with mass. Following mass, the first dance of the day is performed in front of the church in most villages. The statue of the saint is then carried in a procession to the "plaza" or center of the village. Here it is placed in an evergreen-covered bower. Dances are then performed throughout the day on the plaza, and spectators, often numbering in the thousands, observe the event from rooftops and around the plaza. At day's end the saint's statue is returned to the church in another procession. (For dates of the fiestas see the Appendixes.)

Zuni does not celebrate a similar feast day for a patron saint, but holds the Shalako ceremony as an annual event in early December. The ceremony takes place according to the time schedule set by the religious leaders of the pueblo and not on a specific calendar date.

Based upon their economy and fortified with their religious learning and observances, the Pueblos developed their society. Two types of social structure have existed in Pueblo history, and indeed still exist today in many instances. Anthropologists describe such social structures in various scholarly works. What is being related here, however, is an explanation of the evolving Pueblo society that is even now based upon the family. Just as the Pueblos have adopted many principles of Christian society, so, too, have they incorporated much of the Christian social structure. The two types of family structure, the extended family and the nuclear family, exist side by side today. The two overlap, as it were, when there is cooperation within the ancient or extended family, with the eldest man (and sometimes the woman) as the respected head of the extended family.

In the Pueblo nuclear family, the father is the head of the family. With the gradual change from an agricultural economy to one of wage earning, the nuclear family has generally replaced the formerly predominant extended family. Under an agricultural economy, extended families worked together. They might plant wheat or corn together, and later have hoeing bees at various cornfields of the family members. In August, the families would also cooperate in cutting wheat at the various family wheat fields. Wheat, of course, was introduced by the Europeans, but the social structure and the relationships were those carried over from ancient times during the early days following European contact.

Another form of family structure is the clan, a group of people descended from a common female ancestor. Clans may be affected by the conditions and situations of any specific time. Clan bloodlines descend from the mother. But today some Pueblo men are married to non-Indians, and the offspring do not belong to a clan. They are natural members of the father's extended family, however. In some pueblos a woman marrying an "outsider" is expected to make her home wherever the man's home is. In such a case, the offspring maintain the clan bloodline and are still members of the clan, but may reside elsewhere, and may actually be on the tribal rolls of another tribe, or not be enrolled at all.

Still another societal structure is the moiety. In this case, the division is in two groups for ceremonial and social purposes. Membership in a moiety is through the head of the family; often it is by choice at the time of marriage or through ties of friendship.

In some pueblos having a moiety structure, the governor of the village is appointed from alternating moieties each year. Moieties also compete against one another in traditional footraces. During a feast, each moiety takes its turn performing at the plaza for the benefit of the people and the guests of the day. Although the people themselves are aware of the difference between a clan and a moiety, when they discuss these structures with non-Indians the structures tend to be confused due to translation into the English language. Most often (and ignorantly) the moieties are called clans. Because of the religious significance of the moieties, this form will probably remain in Pueblo life for a long time.

Economy

Economic pursuits and changes in economic modes dictate changes in societal structure, and such changes in social relationships brought about by nontraditional forms of economy are evident in every aspect of Pueblo Indian life today. The villages have not disappeared. But they have lost many of their compact characteristics, although they are still principally of adobe construction, which is so well suited to the climate of that area. The former apartment-like family homes are giving way rapidly to planned areas for single-family dwellings.

The ancient apartments made of stone are historically one of the most interesting facets of old-time Pueblo life. Round baking ovens were built on the second floor of the building. Step ladders were guarded carefully and pulled up to the second floor after all the family members were safely home. These precautions were taken against possible raiding parties. Today, there is no need for such security measures; thus we see the gradual deterioration of the multiple housing units, open living, and outdoor baking.

Multistoried housing remains characteristic of Taos Pueblo today, but in other pueblos only a few of such buildings remain, standing as remnants of a historic past. These remaining multistoried houses are used by various societies as their centers of worship and for activities throughout the year.

Pueblo life was built upon a foundation of work, together with religious observances and practices. The people were eminently successful in building a rich and productive life, so much so that the vast Southwest area even today is known as the pre-European "Pueblo culture." They built the first apartment structures in North

Picuris women winnowing wheat, 1935. (Photograph by T. Harmon Parkhurst, courtesy Indian Pueblo Cultural Center Museum.)

America; they constructed complex irrigation systems; and their arts are greatly admired even today.

Farming has always been a precarious occupation in the Southwest. The mountain desert area, where food production and gathering began initially, set certain limits for agriculture. The high altitudes dictated a short growing season, while the arid Southwest usually failed to provide sufficient rainfall for the growing of crops. After the Pueblos' migration to the Rio Grande areas, the supply of water for their crops improved, and the growing season was longer. Trading expeditions with tribes that appeared in the Southwest at later dates also furnished new articles and ideas, enriching their lives. With more water, more food was grown, and the excess supplies were bartered or traded with other tribes. Exactly how far a distance away such trade extended is not precisely known, but evidence exists that sea shells from the Pacific Coast were in use by the Pueblos, and are of the same type as those worn today by male corn dancers. Such shells were unearthed during an excavation in Pueblo Bonito of the Chaco Canyon National Monument in San Juan County. Macaw or parrot feathers have also been used in the social and ceremonial dances of the Pueblos for centuries. These were traded with tribes to the south, and it is believed they came from Mexico.

Corn flour and cornmeal prepared on the metate, and corn pollen as well as corn husks, were trade items. Woven baskets, pottery, and piñon nuts have also been trade items as have eagle, hawk, turkey, and other smaller bird feathers.

Farming was accomplished mainly through cooperation of the extended family. There were "hoeing bees" in cornfields, when the people went from one family to another, until all in the extended family had weeded their cornfields twice during the summer, and hilled them before irrigating. The smaller chile and squash gardens were cared for by individual families, the work being done usually in the early hours of dawn before breakfast.

Irrigating these fields was an all-day affair. During periods of water shortage the official supervised the irrigation of priority areas. Each family took its turn, and often several families together spent the whole night in the task of irrigating. The cleaning of community irrigation ditches was (and is still today) an individual family responsibility. All the able-bodied men and boys of the community or pueblo must and do help in this task. Only by helping with community duties is one identified as a member of the tribe.

37

Pueblo communities held rabbit hunts sponsored by the war captains, and these often occurred before a feast day, after European contact. Elk and deer hunts followed immediately after the harvesting season in ancient times, and continued long after the Spanish contact. Buffalo and antelope expeditions to the eastern plains were held by some of the Pueblos also. This fact causes some merriment among the elders, because the younger generation does not realize that their people knew the buffalo, hunted them, used them, and adopted the Buffalo Dance. Often they ask, "How did we get the buffalo?" Again and again the explanation is made that distances meant relatively little to a people whose neighbors and friends were hundreds of miles away, and that the chance for a buffalo hunt was a lure enough for anyone.

Having settled the vast lands of the Southwest, the Pueblos lived for many eras as the most important if not the only people in the area. Neighboring tribes visited them, traded with them, and often some small groups or some individuals remained with them. With the coming of the horse and the immense change in native economy and mobility, they soon had neighbors. Some intertribal marriages occurred, but not until the encounter with the Spaniards and the conflict that ensued was there any considerable mixture of the tribal bloodlines. Many Pueblo people have Navajo blood, dating from early times when the Pueblos still lived in the Four Corners area. When the Spaniards came and conflict erupted from 1694 to 1696, the Pueblos (especially the Jemez) fled to their ancestral homeland and lived with the Navajos for many years. Some of the Jemez people remained in the Navajo country to become Navajos with Jemez clan membership.

The first known Pueblos to be "relocated" were the Tanos from along the Galisteo Basin, San Cristobal, and San Lazaro, south of Santa Fe. Tano or Thano was the name given to this language group, which we also identify as Tewas today. After the Pueblo Revolt of 1680, some of the Tanos are believed to have moved into Santa Fe to occupy the empty former Spanish homes. Consequently, the return of the Spaniards in 1693 caused many problems for them as they were moved north to the present-day Santa Cruz-Chimayo area. During further attempts to revolt against the Spaniards in 1694 and 1696, these people fled to Zuni, where they remained for a short time. From Zuni they moved to the Hopi country and settled at Hano on the First Mesa, where they remain today. They are known

Old Laguna Pueblo, ca. 1899. (Photograph by Adam Clark Vroman, courtesy Indian Pueblo Cultural Center Museum.)

as the Tewas of Hano, and they still speak the Tewa tongue. There has been little or no change in their language, and they often visit with the Tewas of northern New Mexico, their common language holding together the tribal affiliation. Most Hanos are also able to speak the Hopi language. There were many other Rio Grande people who fled to the Hopi country following the return of the Spaniards after 1692–1693, when they feared retaliation and feudal slavery.

Galisteo Pueblo is often described as having been occupied until October 1780, before moving to Santo Domingo Pueblo. The westernmost village of the Galisteo Basin is San Marcos, whose residents are said to have moved to Santo Domingo Pueblo by February 1792.

Another Pueblo tribe known by the Spaniards and described by them as a large and powerful group was Cicuye. We know them today as Pecos Pueblo people. Since they occupied a marginal position on the eastern edge of the Pueblo country, the people of Pecos suffered continuously from Apache and Comanche raids. Finally, in 1838, the few survivors joined the Jemez people of Walatowa to become one pueblo, as they are today. Their feast day is celebrated annually at Jemez on August 2. Their patron saint is Our Lady of Portiuncula, whom the people call Percingula. The Pecos migrants carried their saint in the white cagelike enclosure in which it remains today. They also brought the "Pecos Bull," which is traditionally seen on the eve of August 1 and the morning of August 2. In addition, they brought one religious society that the descendants maintain even today. Pecos blood is well infused into Jemez Pueblo now. Officially, the two pueblos of Jemez and Pecos were merged by the Act of June 19, 1936 (49 Stat. 1528). The older generation knew a few of, and a lot about, these immigrants, but the younger generation knows very little about them.

The last known immigration was that of the Laguna people to Isleta Pueblo. This event took place about 1879, a year before the railroad came through Laguna. The coming of the railroad brought American engineers and surveyors to Laguna. Three of these white people married Laguna women. Their influence upon the Lagunas soon began to be felt. The result was that the people were split into groups of pro-American "progressive" and anti-American "conservative" factions. The latter were mainly members of various societies and their families, the Kwirina, the Arrowhead, and the Fire societies.

The members of these societies first moved from Laguna Pueblo to Mesita, a few miles east of the pueblo. From Mesita they went to Isleta Pueblo, some fifty miles away on the Rio Grande. They settled at an area called Oraibi, southwest from the plaza at Isleta. This area had other migrants at an earlier date.

The movements of Pueblo people were not a great problem for the Spanish governors de Vargas and his successor Cubero. However, the padres and missionaries were concerned about the "desertion" from the Christian churches along the Rio Grande, and the resulting depletion of their labor force when the people departed. As a result, the Franciscan missionaries spent many years attempting to return the "runaways" to the Rio Grande area, where they might receive "the word of God" and be put to productive work for the missions. Returned refugees from the Hopi country were identified as "Moquinos" by the Spaniards, the term being derived from the word *Moqui,* the Spanish name for the Hopi people. Many Pueblo people of the Rio Grande still bear the surname of Moquino. In 1732, Padre Techungi went to the Hopi country and persuaded five Tiwas to return to the Rio Grande area. These people came to Isleta. Ten years later, Padre Delgado began a series of visits designed to convert Hopis. He was not successful. However, he was able to persuade 441 Rio Grande Pueblo people (probably Tiwas) to return. The returnees also settled at Isleta.

Some years later, an additional 350 Tiwas returned. They settled at Sandia Pueblo. This sparked the refounding of Sandia Pueblo after it was abandoned in 1681 due to the sacking of the pueblo by Spanish Governor Antonio de Otermin.

After initial Spanish contacts lasting more than a century and a half, the Hopis in the far west maintained independence, and had scant relationship with the Spanish. The Spanish governors were unable to muster sufficient strength to cope with the determined and highly conscious Hopis, whose choice it was to live as they wished and to practice their own religion. However, in 1771 a series of dry years with consequent crop failures left the Hopis in a precarious condition. By 1779, many of them had left to go to Zuni. Others joined Tiwa friends at Sandia. In 1780, Father Andres Garcia brought some two hundred Hopis to the Rio Grande pueblos, where they established themselves in various villages. Today, there are Pueblo families at Zia, Santo Domingo, and Sandia bearing the last name of Moquino.

The Lagunas who settled at Isleta were:

1. Francisco Correo, Sun Clan.
2. Maria Correo or Tsi'tiwi, Sun Clan, wife of number 1.
3. Lorenzo Correo, Sun Clan, brother of number 1.
4. Maria Abeita or Shuitia, Sun Clan, wife of number 3.
5. Jose Antonio Correo, Sun Clan, brother of numbers 1 and 3.
6. Lucia Siu'tina, Lizard Clan, wife of number 5.
7. Casildo Velho or Iunai, Lizard Clan, widower.
8. Shauunai, daughter of number 7.
9. Jose Antonio Gayama, son of number 7.
10. Matia Garcia, Lizard Clan.
11. Jose Rita, Lizard Clan.
12. Maria Rita, wife of number 11.
13. Juan Rey Churina or Aute', Lizard Clan.
14. Lupi Churina, Sun Clan, wife of number 13.
15. Jose Marino Churina or Yute', Lizard Clan, brother of number 13.
16. Benina Yuwai, Lizard Clan, wife of number 15.
17. Jose Miguel Churina, Lizard Clan, brother of numbers 13 and 15.
18. Jesusita Miguel, Lizard Clan, wife of number 17.
19. Francisco Torres or Hemish, Sun Clan.
20. Santiago Torres, Sun Clan, brother of number 19.
21. Paulina Torres, Eagle Clan, wife of number 20.
22. Jose Martin, Bear Clan.
23. Josefita Martin or Tsiuyaitiwitsa, or Kwaiye (bear), wife of number 22.
24. Santiago Chavez or Haiuna, Lizard Clan.
25. Juan Pedro.
26. Maria Ts'uku', daughter of number 25.
27. Bitorio.
28. Maria Tsiwakora, daughter of number 27.*

* (The above list is published in *The Pueblo of Isleta,* by Elsie Clews Parsons, Calvin Horn, publisher, 1974, 348–357. However, this writer questions the listing of wives as members of the same clans as their husbands.)

The Pueblo Indians of New Mexico, when the Europeans first met them, were agriculturists, living in established villages and tending their fields of crops. Every kind of corn was grown by the natives of the New World; it was their main crop. Varieties of corn included flint, dent, flour, sweet, and popcorn. From corn they made hominy, succotash, cornbread, and cornmeal mush. Favorites with the Pueblo people were tortillas and tamales. From the beginning of contact, Native American corn outranked all European grains as the favorite crop. The Indians invented the corn crib and used scarecrows to protect their fields and gardens, which were well tended and free of weeds. Their practice of planting beans with corn was restorative to the soil. The United States Department of Agriculture has listed 1,112 species of native plants that furnished food for American Indians in North America, and the Pueblos used many of these wild plant species. Piñons were and remain to this day an important food in New Mexico and elsewhere in the West. Indeed, the extent of the Indians' contribution to the world food supply is one of the best kept secrets of history, and a special study of the Pueblo contributions would amaze many otherwise informed persons. The Pueblos grew chile, squash, pumpkins, and beans— only a partial list of a recognized galaxy of native food plants. Today, the production and merchandising of corn is America's most profitable agricultural pursuit.

An agricultural economy, then, was the Pueblo way of "making a living." They bought no man's labor. They had no slavery. They knew nothing of feudal labor, which ties a human being to a landowner, in exchange for which he receives a place to sleep, something to eat, and enough subsistence to raise a family that then becomes a source of more feudal labor. Each family had its own land for purposes of cultivation. Each clan and tribe gave aid to the others. Whole tribes banded together in hunting, food gathering, farming, irrigation, and care of the land. In spite of the efforts of the Spanish missionaries, outposts of the Spanish Crown, to force the Pueblos into feudal slave labor, the unique type of Pueblo economy persisted well into the height of Spanish domination. In fact, some changes brought by the Spaniards were gladly adopted by the Pueblos, since many of them were found to enrich Pueblo economy. There developed a culture known as the Pueblo-Hispanic culture, and the Spaniards were insidiously, slowly, and inevitably brought to embrace Pueblo ways, including the subsistence pattern of agriculture. Both the Pueblos and Hispanos grew practically the same kinds of crops, producing the basic necessities of life for their own use and for some trade with other tribes. Both groups had Catholic churches, plazas, or village centers where activities took place. The Spaniards had dance halls while the Pueblos had kivas.

After wheat was brought by the Spanish to New Mexico, Navajos took part in the threshing of wheat for the Pueblos, in the 1930s and 1940s, because they had horses. Before threshing machines were available, the Navajos brought herds of horses for threshing use. For the use of these horses they were paid in wheat or wheat flour. Navajos also came to the pueblos to help cut wheat, which was done by hand. The men would remain all through the harvest season, attending pueblo feast days as their holiday after the work was done. Their women often joined them, arriving to visit their men during feast days. During the corn harvesting season the Navajo women came to the pueblos to help with cornhusking. They went to help wherever they were needed. They were paid in corn, corn flour, and husks, and were fed by the pueblos. These Navajo workers often made their homes with their Pueblo village friends. Such friendships often endured, a long-standing, precious possession of both tribal peoples.

The Pueblos of the Rio Grande area had highly prized turquoise available. The Tewas of Tewanangeh (Tewa country), as well as the Keresans, owned turquoise mines in pre-Spanish times. San Marcos, a Keresan village, was located closest to the mines, about three miles north of Cerrillos, New Mexico. Turquoise had been used as a symbol of wealth, and as a trade item for eagle, turkey, and other bird feathers, as well as for baskets and pottery. Strung together with coral and sea shells, the turquoise became even more valuable. These shells were obtained from the south and southwest, probably from Casas Grandes in Chihuahua, Mexico, which is today identified as the Paquime Ruins. Another source was Baja California.

Each Pueblo dialect has its own name for turquoise, but the gem took on the Spanish name of "Chochihuiti," from the Aztec word *Chalchihuitl,* meaning "blue stone."

Salt was also available to the Pueblo people and was used as a trade item until modern times. The Tewas obtained their salt for a time near the confluence of the Chama and the Rio Grande rivers. They called it *Ashugeh.* A larger supply was found in the area east of Estancia and Willard, New Mexico, over the Manzano

Mountains from Albuquerque. This region is commonly called the Salinas, or salt lakes. The old people told many stories of journeys to the Salinas in the east and southwest. They described these trips as they would religious ceremonies, saying they took prayer feathers to Mother Earth so that she could be appeased and continue to supply the salt. Another large source of salt was found about forty miles south of Zuni Pueblo. There were similar pilgrimages to these lakes, especially by the western Pueblos of Acoma, Laguna, and Zuni. In this connection, too, there are endless stories about trips after the salt, with the use of donkeys to bring back the precious mineral, which was used not only as seasoning, but also to preserve food. Salt was personified as an old lady who gave herself freely to those who came to seek the mineral. The Tewas called her *Onyang-kwiyo* (Old Lady Salt), while the Keresans called her *Mina-coya* (Salt Mother).

Aside from the religious differences between the Spaniards and the Pueblos, and the foreigners' attempt to impose a strange and unwanted religion upon the native people, the greatest source of conflict with the Spaniards, and with the Anglos who came afterwards, was the clash between a sedentary, agricultural economy and an economy dependent upon technology, land ownership by individuals, and labor that could be bought and sold.

The nature and process of the Spanish incursion into the land of the Pueblos provide further insight into Pueblo history.

THE FIRST TWO
SPANISH EXPEDITIONS

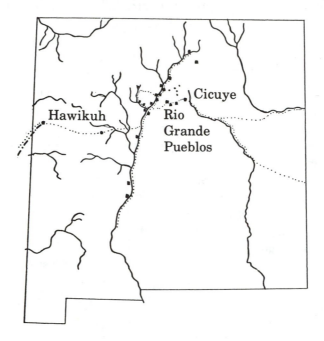

Hawikuh

Cicuye

Rio
Grande
Pueblos

─·─·─·─· Friar Marcos and Estevanico,
1539.

· · · · · · · · Coronado, 1540–41.

✤ 3 ✤

Spanish Conquest and Pueblo Revolt

EUROPEAN ENTRY INTO the Pueblo world did not take place until 1539, after the abortive attempt of the Spaniard Pamfilo de Narvaez to settle Florida in 1528. The efforts of Narvaez and his company were futile. They were shipwrecked near the present site of Galveston, Texas. Only four survived, of the estimated total of two hundred and fifty in the company. The survivors were Alvar Nunez Cabeza de Vaca, Andres Dorantes de Carronca, Alonzo de Castillo y Maldonado, and Esteban, a black Moorish slave of de Carronca.

On their journey west towards Mexico they were captured by hostile natives. In time, they escaped, only to be captured by other natives. Some years intervened while they made their way to the European civilization of New Spain. Traveling across what is now Texas, they reached and crossed the Rio Grande del Norte around the "Big Bend" country and came to Chihuahua. They arrived at San Miguel de Culiacan, Mexico, April 1, 1536, in desperate condition.

They had been gone from the world of their contemporaries for eight years. Now, puffed up with the experience of their adventures, their imagination overtook their good sense, and their tales became exaggerated until only a small semblance of truth remained. They described large settlements of natives who possessed great quantities of precious metals. To the gold-hungry Spaniards, they created a mirage of the mysterious Seven Cities of Cibola, which wavered as a golden haze across the sands of the north, darkened only by the stampede of the millions of huge animals they called *cibolos* (buffalo), and many other game animals. This magnificent myth of an El Dorado, wrought out of the substance of dreams, fascinated the Spanish soldiers and adventurers. Although many previous expeditions had ended in disaster, there were just enough successful ones to keep the dream alive, and the Spanish mind was conditioned to the idea that in the un-explored land there lay great wealth. An impoverished nobleman, or a second son, or an ambitious peasant could dream of rich conquests and of returning to Spain draped in honor, glory, and wealth.

The grandiose tales of available riches related by the four survivors prompted Don Antonio de Mendoza, viceroy of New Spain, to appoint one man to lead a new expedition. Verification of the survivors' tales was its goal. The Franciscan friar Marcos de Niza now entered the Pueblo world, causing jealousy among the mercenary soldiers by being named to lead the expedition.

For his guide and companion, Esteban, the fanciful black Moroccan slave from Azamore, was purchased from de Carronca, "for the service of our Lord, and the good of the people." With native guides, the strangely assorted party set out from Culiacan early in March 1539. Another friar, who was assigned to accompany de Niza, soon fell ill and was left behind. When Holy Week arrived, de Niza stopped at a place called Vacapa. He sent the Moor on ahead, accompanied by some native companions, carrying the famous instructions about "sending back a cross." There are many versions of this story, but the following is a simplified one:

The friar instructed Esteban that if nothing of note was found, a cross was to be sent, the length of a man's hand. If any great discovery was made, one that was twice as long as a man's hand should be sent. And if the country was as fine as New Spain, a really large cross was to be sent back.

Consequently, four days after the departure of the advance team, the friar received a cross as tall as a man. With the bearer of the cross came a native from the New World, who was to furnish a description of the wonderland they were seeking and the location of the precious metal they hoped to find. For whatever communications were exchanged, we must rely on early Spanish chroniclers, who reported that the inhabitants of the New World wore jewels of turquoise in their ears (as they still do), and draped around their garments they wore necklaces (as they do today). Their houses, it was reported, were of stone, three or four stories in height.

The arrival of the Moor among the natives has been described by Ralph E. Twitchell (Spanish Archives of New Mexico):

> *Carrying with him a gourd decorated with two bells and feathers, one white and one red, he sent messengers ahead, displaying the gourd as a symbol of his authority. He was attended by a large number of handsome women, whom he had attached to his party along the route. He also carried turquoise, and the natives who accompanied him were fully convinced that while in his company and under his protection, no danger or ill could befall them.*

Plaza, Zia Pueblo, ca. 1935. (Photograph by T. Harmon Parkhurst, courtesy Museum of New Mexico, Negative No. 45998.)

However, upon reaching one of the "Seven Cities of Cibola," which was really the Zuni village of Hawikuh, his retinue was denied entrance. Further information on the Fray Marcos-Esteban expedition is furnished by F. Ross Holland, Jr. (Holland 1969, 7). As they left Culiacan, Holland relates,

> *It soon became apparent that Fray Marcos and Esteban were not going to get along. Esteban was a flamboyant, confident individual, who affected an air of colorful superiority and wore bright feathers and bells at his wrists and a crown of plumes on his head. As the party made its way northward, the black man accepted gifts of coral and turquoise and pretty maidens from the natives. Marcos's dull piety caused him to be shocked by this behavior, and his chagrin increased as Esteban's entourage of females grew in size. Esteban's conduct became more than the priest could bear, and he ordered the Negro, after only sixty leagues of travel together, to explore the land ahead and keep him posted on what he found.*

Esteban was killed by the Zunis, but not for the reasons some people have relished. It is told by the Indians that Esteban offended the Zunis, before he even appeared on the scene. As was his routine, Esteban sent to Zuni by messenger his colorful calabash (rattle) with some rows of feathers, one red and one white. The Zunis were angered by this symbol, and the head man threw it to the ground, saying he "knew what sort of people they were, and that the messengers should tell them not to enter the town, and if they did so, Esteban would be put to death." Instead, Esteban further offended the Zunis by demanding presents and women. He informed them that he was the advance representative of a large party having considerable arms. Upon hearing this, the Zuni leaders conferred, and then decided to kill him, "so that he would not reveal our location to his brothers."

Thus did the "discoverer" of the Pueblo Indians of New Mexico in 1539 pass from the stage of history. However, Esteban is well remembered today. The Pueblos often say, "The first *white* man our people saw was a *black* man." Every year, on the annual feast day at Jemez Pueblo, the two historical figures are portrayed. One

LATER SPANISH
EXPEDITIONS

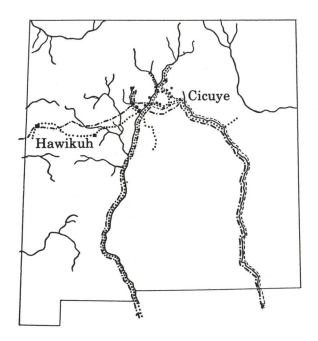

.... **Chamuscado-Rodriguez,**
           1581-82

–.–.–.–   **Espejo, 1582**

- - - - - - **Costano de Sosa, 1590-91**

figure wears a white skull cap, and his face is painted white. He wears a long black coat with a knotted white rope tied around his waist in the fashion of a Franciscan priest. A black sheep pelt covers the head of the other figure to indicate curly hair. His face is painted black, and he carries a snare drum that he plays whenever the friar walks about. One wonders if Jemez people saw the two explorers at Hawikuh, or had the two figures traveled further east and reached the Jemez province?

The friar eventually arrived at Hawikuh. He ascended a mountain to view the town from a distance. Then he raised a cross upon a mound of stones and "took possession" of the land for Spain, calling it "The Kingdom of Saint Francis." After this brief ceremony, his party made its way back to New Spain, and the friar made his report.

The Coronado Expedition

Again the adventurers were inspired with a fierce desire to go to the north. The viceroy organized an expedition at once. This time he selected his friend Francisco Vasquez de Coronado as captain general of the expedition. Coronado had been the governor of Nueva Galicia, and he designated the town Compostella as the point of departure.

And so, on July 17, 1540, another party of Europeans arrived in the Pueblo country. The Coronado expedition explored the Southwest with more care than de Niza had been able to do the year before. Although Coronado used the same route and arrived in Zuni country before sending his subordinates in various directions to see for the first time such places as the Grand Canyon and the Llano Estacado, the main force went as far east as what is now Lyons, Kansas, after visiting all of the Rio Grande pueblos.

Today, most of the pueblos still commemorate the arrival of Coronado's party, portraying him on their feast days as a figure on a dancing horse, holding a sword in his right hand. Another figure plays the snare drum, and the horseman dances to the tune of the drum. In some villages the horseman is called "Santiago," who appears to have been the conquistador's patron saint. Thus do the Pueblo people work their history into living ceremonies. In this way, they gain a wry revenge upon their persecutors. One waits to see what the role of the Anglo in Pueblo historic observances will be.

Upon returning to New Spain, Coronado reported on the expedition. They did not find the heralded city of Quivira, nor did they

Santiago painting on hide by Molleno, New Mexico, 1830s. (Courtesy Museum of New Mexico, Museum of International Folk Art Collection.)

discover gold, the primary object of their travels. In fact, the expedition was considered a failure. The Coronado expedition destroyed all hopes that another storehouse of treasure, like that found in the fabulous Aztec country of Mexico, was available in New Mexico. There was no further interest in exploring the northern frontier, and the natives were left undisturbed for the next forty years.

Nevertheless, the Spanish mining frontier slowly edged northward, as prospectors and slave hunters, who toured the outlands seeking native slave labor, heard stories of settled peoples far to the north.

For a slightly different reason, another Franciscan, a lay brother named Augustine Rodriguez, now proposed a missionary expedition into the area in 1581. Two other friars, Juan de Santa Maria and Francisco Lopez, accompanied Rodriguez, with nine soldiers. All were under the command of Francisco Sanchez Chamuscado. The expedition was served by nineteen natives of New Spain. Unlike de Niza and Coronado, the Rodriguez-Chamuscado party took a different route from New Spain to the Pueblo country. They marched directly up the Rio Grande del Norte.

The avowed intent of the friars was neither domination nor plunder, as had been the purpose of their countrymen, but rather by peaceful means to bring the natives to the Catholic church and the Spanish dominion. When the soldiers returned to New Spain, the friars chose to remain behind. However, all these friars were eventually killed by the suspicious natives, who were determined to keep their land inviolate.

When the decision of the three friars to remain in Pueblo country became known in New Spain, the Franciscans immediately began to organize a "rescue party." As a testimony of his devotion to the church, a wealthy mine owner and rancher volunteered to accompany them with an armed escort. He was Antonio de Espejo. In reality, the "volunteer" was a fugitive from the law. He had been charged with two murders in the spring of 1581, and had fled central Mexico, where he owned a mercantile business in Mexico City, and another in Texcoco. In Tacuba he owned a stockyard, where he had a contract to supply meat to the municipal slaughterhouses. From here he escaped to the northern frontier of Nueva Vizcaya, after a preliminary trial in which his uncle was his legal representative. No wonder he was a Johnny-on-the-spot when the friars were planning the rescue journey.

This group also followed the Rio Grande del Norte on their way to the north. They, too, visited most of the pueblos before returning home by a new route, along the Pecos River in eastern New Mexico.

Espejo reported favorably upon conditions on the northern frontier, and petitioned for a contract to lead a colony of settlers into the Pueblo country. His reports led the Spanish Crown to plan a permanent settlement in New Mexico. But before the authorities could act, Gaspar Costano de Sosa, lieutenant governor and captain general of Nuevo Leon, decided to lead a colonizing expedition, to start in 1590.

This party of 160 to 170 persons followed the Pecos River and established headquarters at Cicuye, or Pecos. They also explored all the Rio Grande pueblos and performed one special act entitling them to some sort of fame among present-day Pueblo Indians. They erected a cross at each pueblo, although no churches had yet been built. De Sosa also appointed *alcaldes* (district area leaders or representatives) and *alguacils* (police, constables); the latter are a part of Pueblo civil government today. Since this expedition was unauthorized by the viceroy of New Spain, a military expedition under the command of Captain Juan Morlete was sent after them to New Mexico. Costano de Sosa and his party were arrested and returned to New Spain in 1591. Two years later, the Spaniards Leyva de Bonilla and Antonio Gutierrez de Humana tried to establish a colony at San Ildefonso Pueblo, but Bonilla and his party were killed by Humana. Later, Humana met the same fate at the hands of another, while on an exploring expedition into Llano Estacado (the Staked Plain).

Although the goals of the various ventures were not attained, all the expeditions helped to make possible a more productive colonizing effort for each succeeding group. In 1595, a contract for the colonization of New Mexico was awarded to another wealthy miner, who owned some of the richest ore deposits in New Spain. He was Don Juan de Oñate. He began immediately to recruit prospective settlers, soldiers, and local natives as servants, who generally performed all tasks necessary for expeditions. It was three years before the colonizing party could start the journey north. The group finally left southern Chihuahua on January 15, 1598. Among them was a conglomeration of adventurers whose descendants we will read about in other chapters. They traveled up the Rio Grande del Norte and arrived in the Pueblo country of New Mexico late the same year.

JOURNEY OF JUAN DE OÑATE AND THE
FIRST COLONIZERS,
1598.

Before we proceed with actual events, let us consider a Catholic prophet who had something to say about the history of New Mexico.

In the *Relaciones* by Franciscan Father Geronimo de Zarate y Salmeron, written in 1626 or 1627, the prophecy of Fray Diego de Mercado is quoted. Salmeron was the second missionary to Jemez Pueblo. Mercado is described as "a religious of this seraphic religion, son of the province of the Holy Gospel," who said, as he viewed the troop of people going through the town of Tula, Mexico, when Juan de Oñate was preparing the expedition to settle New Mexico:

> *God certainly does have great riches in these remote*
> *parts of New Mexico, but the present settlers are not to*
> *enjoy them, for God is not keeping these for them; and*
> *so it has been, for all the first people have died without*
> *enjoying them, and amidst great suffering, because they*
> *have always come with these desires and greediness for*
> *riches, which is the reason they went there to settle, and*
> *they spent their fortunes.*

Accompanied by this prophetic warning, the Spaniards departed upon their colonizing venture. They were later expelled from New Mexico by the natives, as we shall see.

It is recorded that eighty-three heavy wheeled oxcarts comprised the supply train, with a herd of several thousand head of stock driven in the rear. As might have been expected, food and water ran short in the inhospitable region. Their way lay across the desert, later to be called, ominously, "Jornado del Muerto" (Journey of Death). Oxcarts stalled in sand-choked dry washes or arroyos. The people were starving. The animals were dying of thirst. Then, like a miracle, from a pueblo in the north along the Rio Grande del Norte, says a legend, help came in the form of the lifesaving gift of corn from the Piro Pueblo Indians. So the Spaniards named the place "Socorro" (succor), a memorial that exists to this day in the form of a town about seventy-five miles south of Albuquerque.

Upon arrival, Oñate met with various Pueblo leaders, requesting permission to settle his people among them. Authentic information is not available about this event, but some literature indicates that Oñate met with the Pueblo leaders in the "Queres" (Keres) country, probably in Santo Domingo. Others say Oñate met with them in the Tewa country north of Santa Fe. It is also said, but without

Jemez Pueblo, ca. 1885. (Photograph by Ben Wittick, courtesy School of American Research Collection in the Museum of New Mexico, Negative No. 16097.)

definite proof, that at this meeting Oñate established the system of civil government for the Pueblos and introduced the Spanish canes that the pueblo governors possess today.

Eventually, Oñate settled his group across the Rio Grande from San Juan Pueblo, which the Tewas called Yunque-Yungeh, and the colonists named San Gabriel. Thus San Gabriel became the first Spanish capital, and remained so for several years, until the next governor moved the capital to Santa Fe in 1610, where it has been ever since.

The Spaniards introduced many new things that were accepted by the Pueblos. Among new food crops were wheat, grapes, fruit, and chile from southern Mexico. They also brought horses, mules, donkeys, goats, sheep, and chickens. It became known very soon, however, that the Spaniards practiced an entirely different religion from that observed by the Pueblos. This provided only mild curiosity among the Pueblo people at first, but matters changed radically when it became perfectly clear that the foreigners intended to force the new religion upon the native people. The padres who accompanied Oñate were immediately assigned to various provinces, where they began the task of constructing many of the churches that continue to be used by the Pueblos after being later rebuilt. The Indians also learned very soon that the foreigners, whom they had accepted as their guests, were introducing an economy completely alien to their way of life.

The Encomienda and Repartimiento Systems

As Edward H. Spicer explains these systems (Spicer 1967), in order to encourage colonization, grants of land were made to soldiers and other colonists who participated in the conquest. These grants, or *encomiendas,* carried with them the right of *repartimiento,* that is, the right to employ Pueblo Indians living near the grants. The produce of Indian labor went to the *encomendero,* recipient of an encomienda. Lands believed not in use by Pueblo Indians, often adjacent to Indian land, were parceled out to the Spaniards. As an example, two interpreters, along with eighteen other Spanish men, were given the Canon de San Diego de Jemez Land Grant. This land grant abuts the north Jemez Pueblo Spanish land grant boundary. About three miles away, on the south boundary, the San Ysidro Land Grant also locks in Jemez Pueblo land and separates it from the aboriginal holdings beyond the San Ysidro grant.

According to the *Recopilacion de leyes de los reynos de las Indias,* the encomenderos were not permitted to live on the lands that they held as encomiendas, but in New Mexico this law was largely ignored. The result, recorded prominently in connection with encomiendas in the vicinity of the Tewa villages north of Santa Fe, was persistent conflict between Spaniards living on their grants, and the Indians; and between the settlers and the missionaries.

The encomienda system required the Pueblos to "donate" proceeds from their farm labors to the Spanish leaders. The Pueblo people often assisted their own leaders through donations of food. Their system of mutual help also involved the practice of helping their own, so that if a family did not have the necessary amount of produce, someone from the extended family loaned them the corn (or later, the wheat) until the next growing season Or labor was exchanged in payment.

The encomienda system, however, exacted tithes (actually taxes) from the Pueblos. Not only were they forced to pay tithes to the church, but they also were compelled to pay the civil leaders in Santa Fe, and the alcaldes in the alcaldias. The fiscales and their aides went about the villages to collect *permitias* after the harvests. During All Saints Day of November 1, the people were invited to bring offerings of wheat and corn to the church, in return for pulling the long rope placed in front of the church that rang the bells or chimes. The fiscales then stored these offerings in the corn bins or wheat storage boxes of the religious for their use during the coming year. Other taxes, in the form of various produce, were imposed for the alcalde and the governor, and were collected by the village governor, who then passed them on to the Spanish governor's agents, to be hauled by two-wheeled oxcarts to Santa Fe. A most serious change in the economy developed when the land was taken for grazing the Spanish cattle. Life in New Mexico, even today, depends upon water. If there is not sufficient snow in the mountains for the annual runoff, or if water is otherwise scarce, the possibilities of drought develop. But the problem did not exist for the Pueblos prior to the coming of the Spanish. Now there was the serious problem of overgrazing and soil erosion; water shortages for their farmlands became a bitter reality.

Spaniards Versus Spaniards

As has been stated by other historians, the Pueblo Indians were ordered to do one thing in the name of the Crown, and to do another in the name of the church; they considered all this and waited patiently for their time to come. Both the civil authorities and the missionaries contributed to a more serious conflict within the Spanish colonial system as it manifested itself in a variety of ways in the province. A few governors accused the missionaries of forcing Pueblo Indians to labor for them on their churches, in their fields, and with their livestock. The missionaries countered with charges that the governors forced Indians to work for them without wages, purely for the governors' profit.

The civil authorities also accused the missionaries of whipping Indians who failed to participate in Christian religious activities. And numerous cases of severe punishment of Indians by the missionaries were brought up in various investigations that took place in New Mexico between 1620 and 1680. Many of the charges were proven, and the governors complained that this was a major cause of the growing unrest. In turn, the missionaries charged that the governors and their aides had not only physically abused Indians but had been guilty of setting bad examples for the Indians by their own immoral behavior; and in some instances evidence was produced to substantiate these charges.

Thus there was corruption among both state and church officials. Governors who were perhaps particularly corrupt were Juan de Eulate (dates of office, 1618–1625); Luis de Rosas (dates of office, 1637–1641); and Diego Dionisio de Penalosa (dates of office, 1661–1664). Rosas was probably the most tyrannical, since Kessell describes him as "a tough, two-fisted, damn-the-hindmost officer who would knock down the man, colonist, or missionary who got in his way" (Kessell 1979, 157).

One priest who was Rosas's equal may have been Fray Isidro Ordonez. He has been described as everything a friar should not have been: personally ambitious, hot-headed, and scheming. Other friars who were as repressive as the governors mentioned were Fray Esteban de Perea (1616–1638?) and Fray Alonso de Posada (1656–1665). It was Posada who forbade Kachina Dances by the Pueblo Indians and ordered the missionaries to seize every mask, prayer stick, and effigy they could lay their hands on and burn them (Kessell 1979, 182).

The new economic system and the forced religious practices became heavy burdens when the Spaniards also began a continuing practice of cruelty, harassment, and punishment for infraction of Spanish religious and secular rules, or for failure to provide the tithes; they dominated all sectors of Pueblo life. Such punitive actions were generally taken against the war captains of the Pueblo villages, who were the overseers of ceremonial and other activities. War chiefs may have been harassed also, but not the medicine men, since Pueblo people do not reveal who these religious people are. Thus did the Spaniards enslave and dominate the Pueblo people and enforce a feudal economic system and religious intolerance, fortified by a system of punishment for transgression. In matters regarding their religion, the Pueblos of the seventeenth century were not much different from those of today. To give up their religion would have been like giving up life itself.

After coexisting for eighty-two years with the Spaniards under an odious system, the Pueblos' patience was finally exhausted. They remembered all the hated experiences they had been subjected to under Spanish domination. The Tiwas remembered the rape of an Indian woman in the Bernalillo area during the first Spanish contact in 1540, when men of the Coronado expedition advance party arrived. The Keresans of Acoma remembered the massacre of 1589 by the nephew of Juan de Oñate, named Vicente.de Zaldivar, who had led a punitive expedition to the pueblo to avenge the killing of his brother, Juan de Zaldivar. Juan had been on a trip in search of the South Sea, when he stopped his troops at Acoma and at tempted to obtain provisions by force.

During his reign the violent and greedy Governor Luis de Rosas (1637–1641) attempted to enslave Apaches living on the plains east of Pecos Pueblo. When he failed to capture them, Rosas slaughtered the Apaches and maliciously created ill feeling between the people of Pecos and the Apaches. In the same spirit, Governor Fernando de Arguello Caravajal (1644–1647) accused the Jemez people of working with Apaches and Navajos against the Spaniards. He hanged twenty-nine Jemez leaders.

The next governor, Hernando de Ugarte (1649–1653), killed nine more leaders, from Jemez, Alameda, and Sandia pueblos (Hackett and Shelby 1942, 299).

Many other, seemingly minor episodes compared to those de-scribed above took place, involving individuals who were not leaders, who suffered silently, unreported and unknown except to their families and the people of their pueblos. Indignity was heaped upon indignity; and the Spaniards became repugnant to the people, for their indifference to human suffering, as well as for their ceaseless demands for produce, labor, and services.

The event that may have accelerated the movement for the revolt that followed these years of Spanish domination probably took place during the reign of Governor Juan Francisco de Trevino (1675–1677).

During his first year as governor, de Trevino accused forty-seven Pueblo people of "sorcery." The men were charged with bewitching the ailing Fray Andres Duran, guardian of San Ildefonso Pueblo, and three other persons. The men were brought to Santa Fe for trial, bound, and subjected to taunts and abuse by the Spaniards. They were also accused of killing seven friars and three Spaniards. They were found guilty, and four of them were condemned to die by hanging. However, one man hanged himself in his cell. The remaining three were taken to their villages and hanged publicly before their people, as an example to the others. These three men were from the Nambe, San Felipe, and Jemez pueblos. The memory of this incident sparked the first flames of revolt; it lives in the hearts of the people even now.

The forty-three others accused as sorcerers were either sentenced to prison, to years if not life servitude, or to lashing (Kessell 1979, 226). Among those enduring the shame of a public whipping was a man from San Juan Pueblo by the name of Popé. It was he who (tradition has it) united the Pueblos in an effort to expel the hated Spaniards, resulting in the first American revolution in 1680. The revolt was planned by the Society of Opi, together with the subordinate war captains.

A Revolt Is Planned

The Spaniards had heard rumors of an impending Pueblo revolt, but could not pinpoint the plan or date for it until two young men from Tesuque, Nicholas Catua and Pedro Omtua, were apprehended bearing a rope with two knots. They were arrested by Maestro de Campo, Francisco Gomez Robledo. The meaning of the rope was the following: A knot was to be untied each morning until the last knot was untied. This was to be the date when the campaign to expel the Spaniards would begin.

Archaeologist David Snow at the first verified site of remains of the 1680 Pueblo Revolt, 1991. (Photograph by Kitty Leaken, courtesy The New Mexican.*)*

Governor Antonio de Otermin had taken precautions to avoid such a conflict. But the Pueblos disclosed that his henchmen, with his secretary, Francisco Xavier, as well as Diego Lopez Sombrano and Luis de Quintana, were traveling from pueblo to pueblo interrogating and harassing the people. These events caused tension on all sides. One critical night, Padre Juan Baptisto Pio, of Tesuque Pueblo, went to Santa Fe for his safety. The next morning, when he returned "to his children," they were not in the village. Presently they appeared in the hills, where Padre Pio went to address them. His soldier-guard saw the padre go into a ravine with the Pueblo leaders. The padre never came out. This was the beginning of the Pueblo struggle to free themselves from the Spanish yoke. Throughout the villages, the padres and the Spaniards were requested to leave the provinces, with assurances that serious consequences were the alternatives. Out of thirty-two religious, twenty-one refused to leave. But many more Spaniards, and a few religious, started a disorganized trek towards the south after gathering at Isleta Pueblo.

In Santa Fe, Governor Otermin attempted to put up resistance. But after a few days, when the natives cut off the water supply, Otermin also decided to leave. The revolt of the Pueblos in 1680 is not generally known to those of the new generation. Descendants of the people involved know little of this spectacular event that, without doubt, was the point of highest drama in the state's history. The date of August 10, 1680, is not celebrated today. Its historic importance is not observed. That is the date when the Pueblo tribal religious leaders united and expelled the Spaniards, who were trying to force their religion and economic slavery upon the people. What we can observe in retrospect is that, although Ruth Benedict, in her book *Patterns of Culture,* classifies the Pueblos as predominantly peaceful in nature, the Pueblo people will defend themselves and have in the past. Their main political weapons have been organization, alliance, effective tribal policies, and good faith.

In the following year, 1681, Otermin made a fast trip through the Pueblo country, in an attempt to determine the causes of the revolt and to learn who its leaders were. Some of the captives he took gave him an answer. Their response is still related as a legendary joke. The Spanish governor interrogated some captured Pueblo men and demanded, "Tell me, who was the leader of the revolt?" A Keresan captive replied, "Oh, it was Payastiamo." The governor asked further, "Where does he live?" The Keresan said, "Over that

Sandia Pueblo, ca. 1880. (Photograph by John K. Hillers, courtesy Museum of New Mexico, Negative No. 3371.)

way," pointing towards the mountains. A Tewa or Tano man responded to the same question, saying, "The leader's name is Poheyemo. He lives up that way," pointing in another direction towards the mountains in the north. A Towa man replied, "His name is Payastiabo, and he lives up that way," pointing in another direction towards the mountains. The joke consists of the fact that these three names, Payastiamo, Poheyemo, and Payastiabo, are the names of deities whom the Pueblos address in their prayers to intercede for them with the One above beyond the clouds. He generally lives to the north, in the highest mountain, or in the clouds. But the Spaniards concluded that he was indeed the leader of the revolt.

Otermin was able to report a significant "accomplishment," however; he ordered and carried out the burning of Sandia Pueblo. It was then that the Sandia people, forced to abandon their village, went to the Hopi country. They did not return until the 1740s, some sixty years following the merciless sacking of their homes. The year 1681 is burned into their historic memory.

Seven years later, in 1688, the new governor (in absentia), Pedro Reneros de Posada, made another foray into the Pueblo country with a similar purpose, but this expedition also failed to obtain the names of leaders or particulars of the revolt. However, the Spaniards continued to plunder, kill, and burn the Pueblo villages.

The following year, in 1689, still another governor visited the Pueblos. He was Domingo Jironza Petriz de Cruzate. He also managed to destroy Pueblo villages, and forced the Zia people to flee their homes to a place west of present-day Jemez Pueblo. This time he picked up a Zia man, Bartolome de Ojeda, who became a valuable informant to the Spaniards. Upon Cruzate's return to Guadalupe del Paso that fall, he decided to issue land grants to the pueblos. With Ojeda testifying as to the loyalty of the various pueblos to the Crown, Cruzate distributed the land grants. He had been given authority by Spain as early as 1684 to make these grants. This strange spectacle, of "conquerors" who had been evicted making gifts of parcels of land belonging to their victims, can only be explained by the fact that the Spaniards had not given up their efforts to colonize the land owned by the Pueblo people.

The following is conjectural, but it is probable that Ojeda returned to his pueblo after the land grants were distributed, and began a campaign for the return of the Spaniards to New Mexico.

In explaining the Spanish view of the Pueblo Revolt, historical literature generally credits the San Juan Pueblo man Popé as the leader. However, as in most Pueblo endeavors, there were representatives from each village who helped plan and execute the revolt. Popé may have been Po-'png (pumpkin mountain), of San Juan, who was only one of the leaders. The Spaniards themselves had appointed Luis Tupatu of Picuris as their official interpreter and friend, in the area of Santa Fe or Rio Arriba. In the Rio Abajo area there was Antonio Malacate, a Keresan from La Cienega de Cochiti. With them were representatives, many of whom were "coyotes," "mestizos," and "ladinos," who could speak Spanish. Among the known half-breeds were Francisco El Ollita from San Ildefonso, Alonzo Catiti from Santo Domingo, and Domingo Naranjo from Santa Clara. Naranjo was not even a Pueblo; it is believed his parents had settled near Santa Clara after arriving in the area with the Oñate expedition of colonizers in 1598.

Naranjo's father was a black man, an ex-slave who had been included in the household of a soldier, Juan Bautista Ruano, who did not remain in New Mexico. His mother was a Tlascaltec Indian of New Spain, who entered as a servant of Juana de los Reyes, the wife of an original New Mexico settler of the Alonso Martinez family. He was also referred to as Alonso Martin Naranjo. Other leaders were El Jaca (or Saca) from Taos; Lorenzo, the brother of Luis Tupatu, from Picuris; Nicolas Jonva from San Ildefonso; Domingo Romero from Tesuque; Antonio Bolsas from Santa Fe; Crisobal Yope from San Lazaro; many other men of courage from the Jemez area; the Tanos south of Santa Fe and Tewas from Jacona, Pojoaque, and Nambe; and, of course, the Keresans of Rio Abajo.

The Pueblos did not mourn the departure of the Spaniards. The churches were destroyed and left to the elements to deteriorate. And the people began again to practice their religious observances in peace. But this euphoric situation did not last very long. Intersociety quarrels developed, and some societies were expelled from villages due to personality friction or the actions of some men. Native legends relate that there was a movement of society men and their families to other areas. Besides the intersociety quarrels, another more serious danger was the increase of plundering by the Apaches and Navajos, who were now on horseback. The Spaniards, with their horses and guns, had been a deterrent to the marauders. Now the Pueblos were at the mercy of the raiders. Dry years were the most difficult for all the people in the Southwest. Food became scarce; famine was a certainty; and these were the years when the raids became more and more frequent. Special precautions were taken to protect the Pueblos' food supplies and even their women and children.

By 1691 or 1692, a group of Pueblo men from Jemez, Zia, Santa Ana, San Felipe, Pecos, and some Tanos went to Guadalupe del Paso to parley with the deposed Spaniards. According to tribal history, these Pueblo men invited the Spaniards to return.

At a convent not far from Puebla, Mexico, where he was the superior, Fray Juan de Escalona was praying during the ringing of the Ave Maria. When the prayer was ended, all the religious stood up except the holy man de Escalona, who remained in prayer, carried away in spirit during the Ave Maria. After a while, the other religious observed that he began to cry out, saying, "Beati primi, Beati primi" (blessed are the first).

The holy man said no more. When the ecstasy was over, the religious asked what those voices had been. But he refused to speak. The next day, when de Escalona was going to confession, his confessor begged him earnestly, under the protection of confessional, to tell what those voices of the day before had been. De Escalona replied, "Under the condition, my dear Father, that as long as I live, no one will know about this, I will tell you." The confessor gave his word, so de Escalona said:

> Yesterday afternoon, when we were praying the Ave Maria, God our Lord revealed to me all the riches and worldly possessions that he is keeping in the interior land of New Mexico to the north. It was also revealed to me that some religious of my father, Saint Francis, are to explore it. And as the first ones who will enter there, they are to be martyred. These religious appeared before me and I saw them being martyred in spirit, and because I was joyful to see them suffer martyrdom with so much spirit and courage, I said, "Beati primi, Beati primi." It was also revealed to me that when this happens and after that land is sprinkled with the blood of these martyrs, the Spaniards will go in there to enjoy the many riches that are there.

69

Return of the Spanish

Twelve years later, after twenty-one friars and a number of Spanish families had been killed during the Pueblo Revolt, the Spaniards were back to enjoy "the many riches" that were there. There were further clashes with the natives in 1694 and 1696, but the Spaniards were never again expelled. The fate of Fray Juan de Escalona is described in the following manner:

> *And this holy man, Fray Juan de Escalona, with this good desire entered New Mexico with the second expedition of religious who came during the time of Juan de Oñate, and he began baptism in the Pueblo of Santo Domingo on the banks of the Rio del Norte (Rio Grande), among Indians of the Keres nation, and in which pueblo he ended the days of his life as a saint* (Salmeron 1966, 100).

Bolstered with the knowledge that there were some Pueblo leaders seeking their return to the scene of their eviction twelve years ago, General de Vargas left Guadalupe del Paso on August 16, 1692. There were with him one hundred native allies, including Piros from Socorro and Senecu, and Isletas who had fled with the Spaniards in 1680. Their descendants still live at Ysleta, Texas, today.

During a four-month campaign, General de Vargas restored to the Crown twenty-three Pueblo villages, while the padres baptized 2,214 Pueblo natives, mostly children. De Vargas boasted that he performed this feat "without wasting a single ounce of powder, unsheathing a sword, or without costing the Royal Treasury a single maravedi," [*sic*]. All this he compared to Cruzate's expedition of 1689, when at the one village of Zia he lost six soldiers and killed many *Ziaros,* with the result that the survivors all became hostile, while costing the Crown three thousand pesos.

General de Vargas entered Santa Fe on September 14, 1692. From Santa Fe, he went about the pueblos, up and down the Rio Grande. At this time the Zias were still atop Cerro Colorado, a site two miles west of Jemez Pueblo today. They had fled their home after Cruzate burned and destroyed it in 1689. After visiting the Zias, de Vargas and his troops went to visit the Jemez on top of San Diego Mesa. They were received by three hundred armed warriors who mingled unafraid among the Spaniards. The Jemez warriors threw dirt in their eyes, and when Captain Roque de

Madrid told them to desist, they said it was only in the spirit of rejoicing. The general returned to Guadalupe del Paso on December 20, 1692, after visiting all the Pueblos, including the Hopis.

Plans were made at once to return the colonists to New Mexico. When de Vargas returned in 1693, seventy families, among them twenty-seven blacks, traveled with the Pueblo men in the advance group, to pave the way for the colonists and de Vargas. The Pueblo group, under the leadership of the Zia man Ojeda, carried with them rosaries that they presented to the Pueblo leaders and a letter that they interpreted for them. The letter read:

> *Jesus and Mary. My son and beloved Brother. This is to notify you that I am near and about to enter your city. I am very desirous to greet you and all those sons to whom you will make known my message. Tell everyone that the friars and all the Spaniards and many others who they do not know are coming with their wives and children and that consequently they should be very happy for they will live happily with the Blessed Virgin, our Lady and our Mother, and with God. My son, may he spare you many seasons. As a sign of my love I send you a rosary.*
>
>

Don Diego de Vargas
Zapata Lujan Ponce de Leon

The return of the Spaniards caused more uprisings among the Pueblos. However, much of the unity that had existed earlier was gone. While some Pueblos still resisted the Spaniards, others cooperated with them. The Spaniards had returned for good. A period of turmoil ensued, in which many Pueblos refused to support the Spaniards. In one situation there was considerable misunderstanding between the Jemez and their Keresan neighbors of Zia and Santa Ana, during 1693 and 1694. This was principally due to the Keresans' fidelity to the Spaniards. In 1693, de Vargas visited the Jemez province to show his support of the Keresans. During this visit, the padres baptized one hundred and seventeen children. Despite this visit, the Jemez continued to oppose the Keresans and raid their livestock. After four Zia men and one Jemez man were killed, de Vargas made a punitive foray against Jemez. On July 21, 1694, one hundred and twenty Spaniards, with Zia, San Felipe, and Santa Ana auxiliaries, arrived in the Jemez country and camped at the confluence of the two canyons, the San Diego and the Guadalupe, below Pato-kwa, a Jemez village.

On July 24 they stormed the San Diego Mesa with Brother Eusebio de Vargas in charge of twenty Spanish soldiers and some of the Keresan warriors. They were to go up to the San Diego Gorge and climb the mesa up a steep trail in the rear of the highest plateau. Meanwhile, Governor Diego de Vargas, with another military group, was to climb from the southwest, on the Guadalupe Canyon side, near Pe-buli-kwa, a Jemez village.

The strategy, bolstered by the use of firearms, succeeded only after a desperate engagement. Three hundred and sixty-one women and children were captured, and eighty-four Jemez were killed, of whom five were burned to death and seven were lost down the cliffs. According to Jemez legend, it was probably during this attack on the Jemez in the summer of 1694 that some people jumped over the cliffs to avoid capture. Following this event, a likeness of San Diego soon appeared on the cliff. After that, those who jumped landed on their feet, and did not die. The likeness of San Diego is still visible today on the red rock cliffs on San Diego Mesa, facing east, midpoint between Jemez Springs and the southern point of the high mesa. It is especially visible from mid-morning until near noon.

The conquerors camped at A-stio-la-kwa, and remained upon the mesa for sixteen days, to remove the stores of booty as well as the women and children captives. After destroying the villages at the mesa's summit, de Vargas and his troops descended to Pato-kwa, then to Walatowa, and finally returned to Santa Fe. At Walatowa, two Indian informants told de Vargas of the fate of Fray Juan de Jesus Morador on August 10, 1680. De Vargas located and exhumed the remains of Fray Juan. Of the booty collected at Jemez, the greatest portion of nearly five hundred bushels of corn was given to the Keresans who had helped de Vargas. One hundred and six of the one hundred and seventy-five head of cattle were given to Fray Juan de Alpuente for his use at the Zia mission. Loaded mule trains of Jemez booty went to San Felipe Pueblo; from there it was relayed in oxcarts to Santa Fe.

On August 8, the prisoners were taken to Santa Fe. Six days later a few He'mish (Jemez) leaders came to Santa Fe to appeal for mercy for their families. They were told to return to their old pueblo of Walatowa (Jemez Pueblo) and rebuild their church. To prove their good faith, the Jemez were asked to assist the Spaniards in their battle with the Tewas and Tanos. After helping to conquer the

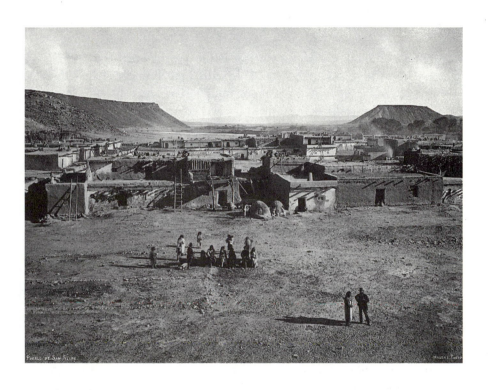

San Felipe Pueblo, ca. 1880. (Photograph by John K. Hillers, courtesy Museum of New Mexico, Negative No. 16094.)

Tewas at Black Mesa, north of San Ildefonso, the prisoners were pardoned. On September 11, 1694, the former prisoners returned to their homes at A-stio-la-kwa, on San Diego Mesa.

The Revolt Continues

Those who survived the burning of Jemez Pueblo probably scattered to the other villages, most of them returning to Walatowa.

The village was then occupied, with Fray Francisco de Jesus Maria Casano as representative of the church. The following year, in 1695, the residents of A-stio-la-kwa completed their move to Walatowa. This bloody experience only promised that the future was to be filled with even more bloodshed as well as intrigue. On June 4, 1696, Fray Francisco was killed. Anticipating another punitive expedition by the Spaniards, the people returned to the mesa. From there they sent to other tribes for help: to Indians at Acoma and Zuni, and to the Navajos. A few days later, Luis Cunixu of A-stio-la-kwa (Jemez) arrived at Pecos Pueblo carrying a reliquary, the property of the slain Fray Francisco. Another unlucky visitor at Pecos was Diego Xenome of Nambe. Because they were suspected as rebels, the Pecos Governor Felipe Chistoe took them to Santa Fe, where they were tried. They were summarily sentenced and each killed by three shots from an arquebus (Kessell 1979, 289).

On the same date of June 4, 1696, when the Jemez killed the missionary priest, other pueblos along the Rio Grande rose in rebellion once more. It was rumored to be another general uprising. The story was that Acoma and the Hopis were coming to the aid of the Rio Grande pueblos.

At San Cristobal Pueblo, which was south of Santa Fe, the Tanos, or southern Tewas, killed their friar, Jose Arbizu, along with his visitor, Fray Antonio Carbonel of Taos Pueblo. At San Ildefonso Pueblo Fray Francisco de Corbera and his visitor Fray Antonio Moreno of Nambe Pueblo were killed, along with four Spaniards who had accompanied Moreno.

Then on June 29, there was a struggle in San Diego Canyon in the Jemez area. Captain Miguel de Lara, stationed at Zia, together with the alcalde mayor of Bernalillo, attacked the Jemez, Acoma, Zuni, and Navajo warriors. Thirty-two Indians were killed; among them were eight Acomas, but no Zunis or Navajos. The Pueblo warriors returned home, and after this the Jemez dispersed. In August, Captain de Lara reconnoitered the area and found it deserted.

At this time, some of the Jemez returned to their ancestral homeland in the northwest, in Canyon Largo and Stone Canyon (Gy'a-wahmu). Others went to An-yu-kwi-nu (Lion Standing Place), to the west of Jemez in the Navajo country. These people lived among the Navajos for a considerable number of years. Many also escaped to the Hopi country (Sando 1982, 121).

The revolt lasted until the end of July, with the battle of El Embudo occurring on July 23. The end came when Lucas Naranjo of Santa Clara Pueblo, the leader of the rebels, was shot by a Spaniard, Antonio Cisneros, in the Adam's apple, and the bullet came out by the nape of his neck (Espinosa 1988, 278). When Naranjo fell, Cisneros decapitated him and carried off his head to Santa Fe to Governor de Vargas. But that was not enough; a Pecos soldier also removed one of Naranjo's hands to take to his governor, Felipe Chistoe. Lucas was the brother of Joseph Naranjo, whose biography is covered in a following chapter in this book.

It was a horrendous time for all involved, the Spaniards and the Pueblo Indians. It was Pueblos against Pueblos, even brothers against brothers, like the Naranjos. Friendly with the Spaniards were San Felipe, Santa Ana, and Zia pueblos, under the leadership of Bartolome de Ojeda of Zia; and Tesuque, under their Governor Domingo Romero Yuguaque, often listed as just Domingo Romero in many reports. Pecos was on both sides; the pro-Spanish faction was led by Governor Felipe Chistoe, who hung the Pecos cacique along with War Captain Cachina and two lieutenants. A fifth one called Caripicado (Pock Face) escaped but was later executed (Kessell 1979, 289).

Following the Pueblos' defeat, the Picuris, led by their able leader Luis Tupatu, joined their traditional friends, the Jicarilla Apaches, at Cuartolejo, east of Pueblo, Colorado—today in western Kansas. They were later returned through the efforts of Acting Governor Francisco Cuervo y Valdez. Cuervo had been serving as governor until a governor appointed by Spain, Admiral Jose Chacon, was to arrive in New Spain. Cuervo was appointed in Mexico by the viceroy, a practice common before the reconquest in 1692.

Meanwhile, the Pueblo leaders who carried out the Pueblo Revolt of 1680 no longer remained in power, and the new leadership no longer entertained another revolt. However, mistreatment of Indians continued. This was due to the lack of discipline and formal military training of the soldiers who served on New Spain's northern frontier.

Encomienda appeared to be a thing of the past. However, repartimiento, in a different form, continued to be a source of friction. Although the viceroy had emphasized that the services performed by the Indians had to be voluntary and remunerated, the practice continued. The Franciscan friars reported to the viceroy there was information to indicate that Indians were forced to go to the governor's palace and perform personal services, and that every year in their pueblos they had to plant an allotted area in wheat and corn for the governor and the alcaldes mayores. After harvesting the crop, the Indians transported it to the officers' warehouses. The viceroy wrote to Governor Chacon indicating that due to this kind of employment, the Indians' own fields were not properly attended and the economy of the province was adversely affected (Flagler 1990, 467). One consolation for the Pueblo Indians was that, as a result of this, suppression of religious ceremonies was less evident.

For the Spaniards, a continuing problem was expressed by governors and military officers after the 1680 expulsion, that the province was faced with three basic problems: insufficient military supplies, Apache-Navajo raids, and the source of resistance represented by the Hopis, who refused Spanish help and Franciscan missionaries, and encouraged the New Mexico Pueblo Indians to resist (Flagler 1990, 471).

By the end of 1696, Governor de Vargas was able to secure the submission of all the Pueblos. They were now reduced in numbers because of the flight of many of their people to other areas, as well as by those killed in action. Those who remained submitted to de Vargas and became allies of the Spanish.

Following these episodes, the remaining Pueblos settled down to outwardly peaceful relations with the Spaniards. While de Vargas's methods in pacifying the Pueblos were severe and brutal, he managed to convince the Pueblo leadership to enter into an alliance with the Spanish colonists in defending their villages and farmlands against Indian raiders.

New friends of the Spanish governor who were interpreters, such as Ojeda of Zia and Naranjo, aided him in controlling the Pueblos. The Franciscans and the civil authorities improved their treatment of the Pueblo people in the succeeding century. The harsh, coercive policies gradually gave way to more humane treatment of the Indians, as both the Spanish and the Pueblos made accommodations

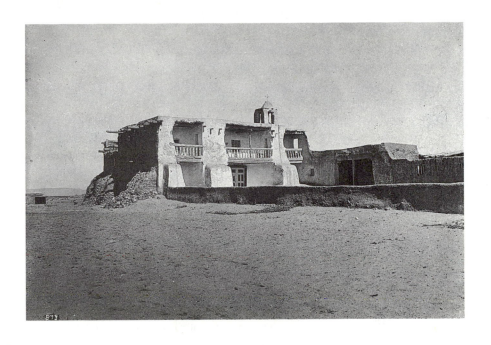

Mission, Santa Ana Pueblo, ca. 1899. (Photograph by Adam Clark Vroman, courtesy Museum of New Mexico, Negative No. 12431.)

economically, culturally, and through intermarriage.

Apparently, as a result of some of the atrocities committed against the Pueblos and his stern rule of the colonists, Governor de Vargas was imprisoned for a time and replaced by Don Pedro Rodriguez Cubero. Cubero became governor in July 1697, when de Vargas's five-year appointment was not renewed. He was fully exonerated of the charges later, however. In 1703, he again resumed his post as governor of New Mexico.

While the forced labor program of the Spanish civil authorities had taken a large toll of Pueblo lives, much of the population loss resulted from migration or flight to the Apache, Hopi, and Navajo tribes. There was also movement into the villages of the Spanish colonists. This was brought about not only by the recruitment of servants for Spanish households, but also by the addition of Hispanicized Pueblo Indians, who, through the efforts of the missionaries, became converts to the new religion and culture, and preferred to live with the settlers.

By the year 1700, the number of Pueblo villages had been drastically reduced. All the Piro settlements were deserted by the end of the century. The Jemez people of the scattered Jemez villages throughout the stronghold of the Jemez Mountains began to migrate to Walatowa. The Tano villages along the Galisteo Basin south of Santa Fe had been abandoned. During the Pueblo Revolt of 1680, de Vargas had executed a number of these villagers, distributed others among the colonists as servants, and sent the rest to live among the Tewas, who were linguistic relatives.

Pueblo resentment of the clergy and the civil authorities remained, however, even after a degree of normalcy was established following the armed clashes. Animosity towards the clergy arose from the strict mission discipline. While there were no longer such large-scale mission building programs as that of the pre-revolt era, repair and maintenance of the missions were now required.

The sacred ceremonial dances were driven underground. Many of these dances at various villages were performed away from the village, usually in a secluded area where guards could be posted. Others held their dances in the kivas at night, and the war captains kept a strict guard.

During this time, no serious attempt was made to compel the Pueblos to cease their native ceremonies, and there is no record of further destruction of sacred paraphernalia or kivas. On the other hand, it may be surprising to note that the custodio and a number of missionaries were supporting not only the right of the Pueblos to bear firearms, but also the Pueblo warriors' right to paint their faces while fighting enemy raiding tribes. Both of these matters were raised in a special meeting called by Governor Flores Mogollon in 1714. The governor and a majority of the settlers opposed the custodio, Fray Juan de Tagle, and priests from Pecos, Santo Domingo, Cochiti, Jemez, Laguna, Santa Clara, and Taos. The custodio insisted that the Pueblos needed the arms to protect themselves. As for painting their faces, the priest pointed out that the Pueblo custom was no different than the practice of the Spaniards, who often painted themselves and put feathers in their hats to wear in church.

A New Alliance

With increased pillaging of both Spanish and Pueblo Indian areas by Indian raiders, the Spanish authorities now attempted to bring the Pueblos into an alliance with the provincial government. A "protector general" of the Pueblo Indians was appointed by Governor Francisco Cuervo Valdez on January 6, 1706, at a meeting in Santa Fe. At that time, Captain Alfonso Rael de Aguilar was introduced to a gathering of influential Pueblos. The practice then began of inviting all newly elected pueblo governors to come to Santa Fe to meet with the provincial governor and to receive official recognition. All the pueblo governors and other leaders, except the Hopis, were present at the January meeting. Don Domingo Romero, governor of Tesuque, and the capitan de la guerra of all the Christian Indian nations of New Mexico were also there and addressed the meeting in good Castilian, as did many of the others, while a few used interpreters. Another purpose of the meeting was to cement the good relations between Spanish authorities and the Pueblos.

And so the alliance between conquerors and conquered was made firm. It lasted until the end of the eighteenth century. Recognition of the new alliance was celebrated with victory dances by both Pueblos and Spaniards. These victory dances are today called Scalp Dances, or Chief Dances; in them a male dancer is dressed as a chief and is followed by a female dancer. The male dancer's family gives away many gifts to the female dancer and throws basketloads of food, household items, and fruit to the singers and to the public. There are four or more of these dancers who perform two

79

at a time, one male and one female, and they all give away or throw to the crowd both goods and food, as a symbol of sacrifice and thanksgiving for the safe return from the campaign against raiding tribes. In order to illustrate some of the ignorance existing today about Pueblo tribal history, a recent incident at a pueblo follows: A Scalp Dance was in progress at a village, and the usual young aides were on patrol around the village. A Spanish man approached the village in hopes of viewing the Scalp Dance. He was turned away as a non-Indian. The Spanish man represented a former ally with whom these dances or victory celebrations were formerly held. Yet, at this same Scalp Dance, a Navajo who represented the former enemy for whom the dances were performed, was left undisturbed and allowed to remain.

As a result of the alliance, we see the Pueblos in the eighteenth and early nineteenth centuries not simply involved in defensive activities, but accompanying Spanish soldiers and settlers in campaigns against the Indian raiders. As the Spanish documents of those times attest, the Pueblos became dependable and courageous warriors. Some chroniclers even indicate that Spanish military leaders reported that the Pueblos were better fighters than the settlers. During the remainder of Spanish rule, every major Spanish retaliatory or punitive expedition against the Apache, Navajo, and Comanche tribes contained Pueblo Indian auxiliaries, usually commanded by a Pueblo leader-interpreter, who bore the title "capitan de la guerra." In these campaigns the number of Pueblo Indians usually exceeded the number of regular soldiers and the men recruited from among the settlers.

Two other men appeared most frequently as capable leaders in the campaigns against the Indian enemies. They were Domingo Romero of Tesuque, and Don Felipe Chisto of Pecos. By 1729, there was no longer any fear of Pueblo Indian uprisings, as unity among the natives and the Spanish became established. The Pueblos furnished numerous forms of assistance, such as scouts, interpreters, and informants, descriptions of terrain, reports of weather, a ready supply of foods and equipment, and their effective fighting techniques, as well as their willingness to offer their villages as rendezvous points for military campaigns. Just as the Apache scouts served to capture the few renegade Apaches, so did the Pueblo auxiliaries serve as the most reliable element in the pacification of hostile tribes and the defense of New Mexico during the eighteenth century. In contrast, as one can gather from the reports of early Spanish governors, from de Vargas to La Concha, the militia in Santa Fe was unreliable, poorly equipped, and often untrained and undisciplined.

One explanation seems appropriate here. The Pueblo people were unique in their peaceful nature before the Spanish conquest, and certainly before the alliance with the Spaniards. Their way of life precluded warfare and conflict. They were hospitable, friendly, and always preoccupied with their agricultural pursuits and their religious observances. During the period of defending themselves against neighboring Indian raiders, they learned the arts of military action, and became as good at warfare as they had been in the pursuit of peace. A false image of the Pueblos as being passive and docile has emerged, as a result of inaccurate books and misinterpretations found in the textbooks. Warfare became an important activity when the Pueblos needed it.

The Spanish-Pueblo alliance also provided New Mexico with unique characteristics that are spreading to other southwestern areas. One unique New Mexico feature still in existence today is the architecture produced by the alliance, which is a combination of the Pueblo style and the Spanish colonial adobe home style. This is only one example of the heritage of the political and cultural alliance that grew with time following the last of the revolts—only to end with the dissolution of the Spanish regime and the emergence of Mexico as an independent nation in 1824.

Santa Clara Pueblo, 1880. (Photograph by John K. Hillers, courtesy Museum of New Mexico, Negative No. 42780.)

❧ 4 ❧

The United States in Pueblo History

AS AN INTRODUCTION to the role of the United States in Pueblo history, we turn to the second nation under whose flag the Pueblo Indians lived. Mexico declared its independence and took possession of the Spanish southwestern domain in 1821. But Mexican influence in Indian life consisted largely of confusing Indian land title, ignoring the illegal taking of Pueblo land, and responding passively when Indian boundaries were violated. Thus were twenty-five years under the rule of Mexico spent. The Indian people were bent on the task of protecting their frontiers, with frustration and disappointment at every turn. They saw squatters on their land, with no protection and no relief from the depredations they wrought. Their landholdings diminished. Under the circumstances it was small consolation to be left undisturbed. However, the new Mexican government, in intent and policy at least, recognized the laws of Spain as they applied to the Pueblo Indians. But the revolutionary government of Mexico, inspired by the desire to institute a system of democracy for all, adopted a body of law that was to cloud the issue of Pueblo rights for nearly a hundred years. A short time before Mexico declared its independence from Spain, the revolutionaries proclaimed the Plan of Iguala (named for the place of the revolutionary army headquarters). The plan stated: "That all the inhabitants of New Spain without distinction, whether Europeans, Africans, or Indians, are citizens of this monarchy, with the right to be employed in any post according to their merit and virtues and that the person and property of every citizen will be respected by the government."

The Plan of Iguala

The declaration was followed, after independence, by the adoption by the Mexican Congress of at least four acts confirming the plan as a principle of Mexican jurisprudence. The doctrine of equal rights, so proudly proclaimed by the revolutionary government, soon became the right for all equally to take Pueblo land. In one of the acts calculated to strengthen the plan, it was announced that "in registration of citizens, classification of them with regard to their origin shall be omitted. . . ."

The contradictions developed by this policy soon became apparent. For, if the Indians were to be accorded the "rights" of all citizens, then they had the right to sell or encumber their land, and others had the right to buy, lease, or use Indian land as collateral, and otherwise reduce or destroy Indian land ownership. As it turned out, corrupt administrators and politicians falsified documents, produced fraudulent titles to land owned by Indians, and were able to alienate Pueblo land, often without the Indians even knowing about it. The protection accorded the Pueblos by Spain, and adopted by the new government of Mexico, was nearly destroyed as a result of this policy. Soon there was a whole array of cases to be decided by the Mexican judicial authorities. According to Herbert O. Brayer, some "items of interest" began to be discussed in journals of the provincial assembly, involving "efforts of the people to secure title to some" of the Pueblo lands. Laxity in enforcement of the laws and the actions of corrupt officials "led to a great many cases of illegal alienation of lands" (Brayer 1939).

The new government of Mexico had other and more pressing problems. Besides the internal difficulties, involving the struggle for power between political factions, Mexico had to be constantly aware of the United States as a threat to its southwestern possessions. The Pueblos received little attention. The ceremonies of the people were held, religion was strengthened, the people planted their corn, harvested their crops, worried about the water supply, and maintained the traditional family life. Clan ties were strengthened, and the ancient customs began to take on new life.

The struggle against church domination then taking place in Mexico bypassed the Pueblos. However, as a result of this struggle, missionary zeal decreased. Catholic church influence waned, while the symbolic church ceremonies and fiestas remained as an adopted part of the colorful Pueblo native ceremonialism. The church, locked in a struggle with the Mexican civil and political factions, was to awaken one year to be accused of "neglect" of its children, the Pueblo Indians. The concept of separation of church and state is alien to the Pueblo philosophy. This doctrine became important with the growth of power for the few, poverty for the many, and the development of a church oligarchy possessing immense riches and exercising political power as a state above the state. Such an oligarchy does not exist among the Pueblos.

By the time of the Pueblo Revolt, Spain had established an autocratic governing structure and a feudal economy based on tithes to the church, taxes to the secular and military echelons of the dominant class, and forced labor for the support of the whole Spanish superstructure.

Religious doctrine and observances were rigidly and harshly suppressed, just as they were, more than two hundred years later, by the United States Government. Disobedience was punished, as it was later by the United States. Homes were raided for evidence of religious paraphernalia, as was done also by the Anglo-Americans after 1846. Feathers used in the beautiful Pueblo dance attire and as headdresses during religious services were confiscated, and punishment was meted out to the offenders.

When Mexican independence was declared, Spanish power in the world was already in a state of decline. But the new nation had to contend with a growing, blustering, power-hungry, and land-hungry United States, bent on expansion. The war with Mexico ended in 1846. Now the Pueblos were to be confronted with a new and more difficult situation. For more than a hundred and twenty-five years they would contend with cultural and political conflicts that would have drained the energies of any people. There was no question now of fighting "the intruders" and successfully evicting them from Indian land, as the Indian revolutionaries of 1680 had done. Nor was it possible to effect an alliance as they had done with the Spanish at the beginning of the eighteenth century, to provide some type of peaceful coexistence between the Pueblos and the Anglos. Of understanding there was none. Of misconception and error in judgment there was a vast quantity. And corrupt officials continued to ply their trade. The United States laid a heavy hand on Pueblo life, religion, economy, and culture.

The Anglo-Americans had already found their way into New Mexico in the years preceding the separation of Mexico from Spain. Lieutenant Zebulon Pike was the most prominent of those few who penetrated the Spanish domain in New Mexico. He claimed to have lost his way when he arrived in 1806–1807. After his capture by the Spaniards, he and his companions were escorted down the Rio Grande and on to Mexico. Like those of the original Spanish adventurers, Pike's reports attracted a good many Americans, especially traders, land-hungry settlers and merchants, and trappers. General Stephen Watts Kearny took possession of New Mexico on August

85

11, 1846. Kearny established civil government in the Territory, organ-ized courts, appointed judges, and convened a legislative body. In December 1847, the Territorial Assembly passed an act titled "Indians." Under this act the pueblos were determined to be "constituted bodies politic and corporate," with the right to sue and be sued, and to have "perpetual succession" in their pueblos. They had the right "to resist any encroachment, claim, or trespass" upon their lands or possessions. This act also refers to the Pueblo Indians as "living in towns and villages built on lands granted to such Indians by the laws of Spain and Mexico." Thus was the fantasy perpetuated, whereby the Pueblo people were not recog-nized as original owners and occupants of their vast southwestern region. But the Territorial Government established by Kearny did recognize the special role accorded the Pueblos under Spanish and Mexican law.

The Treaty of Guadalupe Hidalgo

Formally ending the war between the United States and Mexico, the Treaty of Guadalupe Hidalgo was signed February 2, 1848, ratified May 30, 1848, and proclaimed July 4, 1848. By Article 8 of this treaty the residents of New Mexico were given the choice of retaining their Mexican citizenship by declaring their intention to do so within a year from the date of exchange of ratifications. And, the treaty stated, "those who shall remain in the said territories after the expiration of that year, without having declared their intention to retain the character of Mexicans, shall be considered to have elected to become citizens of the United States." Not a single Pueblo Indian elected to retain Mexican citizenship. Section 9 of the treaty also promised that *eventually* "all the rights of citizens of the United States" would be theirs. *Immediately* upon ratification of the treaty, however, they were to have "free enjoyment of their liberty and property."

Clarity of purpose is certainly expressed in the language of the treaty. For some years after the end of the war, the Pueblos were again left undisturbed, and the Territorial Government enacted legislation concerning Pueblo matters "with such congressional approval as was given by silence" (Cohen 1942). A curious situation now developed. Questions such as these were asked: Are the Pueblo people Indians? Do the Pueblo people have the right to protection

86

San Ildefonso Pueblo, ca. 1912. (Photograph by Carlos Vierra, courtesy Museum of New Mexico, Negative No. 42180.)

under United States law, as Indians? These questions plagued both the Congress and the Pueblo people, as they were shuttled from one lawsuit to another in their persistent struggle to endure as the oldest continuous native inhabitants of North America. During the process of these lawsuits, there were some descriptions of Pueblo life and culture that bear repeating. Indeed, these statements express the strange climate of those years, as the Pueblos won respect and admiration, but were deprived of rights accorded other tribes in the United States.

In rendering a decision that, in effect, deprived the Pueblo Indians of protection of the law making it a federal offense to trespass on tribal lands, the Court stated, with humanitarian fervor, that it would be improper to consign the Pueblo people to the same set of laws and trade "made for wandering savages and administered by the agents of the Indian government." The Pueblo Indians are described as "the most law-abiding, sober, and industrious people of New Mexico." To this adverse decision was added a personal observation:

> *This court has known the conduct and habits of these Indians for eighteen or twenty years, and we say, without the fear of successful contradiction, that you may pick out one thousand of the best Americans in New Mexico, and one thousand of the worst Pueblo Indians, and there will be found less, vastly less, murder, robbery, theft, or other crimes among a thousand of the worst Pueblo Indians than among a thousand of the best Mexicans or Americans in New Mexico.*

Adding some practical information to these complimentary remarks, the justice said that during twenty years "not twenty Pueblo Indians have been brought before the courts in New Mexico, accused of violation of the criminal laws of this Territory."

The judge referred to the Indians of the United States, in this decision, as "wild, wandering savages," a state that certainly could not describe the Pueblo Indians, in his opinion. The Pueblos, said the judge, are a people that have been "living for three centuries in fenced abodes and cultivating the soil for the maintenance of themselves and families, and giving an example by virtue, honesty, and industry to their more civilized neighbors." Chief Justice Watts, who wrote the above decision in the case of *United States v. Lucero*

Our Lady of Guadalupe de Halona Mission, Zuni Pueblo. (Photograph by U.S. Geological Survey, Expedition of 1873.)

(decided January 1869 in New Mexico's Territorial Court: 1 N.M. 422), obviously was ignorant of evidence that placed the Pueblo Indians in New Mexico thousands of years before the Spanish conquest, with walled villages, a sedentary life, and a principal occupation of agriculture.

The decision, despite its laudatory rhetoric, ran against the interests of the Pueblos, and they were to continue their struggle for protection against the taking of their land and resources for another forty-four years, when a ruling in yet another case gave them the right to demand federal protection of their lands and possessions. At this time, however, they were still exempted from the provisions of the Nonintercourse Act, which protected the tribes against trespass and prohibited settlers from entering or settling on Indian land. But, under various appropriation acts by the United States Congress, and actions of the Indian Department, the decision of Judge Watts was, in effect, ignored, as the federal government continued the process of bringing the Pueblos under federal jurisdiction "through the back door," so to speak. Provision was made for an agent to be sent to the Pueblos. Funds were provided for this purpose, and the Pueblos were treated as Indian tribes under the authority of the Indian Department.

The United States Supreme Court upheld the decision of the Territorial Court in 1876 in another case (*United States v. Joseph*). Again the decision went against the Indians, and the federal government was not permitted to apply the Nonintercourse Act of June 30, 1834, to the Pueblos. Here again, the words of the Court bear repeating, for the recognition of historic Indian rights expressed herein.

The Pueblo Indians, the Court said, "hold their lands by a right superior to that of the United States. Their title dates back to grants made by the government of Spain before the Mexican Revolution, a title which was fully recognized by the Mexican government, and protected by it in the Treaty of Guadalupe Hidalgo, by which this country and the allegiance of its inhabitants were transferred to the United States." On the question of whether or not the Pueblo Indians had the right to vote (which was raised as part of the litigation), the Court refused to act, stating they would "decide nothing beyond what is necessary to the judgment we are to render. . . ." The question of the Pueblo right to vote, if indeed citizenship was a reality for them, arose because of an act passed by the legislative assembly of New Mexico under the Territorial Government, stating:

> *That the Pueblo Indians of New Mexico for the present, and until they shall be declared by the Congress of the United States to have the right, are excluded from the privilege of voting at the popular elections of the Territory, except in the election for overseers of ditches to which they belong, and in the elections proper to their own pueblos to elect their officers according to their ancient custom.*

It is interesting to note that the Organic Act of New Mexico (September 9, 1850) provided that the Territorial Legislative Assembly had the right to legislate on all matters "consistent with the Constitution of the United States," but that such acts shall be "submitted to the United States, and if disapproved, shall be null and of no effect." The Congress "acted" by silence as usual, and the primary right of citizenship was thus denied the Pueblo Indians, not to be gained until 1948, and even then following a lawsuit.

New Mexico acquired statehood in 1912, and jurisdiction over the pueblos fell within the province of the federal government through the Bureau of Indian Affairs. In passing, it should be noted that the reference to "pueblos" often made no distinction between Indian pueblos and Spanish pueblos during the days of the Territorial Government, thus causing even more confusion. Some territorial lawyers used this semantic difficulty to the advantage of their Spanish clients.

With the United States' acquisition of New Mexico, still another danger arose, due to the difference in religious beliefs of the Anglo and Indian peoples. Under Spanish rule, some sort of accommodation had been made, in which the Pueblos had managed to retain their religious observances. Many ceremonies were nicely combined with Catholic observances, the result being an interesting combination of some of the two religious practices without loss of the basic fabric of Indian life.

Now the Pueblos were faced by strict, "God-fearing" and proselytizing Christians bent on imposing their own religion upon the Indians. Strict regulations were imposed, both through the administration of the Bureau of Indian Affairs, and through the Religious Crimes Act. Offenses against the regulations were punished. Government agents, superintendents, and federal commissioners made it punishable to practice Indian religious ceremonies. As only one example, Charles H. Burke, commissioner of Indian affairs in 1924, directed that propaganda be carried out against Indian religions. He circulated documents to churchmen, members of Congress, and newspaper editors, asserting that Indian religious observances were sadistic and obscene. He expressed the belief that native religion was a crutch preventing the useful assimilation of the Indian into white society. Burke was in New Mexico one day in 1926, addressing the Taos Pueblo Council on the subject of Blue Lake. At this meeting, the commissioner told the council that they were "half-animals," because of their "pagan religion." Even before this speech, Burke had issued orders to Indian bureau personnel directing them to tell the Pueblo people to rid themselves of their native religion "within a year."

The attacks on Indian religion increased during the early 1900s. The Bureau of Indian Affairs and its commissioner took a leading part in this arrogant and unlawful activity. Reports in minutes, secret communications, and various documents detail this onslaught on Pueblo religion. The response of the Indian people was clear, but has never been publicized. Here for the first time in any publication, is one such response by the Pueblo people themselves (Archives of the American Indian Historical Society):

> The Council of All the New Mexico Pueblos, assembled at Santo Domingo Pueblo this fifth of May, 1924, issues the following Declaration, addressed to the Pueblo Indians, to all Indians, and to the People of the United States.
>
> We have met because our most fundamental right of religious liberty is threatened and is actually at this time being nullified. And we make as our first declaration the statement that our religion to us is sacred and is more important to us than anything else in our life. The religious beliefs and ceremonies and forms of prayer of each of our pueblos are as old as the world, and they are holy. Our happiness, our moral behavior, our unity as a people, and the peace and joyfulness of our homes, are all a part of our religion and are dependent on its continuation.
>
> To pass this religion, with its hidden sacred knowledge and its many forms of prayer, on to our children, is our

*supreme duty to our ancestors and to our own hearts
and to the God whom we know. Our religion is a true
religion, and it is our way of life. We must now tell how
our religious freedom is threatened and denied to us.*

*We specify first the order issued by the Commissioner
of Indian Affairs to Indian Superintendents, dated April
26th, 1921. In that lengthy order, the Commissioner
gives a list of "Indian Offenses for which Corrective
penalties are provided." He places upon local Superintendents the duty of determining whether Indian religious
observances "cause the reckless giving away of property,"
are "excessive," promote "idleness, danger to health, and
shiftless indifference to family welfare." And one of our
present Superintendents of the Pueblos thus states his
attitude in a printed Government report: "Until the old
customs and Indian practices are broken up among this
people, we cannot hope for a great amount of progress.
The secret dance is perhaps one of the greatest evils.
What goes on I will not attempt to say, but I firmly
believe that it is little less than a ribald system of
debauchery."*

*We denounce as untrue, shamefully untrue and
without any basis of fact or appearance, and contrary to
the abundant testimony of White scholars who have
recorded our religious customs, this statement, and we
point out that the Commissioner's order, quoted here, to
be interpreted and enforced by the local Superintendents,
is an instrument of religious persecution.*

*We next refer to the circular addressed "To All Indians"
signed by the Commissioner of Indian Affairs and dated
February 24, 1923. He states: "I could issue an order
against these useless and harmful performances, but I
would much rather have you give them up of your own
free will and, therefore, I ask you now in this letter to
do so. If at the end of one year the reports which I
receive show that you are doing as requested, I shall be
very glad, but if the reports show that you reject this
plea, then some other course will have to be taken." And
on February 14, 1923, the Commissioner addressed all
Superintendents, commending to their attention the*

*proposals of certain Christian missionaries stating that
"the suggestions agreed in the main with his attitude."
Among these suggestions were the following:*

*"That the Indian dances be limited to one each month
in the daylight hours of one day in the midweek and at
one center in each district; the months of March and
April, June, July, and August being excepted (no dances
these months).*

*"That none take part in these dances or be present
who are under 50 years of age.*

*"That a careful propaganda be undertaken to educate
public opinion against the (Indian) dance."*

*We Pueblo Indians of course have not consented to
abandon our religion. And now the Commissioner of
Indian Affairs has just visited the Pueblos, and he went
to Taos Pueblo and there he gave an order which will
destroy the ancient good Indian religion of Taos, if the
order is enforced. He ordered that from this time on, the
boys could no longer be withdrawn temporarily from the
Government school to be given their religious instruction. These boys would stay longer in school to make up
for the time lost, and there is no issue about the Indians
not wanting their children to be educated in the Government schools. But if the right to withdraw the children
for religious instruction be withdrawn, then the Indian
religion will die. The two or three boys taken out of
school each year are the boys who will learn all the
religious system of the tribe, and they in turn will pass
on this knowledge to the generations to come.*

*When issuing this order to the Taos Pueblo, the
Commissioner denounced the old customs and religions,
and he used harsh words about us who are faithful to the
religious life of our race. He called us "half-animal."*

*And now we will call attention to the fact that when
our children go to school, as they all must do and we
want them to do, they are compelled to receive the
teachings of the Christian religion no matter what the
parents or the clans may desire. And the parents, the
clans, and the tribes are not even given the privilege of*

94

saying which branch or denomination of the Christian religion their children shall be taught. Thus a division is made between the parents and the children. And now if we are to be, according to the Commissioner's new order, forbidden to instruct our own children in the religion of their fathers, the Indian religions will quickly die and we shall be robbed of that which is most sacred and dear in our life.

We address the Indians and the people of the United States, and we ask them to read the guarantees of religious liberty which we have received. We came into the United States through the Treaty of Guadalupe Hidalgo, and that treaty guaranteed to all the inhabitants of the Southwest that until such time as they were made citizens of the United States "they should be maintained in the free enjoyment of their liberty and property, and secured in the free exercise of their religion without restriction." And we call attention to the covenant, which was a treaty, made between the United States and the People of New Mexico, whose words were embodied in the enabling act making New Mexico a state and in the Constitution of New Mexico:

"And said convention shall provide by an ordinance irrevocable without the consent of the United States and the people of the said state:

"First:—Perfect toleration of religious sentiment shall be secured, and no inhabitant of this state shall ever be molested in person or property on account of his or her mode of religious worship."

We conclude this statement by asking the citizens of the United States: Shall the Commissioner of Indian Affairs be permitted to revoke those guarantees which the Congress of the United States itself could not revoke under the Constitution? We are but a few people, in the pueblos. We have inherited and kept pure from many ages ago a religion which, we are told, is full of beauty even to White persons. To ourselves at least, our religion is more precious than even our lives. The fair play and generosity of the American people came to the rescue of the Pueblos when it was proposed to take away their lands. Will the American people not come to our rescue

95

now, when it is proposed to take away our very souls?

Most of all we say to all the Pueblos whom we represent—to all of the ten thousand Pueblo Indians, and likewise to the Hopi and Navajo Indians: This is the time of the great question. Shall we peacefully but strongly and deathlessly hold to the religion of our fathers, to our own religion, which binds us together and makes us the brothers and children of God? There is no future for the race of the Indians if its religion is killed. We must be faithful to each other now.

This declaration was signed by leaders and members of these pueblos: Taos, Picuris, San Juan, Santa Clara, San Ildefonso, Nambe, Acoma, Tesuque, Cochiti, Sandia, San Felipe, Santana, Sia, Isleta, and twenty-two Santo Domingo Indians including the leaders.

The Religious Crimes Code, instituted by the United States Government, forbidding most types of religious gatherings and observances, was also applied to the Pueblo Indians, and a period of suppression began that extended through the first two decades of the twentieth century. Indian religious practices were considered "anti-Christian," therefore "un-American." The commissioner of Indian affairs, in order to enforce the code, sent investigators to the pueblos to gather information and report on violations of the edict against the practice of their religion. A campaign of publicity was begun in the newspapers and magazine media, attempting to turn public opinion against the Pueblo Indians. Misunderstanding and misconception proliferated. Strangely enough, the first contact of Anglo-Americans with the Pueblo people gave them the impression that they were devout Christians, because of the Catholic observances they had adopted. Upon closer examination, it was found that these Christian observances had been made a part of Pueblo practices.

Once more the Pueblo Indians took their religion underground, while repressive measures threatened to break their spirit. The result of this suppressive mechanism was a welding of unity among the Pueblos, and the vitality of their religion survived even in the face of government attempts to kill it on behalf of the concept of assimilation.

After the onset of United States domination, Protestant missionaries were sent to the pueblos; they founded some schools and proselytized among the Indians. Thus, in addition to the influence of the Catholic church, influence from other church groups began to be felt.

The Leadership Is Attacked

Still another confrontation with the Bureau of Indian Affairs occurred because of an attack on the timeless All Indian Pueblo Council. This ancient cooperative body of the Pueblo people was not easy to control. They had their own ideas on government, and they insisted upon self-government, in the best traditions of the Pueblos. On October 6, 1926, at Santo Domingo Pueblo, about eighty Pueblo delegates gathered, some traveling hundreds of miles to attend the meeting. The Indians, gathered in their All Indian Pueblo Council, were confronted with a plan of the Bureau of Indian Affairs to thrust aside their council, and substitute federal bureau control. The All Indian Pueblo Council had a distinguished record of accomplishments for the people, one in which gains were being made, and a strong buffer of opposition had been forged against encroachment upon their rights. The council had stood unanimously against repeated efforts to suppress the Pueblo religions and to penalize the education of Indian children who desired to cling to their parental faith. The council had twice sent delegations to the nation's capital, and had carried the people's plea for justice to many cities of America. It provided an outstanding example of the capacity of Indians to organize under a solely Indian leadership, and to maintain complete independence while cooperating with their white neighbors.

Commissioner of Indian Affairs Burke had designated the All Indian Pueblo Council as "unauthorized." He intended to replace it with one that would be "authorized," to meet once a year, on call of the bureau and under its tutelage. Not one Indian spoke an excited or defiant word at this meeting of the All Indian Pueblo Council. Their response was simple, but effective. They unanimously voted to perpetuate and expand the existing Indian-controlled council. Their reply to Burke's denunciations of their culture and religion, and his proposal for a virtual dictatorship, was the adoption of a constitution and bylaws "exemplifying the method of parliamentary work familiar to the Pueblo Indians from a date when the Nordic ancestors of those who follow Burke were cavemen," as one participant at the October 6 meeting remarked. The matter was not yet ended, however. After several meetings with Pueblo leaders, a council of sorts was established, with Frank Paisano of Laguna as head. He was given a budget to operate with, and received promises of cooperation from the Bureau of Indian Affairs. But the Pueblo governors effectively boycotted the new establishment council, and failed to respond to the call of the chairman for meetings. Instead, they continued to meet at Santo Domingo Pueblo, where Sotero Ortiz of San Juan Pueblo was recognized as official chairman of the All Indian Pueblo Council. After a year or so, the United States Pueblo Council, so designated by Burke, ceased to exist. It fell apart for want of public support by the Indians themselves. The All Indian Pueblo Council continued, and continues to this day.

In this climate, issues and complaints increased. But the issue of most dramatic importance was that of Taos Pueblo's Blue Lake. The controversy began in 1906, when President Theodore Roosevelt placed the area under the administration of the newly created United States Forest Service, an agency of the Department of Agriculture. It soon became apparent that the United States Forest Service was attempting to dictate the policies of land use, and to interfere with the Taos religious observances. Taos Blue Lake has always been a sacred and sanctified place for the people. The excuse for placing the lake in so-called protective custody was to protect it from encroachment by mining prospectors and other speculators. The mechanism for changing the status of this ancient sacred area was a proclamation by President Theodore Roosevelt that Blue Lake would henceforth be a part of the Taos Forest Reserve, part of the public domain. It became a portion of the Carson National Forest under an executive order dated June 26, 1908. In 1912, Taos attempted to have the secretary of the interior declare Blue Lake area as an executive order reservation. The attempt failed, because the secretary of agriculture refused to approve the proposal. In 1916, Taos tried again, and failed again. Soon the federal government issued grazing permits for sheep and cattle, made available to non-Indians. By 1919, there was so much encroachment upon pueblo land that the Taos began to physically eject intruders. The struggle continued. An act of 1928 withdrew the area from mineral entry, and helped preserve the terrain as well as prevent further pollution of the Rio Pueblo watershed. However, the act failed to grant the Taos exclusive use and occupancy of the 30,000 acres of their land involved in the Blue Lake controversy. At the same time, non-Indians

Taos Mountain, site of sacred Blue Lake. (Photograph by Marcia Keegan.)

were eligible for permits for sightseeing, camping, and fishing. Outdoor enthusiasts could enter without permits; ranchers were given grazing permits for ten years. The Taos were allocated only three days in the month of August for their ancient religious ceremony, *provided that* they informed the United States Forest Service ten days in advance of their intention to hold the observances.

The Taos Controversy

Through the years, the Taos controversy flared, with Congress proposing legislation, with opposition to such legislation, and with the loud voices of the grazing permittees befouling the issue in the newspapers. Approximately ten bills failed, in one way or another, final passage on behalf of the Taos Blue Lake issue.

In 1951, after the Indian Claims Commission had been established, the Taos people decided to file a claim for the loss of their land. But the commission was only empowered to make a monetary award for lands taken. They waited for bureaucracy to give way to justice. They waited a full fourteen years. The Indian Claims Commission had decided that Taos Pueblo did indeed have valid title. The government was liable for taking land from the Taos. Even this decision was confusing. Somehow testimony had been accepted that this award was for the land lost through encroachment on the town of Taos. The Taos people did not want the monetary compensation; they wanted their Blue Lake returned. Consequently, they began to work for legislation to obtain trust title to the land.

By this time the matter of Taos Blue Lake had become a celebrated cause. Editorials, newspaper articles, feature stories, and television documentaries began to be seen and heard by the American public, and supporters were found in nearly every part of the population. The Taos people set up a well-organized lobby, enlisting the aid of their friends. Finally, on July 8, 1970, President Richard Nixon announced his support of the American Indian. It was a huge boost for Taos. They now had the president on their side. Senator Anderson, therefore, who had been active in proposed Taos legislation, introduced another bill, which appeared to give Taos the use of some of the land. Actually it would have broken it into parcels for various purposes, including logging. When Anderson's bill was reported out of committee on November 16, 1970, it was challenged by Senator Fred R. Harris of Oklahoma, a Democrat; and Robert Griffin of Michigan, a Republican. They introduced an amendment, and the Harris-Griffin Bill passed by a vote of 70 to 12. Thirteen days later, President Nixon signed the bill, and the Taos people had finally won their long fight to regain their land and their sacred lake. Fully sixty-four years had been spent in the effort. Taos Pueblo's struggle to regain its land is one of America's epic stories. It was a symbol of the plight of the American Indian. This long campaign became, finally, the focus of all Pueblo efforts, expanding until it enlisted the united support of all Indian tribes and the people of the world. Through all those years that tried their souls, the Taos people rallied as one to defend their sacred grounds. They fought with courage and persistence, dealing with politicians, lawyers, lobbyists, and opponents with shrewdness and zeal.

Leaders of New Mexico have taken the position that Indians should not be maintained in a legal status different from that of any other citizen of the state, although the state did not classify Indians as citizens of New Mexico except in regard to the right to sell or alienate their land. This is the basis of a persistent controversy concerning federal versus state jurisdiction. Under federal jurisdiction the Pueblos are recognized as citizens of their Indian tribes, as nations with aboriginal claims and rights, with title to their land under the trusteeship and protection of the federal government, and as independent, self-governing entities. Their sovereignty as Indian nations and their rights to their water and natural resources can be protected through such a federal relationship, although it is a continuing struggle to have this lawful protection maintained. The reasoning for this federal-Indian relationship is clear. The land was taken from them, and their economy, which was so well suited to their needs, has been destroyed. The debt owed the Pueblos is enormous, justifiable in law, a debt that cannot be paid in money alone.

Under state jurisdiction, the Plan of Iguala would, in effect, be resurrected, and the Pueblos could only look forward to the misery of alienation of their land. Their resources and their very existence as a race would be destroyed.

It can be said that the Pueblo Indians have dual United States citizenship, with allegiance to the federal government and a voice therein, and state citizenship and allegiance to the state and all its entities with a voice therein. If this relationship seems "peculiar" to the uninformed, so, too, is the illegal and unjust abrogation of Indian rights to their land and resources a "peculiarity" of the position of Native Americans in the context of American society.

The role of the United States in Pueblo history has been only slightly different than it has been in relation to all other Indian tribes. John Collier, head of the Indian Defense Association, a white-dominated organization that fought for many years for Pueblo and other Indian rights, described the situation in these words:

> *Officials of the Bureau of Indian Affairs, with the Secretary of the Interior . . . sell and lease vast properties under rules and regulations of their own making, which they can change or suspend at will. In substantially all matters, they are unreviewable by any court. They are removable by no court. Indian personal life is controlled in the same manner. Regulations by the Secretary of the Interior have the force and effect of statute law. The penal code for Indians, save in the case of eight crimes named in Federal statutes, is made by the Interior Department, is not published, and can be changed or suspended at will. Under that code, or outside it, Indians are arrested, fined, and imprisoned without trial and without court review. Those who trade with Indians are licensed by the Department. . . . The Bureau may at will institute passport requirements for Indians and prohibit the contact of tribe with tribe.*
>
> *The Bureau dictates in the choice of religions. It subsidizes Christian mission boards with Indian moneys. It leaves the Indian family intact, or physically tears it apart, and its decisions are final and its acts, and the method of them short of outright torture or killing, unreviewable.* (Copy in Archives of the American Indian Historical Society. Other information from Hearings on Senate Res. 341, February 23, 1927.)

Although numerous Pueblo Indian men volunteered and served in the United States Armed Forces during World War I and II, they were nevertheless not allowed to vote in either state or national elections until 1948. As a result, their representatives in Santa Fe and in Washington, D.C., began to work for the real needs of the people rather than focusing on the priorities dictated by the Bureau of Indian Affairs. Still, it was not until the 1970s that some light was seen at the end of the dark tunnel created by United States influence over Pueblo efforts to maintain their religion, retain their land, and become an important and independent part of American life. The influence of the United States on Pueblo history, until recently, is clear. It has been filled with suppression, autocratic actions, and a lack of understanding. However, recently some change in understanding is beginning to occur; in recent times, the bureau has employed Pueblo Indian tribal members as superintendents in all the Indian agencies—in Albuquerque and Santa Fe, and at Laguna and Zuni. The more specific aspects of this struggle, as well as some of the issues that cause the struggle to continue, are told in the following chapters. As we shall see, only patience, a unity of purpose, and the will of the Pueblo people make it possible for the future to hold brighter prospects.

Taos elders at the 1971 celebration of the return of Blue Lake to Taos Pueblo. (Photograph by Marcia Keegan.)

5

Land, Water, and Survival

THE MOST CRITICAL TASK facing the Pueblo Indians is the development of an economy capable of sustaining the people. It is not possible to return to the ancient subsistence economy. Nor is it possible, or even desirable, to maintain a viable economy based on a system of federal funding "in perpetuity." What kind of an economy the Pueblos will want depends upon the desires and decisions of each pueblo, working together through the All Indian Pueblo Council. A concrete, long-range plan for such development is still not available at this date. Many ten-year plans have been suggested and anticipated. The Pueblos have heard United States presidents say, "This is the year of the Indian," but as with General Custer, help never comes. Lack of capital and the complexity of tribal-state jurisdictional issues discourage on-reservation investment. Nevertheless, Indian communities contribute greatly to the economic and cultural life of New Mexico, as many tourists can verify.

The one temporary beacon of hope is the Indian Self-Determination and Education Assistance Act (Public Law 93-638), which was signed by President Gerald Ford in 1975. Under this act the Pueblos are financing their own government operations at each village. This is currently beneficial, but when the act expires, or funds are no longer available, then what? Some readers may wonder why the Pueblos are so dependent on the government. The answer is that unlike the land of non-Pueblo Indian tribes, most of the original Pueblo land, especially land with potential resources, was taken over by the federal government before the Pueblo people were recognized as American citizens in 1924; for example, President Theodore Roosevelt declared hundreds of acres of Indian forest land surrounding Jemez and Taos pueblos to be national forest land, announcing that this move was an "unfortunate but necessary sacrifice to progress" (Roosevelt 1889–1896). In general, there continue to be great difficulties to be overcome before real economic progress can be made by the Pueblos. These difficulties involve the nature of the land, and a host of legal problems.

The Land and the People

The Pueblo Indian country is located in the very heart of New Mexico. This region had become the center of Indian populations because of the Rio Grande and its tributaries, on which most of the villages and farmlands are situated. The area may be described as arid and semi-arid. But, within twenty miles or so, there are forest and mountain regions. Rainfall is sparse, approximately fifteen inches per year. While the state has a total land area of 121,666 square miles, its water area covers 155 square miles, less than any other state. On the other hand, there are local high-intensity storms of relatively short duration, especially common on the southern slope of the Rockies. Meteorologists explain that such storms result when the warm, moist Gulf of Mexico air moves inland and becomes unstable over the hot desert terrain of Arizona and western New Mexico, causing heavy thundershowers. The pattern has been that most of these rains fall during the months of June to September. These are also the months that Pueblo religious societies from the traditional villages spend their time in the kivas fasting and praying. Precipitation increases with elevation, especially along that portion of the Rocky Mountains located in north central New Mexico.

New Mexico is the fifth largest state in the union, with Alaska, Texas, Montana, and California taking precedence in size. In the distant past, this region was isolated from the rest of the Pueblo culture. However, since the coming of the Anglo-Americans, the automobile and the airplane have joined the railroad to shorten distances, broaden viewpoints, and change the state's economy. The population has increased greatly and has changed in character. During World War II, many people came to New Mexico's military camps, and returned to settle. Pueblo Indian veterans also returned, with a new understanding of the world, as well as with a pack full of various problems. More recently, many people have come to live in the state from all over the nation, seeking a different and more serene life, surrounded by the beauty of the land.

Within this Pueblo homeland there are some of the greatest masterpieces of the earth. The deepest crack in the earth's surface is here, the Grand Canyon. There are mountains whose snowy peaks act as guides as well as a source of inspiration. The driest of deserts is here, and the Pueblos knew where to find food and water in this desert where others could not. The homeland also contains the Petrified Forest, and the Painted Desert with its glorious rainbows resting on earth. This region, moreover, had the most torrential rivers in America. The awe, love, respect, and veneration with which the people viewed these wonders of the earth caused them to create one of the most beautiful and unique religions in the world. It influenced their arts, which even today are a magnificent contribution to man's cultural heritage. Today, Man in America views these great achievements of a power superior to all others as something to exploit, while Pueblo Man viewed them as a trust to be cared for and used with respect. And so the beauty of the land has combined with the presence of the unique Pueblo people to create a great increase in population.

New Mexico has a common boundary with Colorado on the north, Oklahoma and Texas on the east, Texas and Mexico on the south, and Arizona on the west. The northwestern corner of the state touches corners of Arizona, Colorado, and Utah. This is the only place in the nation where four states meet. The state's common boundary with Mexico is also unique, for many of the people in that country are of the same racial heritage as the Indians of New Mexico.

Looking at the Pueblo culture map (page 3), one becomes aware that such boundaries as exist today are *political* boundaries. The *natural* boundaries of the Pueblo people encompassed nearly all of the area shown on the map. In this land the Pueblos developed their culture and economy. It is the oldest civilization in North America.

The Pueblo Land Grants

Many non-Indians (and Indians) often make the statement that "the king of Spain gave the land to the Indians." Therefore, ownership of the land they hold today dates from the time that Spain dominated the region. It is seldom remembered that the Pueblo people are the oldest known inhabitants of the United States and that they have lived in the same area since ancient times. It would be impossible for the king of Spain to "give" them land that they already occupied and owned, and had occupied long before the Spaniards came. However, the Spanish did recognize the rights of the Indians to the lands they were living on, and the waters they had available to them for their economy. A block of land (a pueblo) was set aside for each of the Indian groups. These areas came to be known as "grants."

The Spanish monarchy recognized the rights of the Pueblo Indians, and issued many edicts and ordinances requiring the New Mexico authorities to provide legal protection for them. In his study *Pueblo Land Grants,* Herbert O. Brayer sets forth the general principles of Spain's policy towards the *Indios de los Pueblos* in these terms: "The Pueblo Indians of New Mexico were considered wards of the Spanish Crown. The fundamental legal basis for the Pueblo land grants lies in the royal ordinances. Only the viceroy, governors, and captains-general could make grants to the Indians, and only these officials had the authority to validate sales of land by the Indians. (In the early days of the Spanish dominion, the Indians were permitted to sell their land, under certain controls.) All non-Indians were expressly forbidden to reside upon Pueblo lands. The Spanish government provided legal advice, protection, and defenses for the Indians. Provincial officials had the authority to appeal cases directly to the *audiencias* in Mexico. The Indians had prior water rights to all streams, rivers, and other waters which crossed or bordered their lands. The Pueblo Indians held their land in common, the land being granted to the Indians in the name of their pueblo."

That the reasoning for Spain's concern for the natives was not only a humanitarian one, is explained by the historian and ethnologist Adolph Bandelier: "The Spanish government recognized at an early date not merely that the Indian was a human being, but that he was, after all, the chief resource which the New World presented to its newcomers. The tendency of Spanish legislation is therefore marked towards insuring the preservation and progress of the natives. . . ." (Bandelier 1892)

The first record regarding Spanish land grants dates from 1684, when Governor Domingo Jironza Petriz de Cruzate was given authority by the Crown to make pueblo grants. The following principle was established in making such grants: A grant was four leagues square (17.712 acres), as measured one league in each cardinal direction (Spanish Archives of New Mexico). There appears to be no evidence, however, that land grants had been made prior to 1689. At that time, ten pueblos were given title to their grants, according to some accounts, and these pueblos possess documents

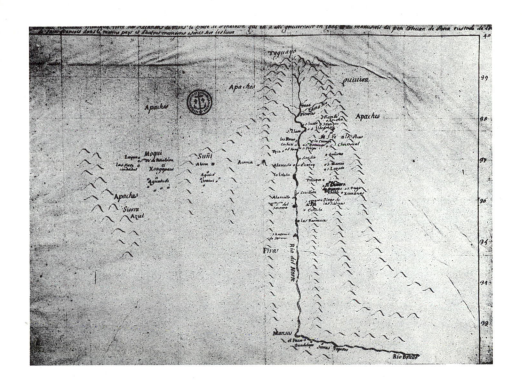

Map of Nouveau Mexique by Penalosa, ca. 1680. (Courtesy of Museum of New Mexico, Negative No. 102249.)

purporting to prove their case. As we shall see, the documents were challenged two hundred years later.

At Guadalupe del Paso, on September 20, 1689, grants were issued to Acoma, Jemez, San Felipe, Santo Domingo, and Zia pueblos. On September 25, Cochiti, Pecos, Picuris, San Juan, and Zuni pueblos received grants. According to some reports, Bartolome de Ojeda, a Zia man, was present at a granting ceremony to testify to the fidelity of the various pueblos. Sandia Pueblo was issued a grant on April 5, 1748. Santa Clara had a small tract granted July 19, 1763. In testimony heard after the United States established domination over New Mexico, it was found that eight other pueblos had lost their original grant papers. These are Isleta, Nambe, Pojoaque, San Ildefonso, Santa Ana, Santa Clara, Taos, and Tesuque pueblos. The Spanish land grants to the pueblos have been recognized both by the government of Mexico following independence from Spain, and by the United States Government.

An interesting adventure in research took place in the 1890s, when Will M. Tipton, an investigator for the Court of Private Land Claims, made a study of the pueblo land grants and declared that all of the Cruzate grants were "spurious." Reference to this study was made by Herbert O. Brayer in his *Pueblo Land Grants.* According to Tipton, the Cruzate grants are invalid and fraudulent for these reasons:

In the first place, Tipton reported, all the grants were countersigned by Don Pedro Ladron de Guitara. No such individual had served as secretary of government and war during the Spanish period. The correct name of Governor Cruzate's secretary was Pedro Ortiz Nino de Guevara. Second, when the signatures of the grant documents were compared with official documents on file in the Spanish Archives of New Mexico and the Museum of New Mexico at Santa Fe, it was found that they were counterfeit. These counterfeit documents were evidently made in the mid-nineteenth century by a group of non-Indians in Santa Fe who were involved in a scheme to defraud many pueblos of their lands. Third, a supposed grant to Laguna was made ten years before the pueblo was even founded. And fourth, Tipton said various parts of these documents were found to have been taken from a book titled *Ojeado sobre Nuevo Mejico,* written by Antonio Barreyro (Barriero) in 1832. However, considering that the Spanish Crown had ordered such

Cochiti Pueblo, ca. 1880. (Photograph by John K. Hillers, courtesy Museum of New Mexico, Negative No. 2493.)

grants to be made by various edicts and ordinances, and that Cruzate had received instructions to do so in 1684, it would appear that Tipton's investigations, while they may certainly be valid, were in effect redundant. A further observation may be made here involving Tipton's probable efforts to make a case for the non-Indian claimants attempting to prove that the Spanish land grants were spurious. The United States surveyor-general approved the grants in 1856, and recommended that Congress confirm them as "Pueblo lands." (Annual Report of the Secretary of the Interior, 1856, 307–334). Congress approved the grants on December 22, 1858. Despite the approval of the United States assigning the land to the Indians, there are still some people who refer to the "spurious grants," as one means of discrediting the Pueblo ownership of the pitiful remains of their vast landholdings. If one wishes, however, to establish the historically legal position of the Pueblos and their land grants, the royal ordinances of Spain supply such authentication.

It is useful at this point to briefly review the main course that the United States has followed in dealing with Pueblo land problems. The United States recognized the rights implicit in the Spanish land grants, which were made a part of the Treaty of Guadalupe Hidalgo. About the year 1849, these holdings were surveyed to establish the boundaries of the various pueblos. The original surveys were made by contract with private individuals and contained many errors. Another survey was made in 1913 by the United States General Land Office more accurately describing the boundaries of each pueblo. In several places, however, there were overlappings of the individual pueblo boundaries in the latter survey. These overlappings remained, were shown on the maps, and the problems were not resolved. Congress established the office of surveyor-general for the Territory of New Mexico July 22, 1854. This person had the task of administering the provisions of the Treaty of Guadalupe Hidalgo. He made three reports, based on the Spanish grants and on the testimony of the pueblos, on September 31 and November 30, 1856, and on January 6, 1867.

On the basis of these reports, Congress confirmed the original land grants of all the existing pueblos, except Laguna and Zuni, which were subsequently confirmed and patented in the acts of December 22, 1858, and February 6, 1869. President Lincoln issued patents to all the pueblos whose grants had been confirmed in 1858. Acoma was confirmed November 1, 1864, and was patented

November 19, 1877. Laguna was confirmed on April 20, 1898, and patented November 16, 1909. Zuni was confirmed March 3, 1931, and patented February 15, 1933.

Land and the Legal Process

Congress established the Court of Private Land Claims on March 3, 1891. This court took over the functions formerly exercised jointly by the surveyor-general for New Mexico and the Congress. It conducted investigations and hearings, and rendered decisions in the form of decrees. Through this court, the grants of Laguna, Santo Domingo, San Felipe, Santa Clara, and most of the Pueblo tribally held lands outside of the original grants, were confirmed.

Despite these legal decisions, infiltration and trespassing on Pueblo land continued. One method of Pueblo land loss can be described. Land speculators would purchase privately owned land near the pueblos, at high prices the Indians could not afford. The speculators sold the land, usually to a Spanish individual for grazing purposes. The Spanish stockman would approach his Pueblo governor friend, asking if he could graze his sheep or cattle on Pueblo land "for a year or two," generally during years of drought. The friendly Pueblo governor was willing to help his neighbor and agreed to the use of the land for grazing. The "one or two" years became four, six, or eight. After a time, the stockman was firmly established on Indian land. The chances are that no one remembered how the Spaniard came to be occupying Pueblo land. During the administration of the United States, the Spaniard or his descendants would be paying taxes on the land, and the land office in Santa Fe recorded the land as belonging to the Spanish interloper. If the Spaniard failed to pay taxes, an Anglo-American connected with the land office could be expected to move in.

That is one way the loss of land occurred—through habitual trickery. Other insidious ways were found, both by the Spanish and by Anglo-Americans, to usurp Indian land. The story of these shady deals makes a litany of incorrigible corruption practiced upon the Pueblo people, most of whom could not read in those times.

In more modern times, however, under United States federal jurisdiction, small parcels of land have been added to one or another pueblo. It is usually not noted that such parcels of land are actually aboriginal Pueblo homelands. The federal government is only returning the merest fraction of what once was Indian-owned.

A whole parade of lawsuits occurred during the last quarter of the nineteenth century, before New Mexico acquired statehood in 1912. Of great importance was the case of *United States v. Joseph,* which involved federal protection of Indian land against trespass and non-Indian settlement. In 1876, the *Joseph* case was decided against the Pueblos by the Supreme Court. In 1891, the United States attorney general ruled that federal statutes authorizing the commissioner of Indian affairs to regulate Indian traders had no application to the Pueblos. In 1894, the Department of the Interior ruled that laws relating to the approval of leases of Indian tribal land had no application to the Pueblos. In 1900, the Territorial Court, in a suit to suppress title brought by one who claimed to have legally acquired some Pueblo land, issued a decree against Nambe Pueblo, stating that the pueblo had actually granted away the land. In 1904, the Territorial Court decided the Pueblos were liable for taxes (reversed later by a congressional act).

Finally, in 1913, a case was decided by the Supreme Court that clearly shifted the center of control over the Pueblos from Santa Fe to Washington. Until then, under the Territorial Government, the Pueblos were generally treated, in the legal sense, like any other municipal corporation of the Territory, as distinguished from most other Indian tribes under federal jurisdiction and trusteeship. This landmark case is known as *United States v. Sandoval.* The ruling of the Supreme Court was that the federal government had the right of jurisdiction over the pueblos. The Court declared that the *Joseph* decision had been made as a result of error and misinformation provided by the Territorial Government.

The effect of the *Sandoval* decision was "to spread consternation among the people of New Mexico who held lands to which the Pueblos laid claim" (Cohen 1942). Constant friction now developed between the non-Indian claimants of Indian land and the Pueblo Indians. This culminated in an investigation by the Sixty-seventh Congress. The investigation disclosed that there were approximately three thousand non-Indian claimants to lands within the boundaries of the pueblo grants, aggregating about twelve thousand persons. Congress was confronted with the necessity of finding a solution. Senator Holm O. Bursum of New Mexico, a champion of his Hispano and Anglo-American constituents, introduced a bill entitled "An Act to Quiet Title to Lands within Pueblo Indian Land Grants." A solution to a vexing problem had been found, it was thought.

*A Pueblo delegation to Washington, D.C., February, 1913, representing
the All Indian Pueblo Council. Standing, left to right: Francisco Montoya,
Cochiti; Juan Sarracino, Acoma; Francisco Naranjo, Santa Clara; Ambrosio
Martinez, San Juan; Jose Martin, Acoma; Victoriano Sisneros, Santa Clara.
Seated, left to right: Antonio Romero, Taos; J.M. Abeita, Isleta; Pablo
Abeita, Isleta; Juan Naranjo, Santa Clara; Santiago Quintano, Cochiti.
(Photograph by DeLancey Gill of the Bureau of American Ethnology, 1913, courtesy
Smithsonian Institution.)*

But a more thorough examination of the Bursum Bill showed it would result in giving non-Indians a way by which they could obtain secure title to Indian lands. The burden of disproving the right of the private landholders would be placed upon the government, a process that would reverse the usual legal procedure with regard to land claims. Mr. Leo Crane, an Indian agent for the Pueblos, took his courage in his hands and charged that Senator Bursum and Secretary of the Interior Albert B. Fall of New Mexico were attempting to provide a path through Congress by means of which the non-Indians could walk in ease with Pueblo land ownership as a final goal. This bill received the approval of the Harding administration, and seemed assured of enactment.

Section 10 of the Bursum Bill, containing one sentence of 190 words, was a monster in the cloak of deceptive language. The true intention of this section was revealed in the last few lines: ". . . any further and additional use of such (Pueblo) waters and the appropriation thereof shall be acquired, determined, and adjudicated according to the laws of the State of New Mexico governing the appropriation and use of waters for irrigation purposes." The intention was clearly to seize Pueblo waters by causing jurisdiction over allocation to be placed with the state, instead of the federal government.

Into this situation a new element was now injected. There occurred a boiling up of public indignation over treatment of the Indians. The incredibly harsh conditions being experienced by the Indians on reservations received widespread publicity. The power of the Bureau of Indian Affairs was the very life and death of the Indian; the outrageous autocratic controls exercised by the bureau became a matter of public concern. National magazines such as *Sunset* and *Colliers* had continuing feature stories about the Pueblos, exposing the conditions. The social climate had changed.

Bursum Bill Opposition

Still another factor should be considered. Indian people had been coming to the forefront nationally, since the beginning of the century. The Society of American Indians had been founded, and it held a high-level convention in 1911, showing the Indian as a professional, a scholar, one learned in the ways of the general society as well as in the Indian culture. The very existence of an organized body of Indian doctors, engineers, teachers, and professional people developed considerable respect for Native Americans.

Mass organizations came to the support of the Pueblos. The Federation of Women's Clubs with its two million members, the Indian Rights Association, based in San Francisco, organizations in New Mexico with social and cultural interests, and many individuals with expert professional standing were enlisted in the campaign against the Bursum Bill. A women's group employed Mr. John Collier as field representative. The Pueblo Indians themselves embarked on the lecture trail, alerting the public to the violations of Pueblo rights and the impending disaster that would result from the proposed legislation. Seventeen Indian leaders gave themselves wholly to the campaign, and the people at home gave full support. The struggle against the Bursum Bill received the complete support of the nation's tribes, and indeed this issue sparked a new movement for Indian rights among many of the tribes.

The efforts of certain members of Congress to seize Pueblo land through legislation resulted in the strongest united action of the Indian people in modern times. An appeal was written by the Pueblos describing the deception used by Senator Bursum and his colleagues on November 5, 1922, which was sent to all Indian tribes and the general public. Its main text follows; it is perhaps the best description of the history of those times.

The Pueblo Appeal

The main text of the appeal to the Bursum Bill reads as follows:

> *We the Pueblo Indians, have always been self-supporting and have not been a burden on the government. We have lived in peace with our fellow Americans even while we have watched the gradual taking away of our lands and waters. Today, many of our pueblos have the use of less than an acre per person of irrigated land, whereas in New Mexico ten acres of irrigated land are considered necessary for a white man to live on. We have reached a point where we must either live or die.*
>
> *Now we discover that the Senate has passed a bill, called the Bursum Bill, which will complete our destruction, and that Congress and the American people have been told that we, the Indians, have asked for this legislation. This, we say, is not true. We have never asked for this legislation. We were never given a chance of having anything to say or do about this bill. We have*

studied the bill over and found that this bill will deprive us of our happy life by taking away our lands and water and will destroy our Pueblo government and our customs which we have enjoyed for hundreds of years, and through which we have been able to be self-supporting and happy down to this day.

The bill will take away our self-respect and make us dependent on the government and force us into court to fight over and settle things which we have always settled among ourselves without any cost to the government.

Before this bill passed the Senate we had trusted the government, and now we find that unless this bill is beaten, the government will betray our trust. We cannot understand why the Indian office and the lawyers who are paid by the government to defend our interests, and the Secretary of the Interior have deserted us and failed to protect us this time. The Pueblo officials have tried many times to obtain an explanation of this bill from officials of the Indian office and the attorneys of the government, and have always been put off and even insulted, and on one occasion when a Pueblo Indian talked with the government attorney who drew the Bursum Bill, he was told he was "ungrateful" and "no good." Knowing that the bill was being framed, a delegation from Laguna, the largest pueblo, waited eleven hours for a chance to discuss it with the Commissioner of Indian Affairs at Albuquerque. At the end of this time, the Commissioner granted ten minutes, in which he answered no question that the Pueblos had come to ask.

After we failed to get an explanation from government officials who are supposed to help us, we have ourselves studied what this bill will do to our life and our land, and have come together today to make a move by which we can appeal to the American people.

The Pueblo, as is well known, existed in a civilized condition before the white man came to America. We have kept our old customs and lived in harmony with each other and with our fellow Americans.

This bill will destroy our common life and will rob us

of everything which we hold dear, our lands, our customs, our traditions.

Are the American people willing to see this happen?

Signers of the appeal were the pueblos of Taos, San Juan, Santa Clara, San Ildefonso, Nambe, Tesuque, Cochiti, Santo Domingo, San Felipe, Santa Ana, Zia, Jemez, Pecos, Sandia, Isleta, Laguna, Acoma, Picuris, Pojoaque, and Zuni.

The Indian tribes made known their support to the Pueblos. A strong coalition of Indian and non-Indian forces brought powerful pressure upon Congress. Evidence was presented to Congress proving the adverse effects of the bill upon Pueblo life. It became clear that the bill was an undercover effort to seize Pueblo land, and the Bursum Bill was finally defeated.

The Pueblo Lands Act

A new measure was introduced in Congress on June 7, 1924, calling for the appointment of a commission to investigate Pueblo land titles, and to provide legal solutions to the thousands of non-Indian claims against Pueblo land. Known as the Pueblo Lands Act, the legislation provided for a lands board, with authority to determine the exterior boundaries "of any land granted or confirmed to the Pueblo Indians of New Mexico by any authority of the United States of America, or any prior sovereignty, or acquired by said Indians as a community by purchase or otherwise." To enforce the act, the attorney general was instructed to bring lawsuits to quiet title to all lands listed as Pueblo lands by the Lands Board. One section of the act required non-Indian claimants to demonstrate a proper claim by these means: Either to prove continuous adverse possession under "color of title" since January 6, 1902, supported by payment of taxes on the land; or to prove "continuous adverse possession since March 16, 1889, by payment of taxes but without color of title." A finding that Indian title had been extinguished (which meant that Indians had lost their land) required a unanimous vote of the board. Land lost to the Pueblos because of the failure of the United States to prosecute illegal settlers or trespassers was to be "reimbursed" to the Indians by means of a monetary payment, according to the fair market value of the land and water rights.

On May 31, 1933, the Pueblo Lands Act was amended to implement the original law. These provisions included the purchase of land and water rights for the Indians, and arrangements for the payment of monetary awards to both Pueblos and non-Indians who had failed to prove title to Pueblo land that they had illegally occupied; they also stipulated the way in which the secretary of the interior could disburse funds awarded to the Indians in purchasing lands, water rights, and other assets. This part of the act is particularly significant, since it spells out the policy of Pueblo control in the utilization of their funds:

> ... the Secretary of the Interior shall not make any expenditures out of Pueblo funds resulting from the appropriations set forth herein or prior appropriations for the same purpose, without first obtaining the approval of the governing authorities of the Pueblo affected.

But a contradictory policy was also established that foretold the compelling problems that would arise in the future; according to this contradictory policy, the Pueblos, while being allowed to initiate the purchase of lands and water rights, and to authorize the expenditure of funds, could do so only with the "approval of the Secretary of the Interior."

The New Mexico Enabling Act (congressional legislation admitting the state to the union) contained language recognizing the Pueblo people as "Indians," subject to the same regulations, controls, and rights as other Indian tribes. The Enabling Act was further strengthened in the *Sandoval* case, and the Pueblos were finally recognized as Indian tribes under federal trusteeship. There was now an increase of services provided to the Pueblos. There was also, together with the extension of such services, the imposition of various debts and liens against the Indians. The "increase of federal services" included irrigation, drainage of Pueblo lands, educational facilities, construction of bridges and roads, and the establishment of a sanatorium. The federal government did not hesitate to charge the Indians for such things as irrigation. In some cases, irrigation ditches were dug where there was no water; tribes were charged for them; a lien was placed against the tribe for these charges; and the Department of the Interior as well as the Bureau of Indian Affairs soon forgot the ditches. There was no provision nor appropriation made for their maintenance, and soon such ditches filled in and were of no use even if there had been water with which to fill them. The question of these liens became a matter of considerable controversy. Years later the liens were lifted due to the opposition of the Indian people and their non-Indian friends in Washington.

The Pueblo Lands Board began its work in 1925 and completed it in 1938. However, during these crucial years the Pueblo Indians came out losers. A former territorial governor of New Mexico, Herbert J. Hagerman, was appointed to represent the Pueblos on this Pueblo Lands Board; but it is clear that Hagerman did not adequately represent the Pueblo Indians while on this board, since after he was later appointed special Indian commissioner to negotiate the value of lands lost by Indians in New Mexico, Colorado, and Utah, he was charged by the Senate with neglect of duty and with misconduct. It was at this time that his inattention to duty on the Pueblo Lands Board also became evident. While serving on the Pueblo Lands Board, Hagerman failed and refused to find the fair market value for land, and to award fair compensation to the Indians for land and water rights that had been owned and forfeited by them.

During this time, and even following adjudication of Pueblo land titles, the Indians' attorney had the enormous job of ejecting those claimants whose titles had been declared invalid. Even now, an occasional claimant continues to present his Spanish or Mexican land grant papers against property returned to the Pueblos or purchased for them by the federal government or exchanged or deeded as executive order land either by the president or the Congress of the United States. Although the Pueblo Lands Act is no longer applicable to the present-day situation, through the courts, or by purchase, three western pueblos have added a good bit of land to their reservations in recent years; these pueblos are Acoma, Laguna, and Zuni.

In general, the policy evolved by the United States Government with respect to the Pueblos since the end of the war with Mexico can be summed up in these general statements:

The Pueblo Indians of New Mexico are wards of the United States Government, the federal government having a trusteeship relationship and jurisdiction over Pueblo lands, water, and assets.

The Pueblo Indians, it was recognized, have a communal title to their lands, originally granted by Spain, recognized by Mexico, and confirmed by the United States. While this policy recognized only the land grants, ignoring the aboriginal ownership, the Pueblos work within the legal structure of the land grants formula, but insist that this does not totally determine their rights as original owners of the land.

As "wards" of the United States, the Pueblo Indians may not alienate their lands without the consent of the government. Simply put, this means that the Pueblos may not sell or encumber their land without the consent of the secretary of the interior.

A Question of Survival

Only the vigilance of the Pueblo people has made it possible for them to protect their land and preserve it from destruction. A far greater threat now confronts the Pueblo people, the loss of water through illegal seizure by non-Indians, aided and abetted by the agencies of the federal government. While the loss of their water has been a threat since the advent of the Europeans, it has become the gravest of dangers now that New Mexico has experienced a vast expansion of its population.

As the population grew (described by historians who tilt their history to the dominant society as "westward settlement"), the newcomers created a law to benefit themselves. This law, it is claimed, grew out of the concept of "prior beneficial use," also known as the doctrine of prior appropriation. The main feature of this doctrine is the priority of rights to the waters based upon actual historic and current use. The mass encroachment of Anglo settlers near Indian lands throughout the West finally raised the issue of whether the lands of the tribes were subject to the doctrine of prior appropriation. The issue was answered in still another decision of the Supreme Court, *Winters v. United States,* decided in 1908.

The decision of the Court in this case came to be known as the Winters Doctrine. Briefly it may be defined thus: Indian tribes residing on reservations have paramount and prior rights to the waters of their land, including those waters underground, traversing through, or adjacent to their land. They have prior rights to the water for present and future use. Those rights are not subject to state laws and are paramount above the rights of those water users who claim their rights under state laws. Under this doctrine, the federal government found itself on firm ground when faced with the obligation to protect tribal water rights. However, the history of federal-Indian relationships raised many questions involving conflicts of interest existing within the federal government itself. As one aspect of this most complex issue of water rights, we consider the Middle Rio Grande Conservancy District.

Created in 1925 as a political subdivision of the state of New Mexico, it was designed to plan, construct, and operate a coordinated modern irrigation and flood control project. Within the exterior boundaries of this district are located the six pueblos of Cochiti, Santo Domingo, San Felipe, Santa Ana, Sandia, and Isleta. These six pueblos were incorporated into the district, and the Bureau of Indian Affairs undertook the financial responsibility for the six pueblos' share of the cost of land rehabilitation and efficient water distribution. The pueblos agreed to redistribute their land into larger, revenue-producing farms. However, only Isleta and Sandia have fulfilled the agreement, completing a major part of the project. The reluctance of the pueblos is understandable. No one wants to give up good land that has been in the family's possession for generations. Also, they may be taking a chance on the kind of land they may get when it is redistributed. Still another problem is the tribal officials' unwillingness to pressure the people who do not want to give up their land. If attempted, this would naturally cause great dissension among the members. An additional question was of concern to the six pueblos. The agreement with the Middle Rio Grande Conservancy District (December 14, 1928) provided for "improvements . . . to divert and carry the water to the acreage of Indian lands of the six pueblos approximating 23,607 acres. . . . The new system will carry and deliver to all areas of Indian lands now irrigated an adequate water supply without cost to the Indians other than as herein provided."

This agreement appeared to be highly beneficial. But the six pueblos noticed the manner in which their water rights were "recognized" in the agreement. Clause Number 20 stated:

> The cultivated area of the Pueblo Indian lands approximating 8,346 acres has water rights for such areas that are not subject to the laws of the state of New Mexico, and are prior and paramount to any rights of the District or any property holder therein, such water rights being for irrigation, domestic, and stock purposes. The said District hereby recognizes these water rights . . . as prior and paramount to any rights of the District or of any property holder therein; that in regard to the newly reclaimed Pueblo Indian lands the said District hereby agrees, recognizes, and grants a proper share of

123

water sufficient to adequately and properly irrigate the
newly reclaimed Pueblo Indian lands, as for like District
lands. . . .

The critical part of this clause is "the newly reclaimed lands." These were lands that heretofore had not been cultivated on the Pueblo reservations. Hence, the agreement created two categories of land for the Pueblos: cultivated land and newly reclaimed land. The cultivated land (8,346 acres) was recognized as having prior and paramount rights to water. The newly reclaimed land (15,261 acres) was treated differently. Although this acreage was Indian land, subject to Winters Doctrine rights, the newly reclaimed land was only granted a "share of the water" on the same basis as non-Indian land within the Middle Rio Grande Conservancy District. In the failure to recognize that the 15,261 acres of newly reclaimed land had prior and paramount rights, just as the 8,346 acres of cultivated land, the agreement resulted in a gross seizure of Indian water rights.

The Conservancy District

As parties to the Conservancy District, the six pueblos were now directly affected by the Rio Grande Compact controversies, studies, compromises, and finally, the approval of the compact by Congress in 1939. The Rio Grande Compact was soon engaged in massive studies of the major river systems of the West, including the Colorado and the Rio Grande. In 1937, a report of the National Resources Committee revealed detailed studies of possible water usages and divisions pertaining to both the Colorado River Basin (transporting water from the San Juan River across the Continental Divide) and to the Chama River in the Rio Grande Basin. The total report also included many supplemental projects for developing the Middle Rio Grande Basin.

These plans were by no means isolated operations in the whole scheme of the Department of the Interior's Southwest operations. Seven Rocky Mountain states had been involved in the scheme since 1921: Arizona, California, Colorado, Nevada, New Mexico, Utah, and Wyoming. When these seven states signed a compact in 1922, they included wording in Article VII reading, "Nothing in this compact shall be construed as affecting the obligations of the United States of America to Indian tribes." Subsequent agreements with other states like Texas and Oklahoma concerning the Rio Grande,

San Juan, Las Animas, Pecos, and Red rivers generally carried similar statements about the obligations of the United States to the tribes, and a representative of the federal trustee was usually present to uphold the tribal interest. But despite the benevolent wording, state legislatures have attempted since then to pass legislation that is not beneficial to Indians.

Of the various projects under the compact, the one project that the Pueblos were attracted to was the San Juan-Chama. This project was to divert water from the San Juan River flowing on the west side of the Continental Divide to the east side of the divide, into the Rio Grande water system. This diversion affected the Jicarilla Apaches and the Navajos, whose rivers, the Navajo on the Apache Reservation and the San Juan on Navajo land, were thereby reduced in quantity of flow. It also directly affected the pueblos on the Rio Grande, because it introduced foreign water into their river system, causing difficulties in determining the rights of water users on that river.

An ongoing development that vitally affects the land and water rights of the Cochiti Pueblo people is the Cochiti Lake Project. This scheme involves the building of a recreation area around a reservoir constructed on Cochiti land. (The Federal Water Project Recreation Act of 1965 provided for the development of recreation areas at or around reservoirs. The Cochiti Lake Project is one of those developments, complete with man-made lake, housing, recreation facilities, offices, and a public hall.)

Thus, under the direction of the United States Corps of Engineers, many reservoirs have been constructed at or adjacent to Indian land. The emergence of the "recreation area" at such places has posed various problems for the Indian tribes.

In the case of Cochiti, the Pueblo Indians were induced to sign an agreement with a private developer, promising to deliver 90,000 acre-feet of water per annum for the use of the new development. It was projected that housing construction on the site might increase the population to 45,000. The 1981 population of Cochiti was less than 1,000. It seemed obvious that the time might come when non-Indians could control the affairs of the pueblo through elections, and gain political as well as social influence upon schools and education, health, and welfare, both in local and county affairs. The project itself lacks practicality, since there is not enough water to provide the promised 90,000 acre-feet for the development. The system was already over-committed, with barely enough water available for the pueblo itself.

However, these developments took a turn for the better in 1986, when Cochiti Pueblo bought out the original developer, Great Western Cities. Now Cochiti Pueblo, under the name of Cochiti Community Development Corporation, is the prime developer. This development consists of core areas A and B, of which 356.41 acres is the housing area and 291.98 acres is the golf course. Moreover, even though any increase in population contributes to a shortage of water, as of 1991 fewer houses had been built than had been anticipated. There are only 165 houses with a population of approximately 250 people. The United States Corps of Engineers is in charge of the lake and the shoreline on a ninety-nine-year lease signed in 1965, while the Cochiti Community Development Corporation is in charge of the marina and the boat storage areas. But as the Indians view the situation, the revenue that the core areas A and B brings in is no compensation for the loss of their farmland. This loss of farmland has been the major concern for Cochiti Pueblo, since under the present conditions no one can farm.

There are other pueblos, like Jemez, that might benefit from a flood control dam, since the floods along the Jemez creek each spring haul away much valuable farmland. Santa Ana has a flood control dam on its reservation, but already it is inundated with problems concerning land use by non-Indians surrounding the dam.

In 1966, the state of New Mexico instituted one of six projected suits, involving the United States, four northern pueblos, and hundreds of other non-Indian users. The purpose of the lawsuit was to determine the water rights of the defendants in the "Nambe-Pojoaque River System," a tributary of the Rio Grande. Ostensibly, the suit was instituted to facilitate the administration of the San Juan-Chama reclamation project that was under construction at the time. The state charged that the users of the water in that system, including the four pueblos, had use of the water by virtue of the New Mexico prior appropriation law. The state engineer had made hydrographic surveys of the stream, it was asserted, and the complaint asked that the court define and determine the water rights of each of the defendants. On behalf of the Pueblos, the United States claimed immemorial rights to the use of water, stating that the tribes were entitled to enough water to satisfy "their maximum needs and purposes." But, as an additional and "alternative" claim, water rights for the Pueblo tribes were asserted under historically irrigated lands based on appropriation and beneficial use. This alternative claim would place the water rights of the Pueblos on the same basis as those of the non-Indian users of the Nambe-Pojoaque River, and the Pueblos would have no rights allowing them to claim water for future use. It became obvious that the United States was willing to force the Pueblos into a process of murderous competition for water; the anticipated outcome most assuredly would be against the Indians.

If this alternative were allowed to stand as a basis for Pueblo Indian water rights, then there would be no way for the Indians to develop or to progress economically. Thus it is; the United States giveth, and taketh away! The federal government, as trustee, had the obligation to act as a relentless advocate for protection of the beneficiary's rights. The fact that the trustee, the United States, would even allow consideration of "historically irrigated" acres based on appropriated use as a principle on which to build a case "protecting" the rights of the Pueblos is an indication that the trustee is not honestly executing its full and unqualified effort to protect Pueblo interests. As a result of the filing by the United States of the *Motion to Intervene,* the parties in the suit were re-aligned to place the United States and the four pueblos as plaintiffs. The original suit thus proceeded on the basis of two separate complaints that seem unrelated. Along with the New Mexico complaint, the state engineer prepared a survey showing all irrigated lands within the Nambe-Pojoaque watershed. From this survey the state made "offers of judgment" to hundreds of non-Indian defendants. If the offers were accepted by the defendants, agreements were signed and an order issued by the United States District Court granting water rights to the parcels of land involved. While these offers of judgment were being made, the United States failed to request that the non-Indian defendants be required to prove their land title and rights to use of the water. Even though the non-Indians may have had those rights, the failure of the United States, as trustee, to even examine the non-Indian defendants might have meant an abandonment of Indian rights.

A few months later, Santo Domingo and San Felipe pueblos, located downstream from the four pueblos in the north, filed a *Petition to Intervene* in the suits already instituted, on grounds that their rights were not being protected by the United States in regard to the initial suit. The two pueblos believed that those suits affected waters from the upstream tributaries that fed the mainstream of the Rio Grande that went by their pueblos. The United States responded that the two downstream tribes had no valid interest in the five suits. Since that time in 1970, the United States has continued to oppose the intervention of the two downstream pueblos, thus denying them the right to defend their water rights. The Indians asked: Is the Department of the Interior in a conflict of interests, attempting to protect the interests of the non-Indian water users and doing the worst possible job for the Pueblos?

Trust Responsibilities Breached

The federal government has made many pious gestures and floated much rhetoric about the protection of tribal land and water interests. Yet, through the years, the Pueblos have witnessed a steady deterioration of their land and water resources, both in quantity and quality. Pueblo leaders have seen the federal government give its overt approval to special interest groups, assuring their success in stealing the very resources upon which the existence of the Pueblos depends. Although the younger generation of Pueblos has become more sophisticated and articulate, despite their interest and participation, precedents are being set in the courts, and the battle for justice will undoubtedly continue.

As a result of the current cases at law, the Pueblos believe that the trustee has breached its trust responsibilities and will continue to breach that duty until the United States Government is honest enough to change its policy. A deplorable conflict of interests exists, in which the United States promulgates Bureau of Reclamation projects designed to develop non-Indian interests that usurp Indian water rights. Realizing the conflict of interests, President Nixon stated that "No self-respecting law firm would ever allow itself to represent two opposing clients in one dispute." But the Pueblos see such cases occurring, and are compelled to live with them and fight against them.

In August 1973, United States District Judge H. Vearle Payne ruled in the case of one of the suits (*New Mexico v. Aamodt*). His ruling, issued as instructions to the special master in the water rights suit, stated in effect that Pueblo Indians in New Mexico are subject to the same state water rights laws as non-Indians. Payne wrote, "I do not believe that the decisions of the United States

Supreme Court in the *Winters* case or in the case of *Arizona v. California* are exactly on point because in each of those cases the Court was talking about reservation Indians, and for reasons which I will not discuss, the situation of reservation Indians is not the same as Pueblo Indians." It would appear that the old arguments advocated by the Territorial Government during the *Joseph* case were being used to arrive at this decision against the Pueblos, with some additional flourishes and legal embellishments. The Pueblos decided to follow the procedures available to them, and continue the fight in the courts. As a first step in this direction, on October 4, 1973, a resolution was passed by the pueblos of San Felipe, Santo Domingo, and Santa Ana, stating that ". . . we are confronted with a threat of immediate and continuing irreparable damage from the immediate closure of Cochiti Dam on the Rio Grande and the impounding of the waters of the Rio Grande above this dam."

Damage was also being inflicted upon the Pueblos, the resolution stated, by "the introduction of foreign water from the San Juan River drainage system by the San Juan-Chama Project." The Indians warned that "devastating and shocking consequences will be precipitated by the application of the principles of law enunciated by Judge H. Vearle Payne when he recently determined in the case of *New Mexico v. Aamodt* that the Pueblo rights were inferior to the rights enjoyed by all other western Indians in the United States in that they did not include the dignity of the Winters Doctrine rights, thereby stripping them of the mantle of constitutional protection to which they are historically and legally entitled." The Pueblos also stated that there was an "intolerable conflict of interest," stemming from "the efforts of the attorney general and secretary of the interior in their purported claim to be acting for the benefit of the Indian people but in truth and in fact are really nothing more than a masquerade fronting for giant economic interests whose primary programs are both self-serving and totally confiscatory of all Indian rights to land and their use of water."

The resolution demanded that the president order the attorney general and the secretary of the interior to meet with Pueblo leaders to immediately formulate actions in order to offset the adverse consequences of Judge Payne's ruling. On October 20, 1973, the All Indian Pueblo Council met and passed their own resolution that "strongly supports the resolution passed by the tribes of San Felipe, Santa Ana, and Santo Domingo," promising to "make every effort to ensure that all the Pueblo tribes are informed of the serious water rights problems facing the Pueblo people." The council called attention, in the same document, to the "grave and dire consequences which will irreparably damage the Pueblo land and water rights and make meaningless the exercise of tribal sovereignty," as a result of the Payne ruling. Thus were the Pueblos united once again, as in the days of the Bursum Bill, as in the days of the struggle for religious freedom, and as in the days of the Pueblo Revolt in 1680.

In 1974, at a congressional subcommittee hearing, the Pueblo people spoke again. In the words of Robert Lewis, of Zuni Pueblo, then chairman of the National Tribal Chairman's Association, "Water rights were not given up or ceded. There is an implied reservation of the right to the use of water by and for the Indians in any source of water which arises upon, borders, or traverses Indian land. Water is reserved from use and appropriation by others, so far as the Indian reservations are concerned, and is to be used by them to satisfy their present and future needs. These are private not public rights, and should not be administered as are the rights to the use of water owned by the public as a whole. The Indians want their water rights to be protected, fully quantified, and projects developed at tribal options to put their water to beneficial use."

Frank Tenorio, chairman of the water committee for the All Indian Pueblo Council, said at the same hearing: "The attitude has been that the rights of the Pueblo people are insignificant when put next to the possibility of large-scale land sales to easterners and the reservoirs of the water-skiers and sport fishermen. We did not derive our rights from any sovereign, but these rights are our immemorial rights which our forefathers knew and handed down through the generations to us, to cherish and protect. There is a blatant conflict of interest in the water rights issue. Indian tribes are under the jurisdiction of the Department of the Interior. So, too, is the Bureau of Reclamation, whom we must fight to protect our rights."

In another case, in 1974, Judge Howard Bratton of New Mexico ruled that state laws do have application on Indian land, thus jeopardizing developments dependent on water and placing rules and regulations administered by the tribe in a precarious position. However, a state ruling in 1973 said that local authority cannot apply to Indian land, because the federal government exercises preeminent authority (City of Santa Fe in United States Supreme Court, which rejected the city's bid to impose platting and planning authority over the Colonias de Santa Fe, a political subdivision of the state of New Mexico). It would appear that the government is playing a game of yo-yo with the Indian tribes, the rulings going first one way, then another.

On December 11, 1973, representatives of fourteen pueblos met with government representatives in Washington. In a letter to the secretary of the interior and the attorney general of the United States, the Pueblo people stated that "Judge Payne's opinion can only be defined as the logical consequence of at least a half century of failure on the part of the attorney general and the secretary of the interior to properly represent the Pueblo Indians, and to preserve, protect, and conserve their life-sustaining Winters Doctrine rights to the use of water. A long and tragic history of failure to act, which has even included aggressive action against the Indians, has resulted in the steady erosion of their rights to the use of water, and the present plans threaten to gravely limit those rights to the very meager present use on the tributaries and on the main stream."

The Pueblo representatives asked for "vacating of the trial date, set for March 12, 1974, in the case of *New Mexico v. Aamodt.*" They made specific criticisms of the Justice Department's failure to properly prepare their case in defense of their water rights in the pending suit. The work of this department of the federal government was characterized as "weak and utterly inadequate."

The voice of the Pueblo Indian has been heard in the halls of Congress, in hearings before state and federal agencies, and in the public press. Viewing the long road traversed by the oldest inhabitants of North America for their most elementary rights, one can only judge that the actions of their trustee, the United States Government, have been of a most capricious nature, have failed to meet the obligations of a trustee, and have caused this most tormented people to engage in lifetimes of struggle; and, as yet, there is no end in sight.

If indeed, as previously asserted, the most critical task facing the Pueblo people is the development of a sustained economy, it is dead certain that such economic development cannot be separated from Indian rights to the use of water, which is the most valuable of all natural resources in the arid and semi-arid regions. Without water rights, the pueblos are virtually uninhabitable. The fight for land and water is a struggle for survival of the Pueblo people. Nations have gone to war for food, liberty, freedom of expression, and religion. At this point in their long and heroic history, the Pueblos fight for their very survival. Again and again the voice of the Pueblo Indian is heard, as it was heard in the subcommittee hearing in 1974. "The Indian finds himself in a life and death competition for a water supply rapidly becoming inadequate to meet all demands," said Robert Lewis. "Ours is a cause for survival of a people who only want what is theirs," said Frank Tenorio. Is survival too much to ask from a nation that has become the most powerful in the world? *That these people shall endure upon the earth* is all the Pueblos want.*

* Published sources for the case histories and litigations mentioned in this chapter are: Cohen 1942, chapter on Pueblos; Brayer 1939; Senate Subcommittee on Indian Affairs, hearings, 1974; minutes and resolutions of the All Indian Pueblo Council; Archives of the American Indian Historical Society; reports of William H. Veeder, water specialist, Bureau of Indian Affairs (an independent attorney located in Washington, D.C., serving Indian tribes in their struggle for their water rights). Personal knowledge of events described is an added source.

☙ 6 ❧

Elements of Change

THE PUEBLOS HAVE KNOWN changes throughout their long history. But the tendency of historians and anthropologists has been to treat Indian history as static, disregarding the changes that have occurred. Conditions for change, whether of a positive or a negative nature, involve the choices of the people, as well as the external circumstances with which they are faced. At this period in Pueblo history, the changes occurring amount to a near transformation of the society and its potential for development.

Education: Fulfilling a Promise

The most important new condition effecting a transformation of Pueblo society is the availability of education for the youth. Educational opportunities for the people today are much more abundant than in years past. Twenty years ago, a college education was the great and wondrous exception. Today, there are, at a rough estimate, about seven hundred colleges and universities. More students are completing high school, when it was the exception for them to complete grade school not too long ago. These Pueblo people are preparing themselves to take a large and important part in Pueblo life, and it is not too far flung a prediction to say that their participation in the future will change life for all the people.

Education was the promise made to the Native Americans when the United States took Indian land and resources. In nearly 130 years of Pueblo domination by the United States, this commitment has been unfulfilled. At best, inadequate, overcrowded boarding schools were provided, and the process of forced assimilation nearly destroyed Pueblo culture. The Presbyterian church began to found schools among the Pueblos about 1873. These schools were followed by the government boarding schools in Santa Fe and Albuquerque from 1881 on. Day schools were opened in most of the pueblos by 1929, although the Catholic church had established parochial schools in some pueblos before then. The day schools provided classes up to the sixth grade, and the students attended the boarding schools following this. The boarding schools were the sole means of education beyond the sixth grade level at the Pueblo day school. However, about 1955, Pueblo students began to attend public schools near their homes.

Public schools with Pueblo enrollment today are: Taos, Penasco, Espanola, Pojoaque, Jemez Valley, Bernalillo, Rio Grande in Albuquerque, Los Lunas, Laguna-Acoma, and Zuni. St. Catherine's School in Santa Fe is a Catholic school that has done an excellent job of preparing many Indian students for college, as well as for vocations. Other Pueblo students have attended St. Michael's and St. John's in Arizona. Both are Catholic schools.

Although the government day schools in most of the pueblos opened around 1929, since about 1958 many of these have also taken the public school route. Today, there are government day schools at Taos, San Juan, Santa Clara, San Ildefonso, and Tesuque in the northern area. Among the southern pueblos the day schools are at San Felipe, Jemez, Zia, Isleta, Laguna, and Acoma. Public schools, from the first grade on to high school, are available at Picuris, Nambe, and Pojoaque in the north. In the south, the pueblos with public schools only are Cochiti, Santo Domingo, Santa Ana, and Sandia. Zuni has a parochial school to the eighth grade, along with their high school, from the first to the twelfth grade. Jemez Pueblo has a parochial school to the eighth grade, a government school to the sixth, and a public school from the first to the twelfth grade.

A vocational school is located in Albuquerque, the Southwest Indian Polytechnical Institute. In 1975, the student body was comprised of approximately 900 enrolled at "SIPI." This school is a hotbed of student discontent, and outbursts of student unrest have occurred from time to time. The consensus of Pueblo youth and adults in 1975 was that this school does not serve the Indian youth in any degree comparable to their needs. The curriculum is planned without consultation with the Pueblo people; nor are the students brought into the planning process. It is a prime example of what can happen when the people themselves lose control over the education of their youth. Currently, with Indian administration, the situation is gradually changing. As has been stated, tribal members are now agency superintendents. There are now two school superintendents also: Hayes Lewis, of Zuni, is superintendent of the Zuni public school system, and Joseph Abeyta, Jr., of Santa Clara Pueblo, is superintendent of the Santa Fe Indian School.

Isleta Pueblo, ca. 1915. (Photographer unknown, courtesy Museum of New Mexico, Negative No. 12337.)

All the pueblos have Head Start programs, attended by youngsters from ages three to five. The success of this program can be partially gauged by the children's new fluency in the English language and by the sophistication they display in dominant society behavior. Bicultural classes teach English as a second language in some cases, and in others, teachers work with the students in both English and the native tongue.

Higher Education

Except for two hardy individuals who went on to obtain college degrees much earlier, education on the college and university level was relatively unknown until the 1940s, when half a dozen Pueblo individuals were able to struggle through many obstacles to gain their baccalaureate degrees, mainly in preparation for a profession in teaching.

The two known early college graduates were Suzy Rayos and Miguel Trujillo, Sr., both of the Laguna Pueblo tribe and both teachers.

Suzy Rayos went to the famous Carlisle Indian School in Pennsylvania and from there to Bloomsburg State Normal School (since renamed Bloomsburg State College), graduating in 1906. After teaching at Carlisle for one year, she returned to the Pueblo country and married Walter Marmon. Following a period of teaching at Isleta Pueblo, she returned to her home at Paquate, where she taught school for nearly 50 years. Mrs. Marmon died on April 5, 1988, at the age of 111. Because of her reputation as a lifelong educator, she was honored posthumously by having an elementary school on the west side of Albuquerque named after her. The Suzy R. Marmon Elementary School was dedicated on March 11, 1990; at least two of her descendants work at this school today.

Mr. Miguel Trujillo, Sr., also taught in the Bureau of Indian Affairs system for many years before he retired. Mr. Trujillo died on August 27, 1989. In addition to his teaching, he will be remembered for his contribution to making it possible for the tribes of New Mexico to vote in state and national elections. Prior to 1948, denial of suffrage was based on Article VII, Section 1 of the Constitution of New Mexico, enacted in 1912, which forbade suffrage to "Indians not taxed." On August 3, 1948, a special three-judge federal court in Santa Fe ruled that New Mexico had discriminated against its Indians by restricting the vote on this basis, especially since Indians had paid all state and federal taxes except private property taxes on the reservations. The events that led to the Indians' right to vote began on June 14, 1948, when Mr. Trujillo attempted to register to vote in Los Lunas and was refused by the recorder of Valencia County under the Article VII provision. Mr. Trujillo's ensuing actions helped pave the way for other Indians to vote.

Since then, two other prominent Pueblos have made their mark in the judicial system and in state government. The first Pueblo Indian judge to be appointed was Theresa Ann Gomez of Isleta Pueblo. She was sworn in as a Metro Court Judge on March 22, 1991. New ground was also broken by Representative James Roger Madalena of Jemez Pueblo. He was the first Pueblo Indian to serve in the New Mexico State Legislature. In the spring of 1991, Madalena completed his third two-year term representing District 65, which is in Cibola and Sandoval counties; both counties are heavily populated by Pueblo Indians.

The other early Pueblo graduates from colleges were: Emily Aquino of San Juan, Agnes Shattuck Dill of Isleta, Marion Marmon of Laguna, Grace Paisano Tafoya of Laguna, John C. Rainer, Sr., of Taos, Teofilo Tafoya of Santa Clara, and Jose Toledo of Jemez.

Some years later, two young Pueblo men fought through nearly insurmountable obstacles to gain their doctoral degrees in anthropology. One of them, who died at an early age, was Edward Dozier, a distinguished scholar who taught at the University of Arizona. The other one was Alfonso Ortiz, who is now professor of anthropology at the University of New Mexico, after teaching some years at Princeton University. In 1991, Ortiz had been a professor for twenty-five years, although he had been teaching for only twenty of those years, due to the fact that he received fellowships for five years—fellowships for two years of study at the Center for the Advanced Studies of the Behavioral Sciences at Stanford University in California, as well as a fellowship for three years of work from the John D. and Catherine T. MacArthur Foundation. In addition to these scholars, George Blue Spruce, D.D.S., M.P.H., who became the first Pueblo Indian dentist and spent considerable time as an administrator, was an assistant surgeon general in the United States Public Health Service before he retired. Today, he is a consultant and lectures on behalf of the Association of American Indian Physicians. His brother, Beryl Blue Spruce, obtained his medical degree and became a practicing physician of considerable attainment;

but this gentle, dedicated man died in the prime of his life.

World War II and the GI Bill made it possible for more Pueblo people to gain a foothold in higher education. With these graduates as a nucleus and as models, more and more Pueblo young men and women began to enroll in institutions of higher education. A demand arose for financial assistance, and the Bureau of Indian Affairs started a process of awarding grants to Pueblo aspirants in 1949.

Before this date, the bureau had only made loans available to Pueblo students. A real breakthrough came after 1969, when the education chairman of the All Indian Pueblo Council arranged to take over the scholarship program from the bureau, placing it in the hands of the council under a contract with the bureau. During the school year 1968–1969, under its direction, the bureau had been assisting 165 students. The education committee, with approval of the All Indian Pueblo Council, revised the rules of eligibility, and soon more Pueblo students became eligible to obtain scholarships. Miss Effie Marmon of Laguna was selected to direct the scholarship program, and began her work July 1, 1969. During the academic year 1969–1970, 253 Pueblo students received scholarships (not counting those who were in colleges as armed forces veterans or recipients of private scholarships).

The All Indian Pueblo Council soon added a talent search project, and college enrollment literally began to skyrocket. In the academic year 1970–1971, there were 423 students in college. In 1972–1973, there were 478; and in 1973–1974, 600 students who applied for financial aid to attend college were approved. At the end of the first year under Indian direction, there were 10 college graduates. The next year, there were 37. Some colleges have even requested Pueblo students, saying they are known to be "diligent and patient students."

Currently, a few undergraduate scholarship programs are operated by various pueblos. Since the All Indian Pueblo Council scholarship program began in 1969, some groups, such as the Eight Northern Pueblos, the Lagunas, and the Zunis, have left the original program and started programs of their own.

The number of students entering graduate school is still small. But, compared to the situation in 1975, when there were only four Pueblo students entering law school, by 1990 there were more Pueblo law school students than there were education students. Some law school graduates, after passing the state bar examination, have joined prestigious law firms in New Mexico as well as out of state. Others are serving as tribal judges at their pueblos; as one example, David Yepa, of Jemez, is the attorney for his tribe.

There is no longer a lack of Pueblo models in any field or profession as there was for the Pueblo Indian student pioneers in higher education. Pueblo people are entering education, the health professions, and the social sciences in increasing numbers. The many Head Start programs have employed numerous Pueblo men and women as teachers' aides. And many of these have become teachers, some with A.A. degrees, some with B.A. degrees, and still others by attending summer schools or special off-campus classes offered towards teaching certificates. There are now a few principals, vice-principals, and administrators in BIA day schools and offices, as well as in public schools attended by Indian children. Although the emphasis on choice of professional careers is shifting from education to other professional areas, some Pueblos have succeeded in obtaining Ph.D. degrees in the teaching field. Besides Dr. Alfonso Ortiz, others with Ph.D. degrees teaching at the University of New Mexico are Ted Jojola of Isleta and Joe Suina of Cochiti. The latter's brother, Dr. Sam Suina, is employed by the Bernalillo public school system; and Dr. Mary Toledo Tang of Jemez has worked at the Sandia National Laboratory in Albuquerque for some time.

Many other Pueblos, now trained as health professionals, are serving their people. Michael (Migue) Dozier, M.D. (the son of Dr. Edward Dozier featured in "Some Who Shaped Pueblo History" in this book), is working at the clinic at Santa Clara Pueblo. Paul D. Avritt, M.D., of San Felipe Pueblo, is the physician at the Indian Hospital in Albuquerque. Ronald Lujan, M.D., of Taos-San Juan origin, has been the physician at ACL (Acoma, Canoncito, Laguna) Hospital. Tim Garcia, M.D., Cochiti, is at the Zuni Hospital. Michael Trujillo, M.D., Isleta-Laguna, has been in Rochester, Minnesota, for some time, where he is on the staff of the Bureau of Prisons. His sister, Josephine T. Waconda, B.D.N., C.F.N.P., has been the director of the Albuquerque area Indian Health Service. And Raymond Loretto, D.V.M., has a practice at Jemez Pueblo as well as other parts of Sandoval County.

There are Pueblo students now enrolled in universities throughout the nation, from the prestigious Ivy League schools on the East Coast, to those on the West Coast. Most are attending state universities, such as the University of New Mexico at Albuquerque, the

University of Albuquerque, Eastern New Mexico University at Portales, New Mexico State University at Las Cruces, Highlands University at Las Vegas, the College of Santa Fe, Western New Mexico University at Silver City, and Ft. Lewis College at Durango, Colorado, just over the state line.

The study of American Indian history is being given a place in the curriculum, and programs in Native American studies have in some cases been elevated to a university department. The very presence of the Indian students at any school of higher learning makes it possible to institute courses that are available to both Indian and non-Indian scholars on the history and current affairs of Native Americans.

These are the positive aspects of the transformation of Pueblo life so far as education is concerned. There are many adverse conditions. Universities still refuse to accept the fact that Indian history deserves to be taught (in addition to anthropology), and that Indian current affairs must be studied if one is to understand political and economic affairs in the nation as a whole. The students at universities who are Indian are still confronted with prejudice; counseling is inadequate and incapable of dealing with the native student; and financial aid is on a year-to-year basis, the prospect always being that aid will either be cut off, or severely reduced. Dependence upon financial aid on the federal level is something that cannot be avoided at this time, and aid will probably be needed for years to come. But the advantages of higher education cannot be over-emphasized, for the future welfare of the Pueblos depends upon these young people and their professional knowledge that can be gained only on the highest educational level.

One of the principal concerns of those who are active in Indian education is that the education of Indian youth is not sufficiently directed. When considering the present status of Indian education, the failure of direction is the most serious problem. Pueblo students are entering disciplines and professions without any basic understanding of what lies in store for them. Even more important is the fact that they are entering fields of endeavor without being given an opportunity to consider the alternatives, and indeed without counseling of a sympathetic and professional nature. In many cases, the counselor is discouraging the youth from entering higher education. They are being told, "You won't make it," just as they were told many years ago. A profound change is needed to effectively direct the Pueblo youth into fields where they have a better chance of success, and notably where the people need them. As only one example, the Pueblo people need teachers. But they do not need a thousand teachers. Yet, the number of students who are entering this profession constitutes the great majority of our youth. If this continues, there will be an excess of teachers who will not have a place in which to teach.

The Pueblos need hydrologists, earth scientists, wildlife management experts, forestry workers, range managers, agronomists, planners and architects, writers and editors, historians and anthropologists, doctors and health professionals. Priorities should be set up by the tribal councils, directly through each pueblo, and the people should decide for themselves, together with the students, just what is needed, and how many are needed for each profession. This would be a return to traditional ways, within a modern structure. In the past the Indian people had control and direction over the education and training of their youth, according to the needs of their society, and of course, according to the talents, abilities, and desires of the youth. The other side of the problem is the training of tribal leaders and parents, so that wise decisions can be made, and the best possible advice be made available. At times the tribal leaders and the parents have relinquished their leadership role in education.

It is true that in many areas there are "advisory councils" comprised of parents and interested adults. It is even more important to have the tribe itself take responsibility for guiding the youth. This responsibility has been yielded to establishment schools and establishment counselors. If this were changed, a planned society, which offers the greatest possible improvement in the lives of the people, could result. Leadership and self-government would then be a prospect one could anticipate with certainty. In a few years, the Pueblos will be faced with a large group of college-trained youth, with no place to go except to the cities, away from their people, the enormous effort and financial support given to them lost to the tribe. Certainly the possibility of individual accomplishment and the desires of each individual should be considered. But the choices should be made available, and who is to say that individual accomplishment may not be of greatest success "at home" with the Pueblo people.

The kind of education the Pueblos look to is one that will prepare them to be attuned to their environment, and the main characteristic of their environment at this point in their history is the necessity of living in two cultural worlds. This lifestyle calls for a professional position on the reservation, bordering town, or city. There are Pueblos employed by the Los Alamos National Scientific Laboratory at Los Alamos, and others work in Albuquerque. Still others are employed by various government agencies. Scores of craftsmen are working for construction industries in nearby cities. These people are usually "commuters" who go to work in the morning and return home to their pueblo after work. Some of these commuters are members of religious societies and must meet their society obligations. Others are pueblo officials in a village or governing council. Thus they have duties to be performed that involve spending time away from work. This is one of the serious problems confronting a person who must live in two cultures. Often the pueblo responsibilities cannot be met by people who work outside the reservation. If met, the employee faces discharge from his job, penalty of non-payment of salary, or earning a reputation as an unreliable worker.

The dominant society makes no allowances for these additional duties and privileges of the Indians who must live in two cultures, and this leads to misunderstanding. The Pueblo leaders, the employers, and the Indian workers will need to reach a better understanding and make adjustments.

It is a good omen for the future when one sees the number of Indian students in college. The problems these young people face, however, could largely be avoided if the preparation for life and learning could begin at a much earlier age. Primary, elementary, and secondary school education are extremely serious concerns, for this is where the trouble begins. There are not enough Pueblo teachers, even though there are many who are preparing for this profession. Counselors are not competent enough, and have been unable to deal with Pueblo children in most cases. Curricula still lack courses in Pueblo and general American Indian history. In large part, this is due to a shortage of instructional materials and books. Both teachers and students are hesitant to utilize the commercial textbooks for teaching Indian history, since these have been shown to be ethnocentric in many cases, prejudiced against the Indian, and in some cases actually racist and degrading to the Indian. In almost all cases there is flagrant inaccuracy of the role of the Indian in American history.

Unfortunately, the history of American education appears to reflect the attitude that anything not included in the textbooks is not worth learning. The approach appears to be that only European values and methodology are essential for survival, and needed for knowledge. Until quite recently, dominant American society ignored the values of other ethnic groups. Americans did not learn the languages of other people as a general rule, and most assuredly the Indian languages were considered dead languages not worth studying. We believe this concept is changing even now, and as we view the experiences of other Indian tribes throughout the nation, it becomes clear that the possibility for change is very real. As only one example, the Mohawks of New York State instituted a course in their language, because the parents wanted their children to know the ancient tongue. Although they expected to have Indian enrollment only, surprisingly the class enrollment was twenty Mohawk students and fifteen non-Indian students. It is now becoming accepted, it appears, that Indian languages are beautiful, are living languages worthy of study, and may be learned for sheer pleasure.

The American educational system is successful only in teaching dominant society values, methods, and superiority. We read only of *their* successes and *their* heroes. Perhaps this is because non-Indians write the books. These are the things that turn off our Pueblo children. How many dropouts would the reader guess General Sheridan created since he coined the aphorism, "The only good Indian is a dead Indian"? Indian children do not come to school out of a vacuum. They generally have a positive concept of self when they arrive at school. But the models they read about rarely if ever identify with their culture. In fact, nothing in the usual classroom relates to the child's past experiences at home and in his village. The ultimate result of this experience is that the children develop a negative perception of themselves, their parents, and their culture. Dr. John Aragon, of the Cultural Awareness Center at the University of New Mexico, explains that the children begin to reject all those things to which they attribute their lack of success: their language, their values learned at home, and their social patterns. The traumatic experiences that ensue are generally responsible for their failure at school. The challenge, then, is to find a cure for the ills of the system. Mainly, such a cure involves giving equal recognition to all ethnic groups and their part in the development of the nation. The American educational system teaches only that a continent and its people became a part of the world after "discovery" by Europeans.

The system fails to recognize, in its declaration that America was "discovered" in 1492, that a viable culture and people have lived on the North American continent for ages. There is even a national holiday on the second Monday in October to attest that no one existed in America before October 12, 1492, other than less-than-human "savages." These assumptions are taught our Indian children, preparing them to conclude that the prior civilization of their forefathers and their cultural heritage in America are of no value.

Religious leaders are not immune from falsifying history and imposing ethnocentric concepts upon Indians who know better. Indeed, some of these concepts offered by missionaries to the Indians actually damage their attempt to convert "the heathen." God and Jesus are invariably presented as members of the white race in religious observances and histories. A good example of illogical and ethnocentric concepts was provided one time by a minister who gave the opening prayer before the Cotton Bowl game one New Year's Day. Innocently enough, before millions of listeners on television and thousands in the field, the minister said "Thank God for the land He gave us." Certainly any Indian can win an argument with any European-American that it was the American military and armaments, and not God, who made it possible for the European-Americans to claim all the American real estate.

Educating the Adult

The majority of the Pueblo adults still constitute the greatest number of uneducated and inadequately educated people. Adult education, vocational education (as distinguished from vocational "training"), is a rare opportunity for the Pueblos. Many Pueblo adults feel it is too late to educate themselves, and this concept should and can be eliminated by using examples from the past.

As only one example of success achieved in the acquisition of knowledge by the Pueblo leaders who had a minimum of education, one can point to the Pueblo leadership in pursuing legal rights to land and water. Lawsuits and legislation have hounded the Indian people for two hundred years. The end is not yet in sight. Handling the massive quantities of evidence, documents, and briefs, and being in a position to make wise decisions from such a massive array of

*Dr. Alfonso Ortiz, anthropologist and author from San Juan Pueblo.
(Photograph by Marcia Keegan.)*

legal terminology is a task to befuddle a genius. However, past Pueblo leaders have dealt with this flood of legal decisions, litigation, case law, and conflicts over status by both state and federal government with great competence. Without formal education, without even a concise knowledge of the English language, the people have plunged into the legal battles unafraid. What they did not realize, and what history will accord them with a full measure, is that they had the noblest courage of all, the courage to learn by intelligent observation, the courage to be still when ignorant and eloquent when knowledge is the sword. Untangling the web of lawsuits and the mass of proposed legislation affecting the Pueblos was an incredibly difficult task. Pueblo leaders and active tribal members have literally become "lawyers without portfolio" in the process. But the Pueblo people persist, and therefore they have endured. They learned to "read law." They became adept at giving testimony in congressional hearings and presenting evidence in court. They gave (and still give) their time, with patience and fortitude, to the intolerably lengthy process of untangling the law so that their rights may be protected. They have also become familiar with the long, dreary road of introducing legislation in Congress for protecting their rights as citizens on three levels of government: as citizens of their tribes, of the United States of America, and of the state of New Mexico.

A good example of the Pueblos' ability to deal with the legal system is the response to the Bursum Bill, which was defeated through the efforts of Pueblo leaders. Even the most highly trained lawyer has had difficulty unraveling the mess of verbiage, in order to dredge the meaning out of that infamous piece of legislation. The Pueblo leaders did just that. They alone were the ones who first pointed out the injustices inherent in the legislation. They did not hesitate to ask questions, but they alone were the leaders in the process of unmasking the proposed congressional act, which would have deprived them of their land forever. Help came, certainly. But only after the Pueblo leaders found the truth in the morass of language, and proceeded to shout to the world that they were being destroyed.

This situation is changing remarkably. The Pueblos will very soon have their own attorneys, young people who have grown up at home, know the culture, and come with utter dedication to the task of protecting Pueblo rights to their land and water. If the old-timers, who may be described as "dirt-road" lawyers, have done so well, may we not anticipate the final glory of success, with our own youth in the driver's seat? To the Pueblo adults, this bit of their history is an example of what they could achieve, and what they must achieve with some effort. Adult education is available, but is not being taken advantage of. Beefing up the classes, making more classes available, and enlisting the help of graduate students in the teaching process will make it possible for the adults to gain knowledge with which to change their lives for the better.

A new concept should be developed in educating the Pueblo individual for mechanical skills. A man or woman who chooses to be a bricklayer or carpenter is not necessarily uneducated. Nor is it true that this man or woman has no appreciation of the fine arts. We know many men and women who have not completed high school but who are completely attuned to their surroundings, of high intelligence, and probably more interesting to be with than some professors we know. Self-education is an essential ingredient in the making of a student, worker, or professor, and without it we do not have success in any field. There are many Pueblo youth who will choose a lifestyle in which their labors are those of a woodworker, factory worker, or farmer. The tendency to look askance at these persons is not productive when one considers the human values that are lost in encouraging such negative concepts.

Pueblo Economy

In the 1920s, reports prepared by the Indian Defense Association stated that more than fifty percent of all Pueblo adults were unemployed. The probability is that the figure was closer to seventy percent. However, it is most difficult to obtain accurate or even relative figures on unemployment. For centuries, the Pueblo Indians lived by farming, and many still do. Therefore, when one tills his farm, the statistician may wonder if the farmer is employed, unemployed, or self-employed. Recent conditions show a decrease in farming, and the unemployment has been above the fifty percent mark, the figure even going to eighty percent during the winter months. Strangely enough, there is no evidence of alarm by government agencies at this high unemployment rate. In contrast, when Boeing in Seattle closes, or reduces its number of employees, the fact makes immediate headlines throughout the nation. The same is true of any industry or business. Or, as another example, if a former military base or shipyard is rumored to be phased out, the congressmen of the area begin to campaign, stating they will see to it that the facility continues. If one of these installations does close, the unemployment rate goes from five to six percent. This is considered a catastrophe!

Matters have not really changed much as of 1990. There may be a shortage of funds at present to appropriate for projects on Indian reservations, due to the recession. However, the key to a long-term solution to Pueblo economic problems, according to some leaders, is to forge a cooperative relationship between the Pueblo tribes and the state and federal governments, through which scarce resources of both the tribes and the state or nation can be effectively coordinated and used for the goals of all. Such cooperative ventures have been the hope of Pueblo leaders, but until now both the state and federal governments have tended to view the Pueblos as a minority with minor problems. However, the future may hold some possibilities for improvements. Since 1990 the state of New Mexico has had, in Bruce King, an experienced, friendly, and sympathetic governor, who is well known by the Pueblo Indians. And communication centers for exchange of information are located at each pueblo governor's office. In addition, Regis Pecos, of Cochiti Pueblo and a Princeton alumnus, has done an outstanding job of upgrading the New Mexico Office of Indian Affairs and of bringing tribal problems to the attention of the New Mexico State Legislature.

Traditionally, the Pueblos lived with an agricultural economy, also raising stock after the Europeans came. Today, with the shortage of water, the erosion of grazing land, and the increase in population, a new source of earning a living must be found. The traditional agricultural life of the Pueblos has diminished for a number of reasons. World War II affected the Pueblos when the cream of Pueblo men went into the services. Many returning veterans had learned new trades in the service, or took advantage of the GI Bill to become skilled workmen and professional people. Also, the strange workings of the federal government brought on the soil bank program. The Pueblos were advised not to farm; they would be compensated for their idle lands. A decrease in farming, probably for years to come, or even for all time, is the result. Also, with the limitations on availability of water, there developed a feeling of insecurity as more and more people from other parts of the country settled in New Mexico, demanding a share of the dwindling water supply, of which land developers had promised an abundance. Considering another aspect of the problem, the availability of welfare has created a new kind of Pueblo person, one who does not work. Finally, subsistence farming is no longer practicable.

The time honored vocation of stock raising has reached its peak, since the population is steadily increasing and all the families cannot possibly own unlimited numbers of sheep and cattle with limited grazing lands. Today, only the western pueblos of Acoma, Laguna, and Zuni are involved in the sheep raising industry. Cattle raising is done in all the pueblos, with most choosing improved, choice, and registered herds of Herefords. Cattle associations have been formed at Acoma, Laguna, and Taos that are more capable of controlling the members and preventing overgrazing. Acoma and Laguna also have sheep and wool growers' associations. Other pueblos are reluctant to form associations, however, since that would probably mean a reduction in herds. At these pueblos the tribal councils are not willing to tackle a job that could cause dissension among the tribe's members. Education about the benefits of conservation on rangeland is a long and tedious process, and there are not enough experts who are capable of training the Indians in this field. The Bureau of Indian Affairs is charged with this responsibility, but with a limited budget and lack of adequate personnel, they have not been able to maintain a consistent effort. Two bureau employees are often responsible for as many as ten reservations in the southern pueblos. Only one or two are available for the eight reservations in the northern pueblos. The government could save money by having the pueblos serviced from one office, but it does not deliver the services. In most other Indian reservations of similar size and population, one bureau office serves only one tribe. But with the Pueblos, it has always been a place to "save money" and deliver the least amount of services. The United Pueblos Agency of the Bureau of Indian Affairs served all nineteen pueblos under its jurisdiction in the past. The distances ranged from 135 miles in the north at Taos to 145 miles to the west at Zuni. Today, there are three offices serving the eight northern pueblos from Santa Fe and the ten southern pueblos from Albuquerque; Zuni has its own office.

In the area of multiple services, there is always a demand for service, ranging from one kind at a time to many at once. Should a flash flood occur, four or five pueblos stand to lose their roads or an irrigation ditch. They will all want heavy equipment, and with the limited amount of equipment available, most of the pueblos must wait. This hardship has never been acknowledged by the bureau's Washington office.

Industry on the reservation has been a long time coming. Tribally owned industry would be the answer for the Pueblos, both for convenience of the residents as well as for economic gain. However, there are several hurdles obstructing the development of industry on the Pueblo reservations. A great problem is transportation of the finished product to the consumer area. The costs are high in delivery. The other deterrent is the lack of capital to invest in plant construction and operation. Just two advantages of industry on Indian land are the available tax-free land and a stable labor pool that can be trained by the Bureau of Indian Affairs, or the departments of Commerce or Labor. It will take skilled and sophisticated leadership to guide present Pueblo governments through the process of bringing in and running more businesses on the reservations. However, in some pueblos individuals have established what appear to be profitable business enterprises. Many are small grocery or convenience stores. Others are arts and crafts shops owned by pueblo members.

The northern pueblos have a guide and tourism project. Acoma and Zuni have a tourist project, but tourism and recreation are highly competitive businesses, and it takes skilled, experienced people to develop maximum income. The beautiful Jemez Mountains draw thousands of summer visitors, but it sometimes seems as though everyone in New Mexico earns money from tourism except the Indians. Native arts and crafts are sold throughout New Mexico and the Southwest, but the dealers who profit are mostly non-Indians. Some Indian craftsmen have finally raised their prices, but the non-Indian dealers merely continue to hike the prices to the customary fifty to one hundred percent markup. It is possible they may "high price" themselves out of their only livelihood. Many Indians are fearful that the non-Indians may tire of Indian turquoise and silver and return to their gold and diamonds. It is a sad commentary on the present situation, in which the Indians rely on the traders, to have this kind of reaction develop.

Santa Clara Pueblo is taking advantage of its scenic canyon, and has opened up the area to campers and fishermen, nearly year-round. It has also started an annual day of pan-Indian dances at the Puye Ruins in the canyon in late July. Jemez Pueblo stages an All Indian Track and Field Carnival annually in June on Father's Day in their remarkable new track and field facility. Jemez and Zuni have built picnic benches and tables with attractive back-oven type fireplaces near their fishing ponds, but charge nothing for their use while camping. Old Acoma and Taos are the only places where visiting tourists and feast day visitors are charged a parking fee. They may also permit picture taking for a fee on non-feast days. Picture taking on feast days is not permitted in most of the pueblos.

The other pueblos would also like to develop some kind of a tourist attraction, but since the areas that would have been their resources are generally owned by non-Indians on the reservation borders, they cannot develop such facilities as ponds, fishing streams, or forests. Taos, Santa Clara, and Jemez are the only pueblos having timber resources, and these resources are very limited. The other pueblos have been denied ownership of these resources, and now large corporations own valuable timberland.

Most Pueblos must travel anywhere from eight to sixty miles to Taos, Albuquerque, Espanola, Santa Fe, Grants, or Gallup to shop for necessities. The irony of this situation is that most of their taxes are paid at these towns or cities on purchases of food, furniture, hardware, machinery, and automobiles. The profits from these sales go to the merchants at these towns. Yet, when an area is considered for special projects such as employment, the Pueblos are classed as "out-of-town" people, instead of "suburban," which would make them eligible for such projects.

Department of Housing and Urban Development programs also came to the pueblos. But the main thing that was learned was that HUD is an even bigger bureaucracy than the Bureau of Indian Affairs ever was. In spite of bureaucratic snarls, several block and frame-stucco three-bedroom homes were built. The HUD Department gave the people a choice of traditional flat roofs or pitched roofs. Not surprisingly, many chose the pitched roofs, because they were different, whereas many non-Indians who come to the Southwest select flat roof type dwellings. Some of these "flat-roofers" have criticized tribal leaders for allowing pitched roofs in traditional pueblos. But the fact remains that the people are getting what they asked for. Criticism has been leveled at some of the housing programs for the poor quality of materials and workmanship. Some construction, it is said, will be in a state of decay in a matter of a few years.

On the surface, there appears to be little or no ethnic discrimination against the Pueblo people, because their unique culture is a major part of New Mexico's attraction. However, there is rank discrimination in other areas of economic development. Pueblo people are not represented in the major industries located around their own country. There are some minority groups that practice boycotting against firms that have questionable hiring practices. But if the Pueblo people were to boycott for the same reasons, they would be regressing to a time of some twenty or thirty years ago when they grew their own food and made their own tools. The airport, as an example, has airlines that did not employ a single Pueblo Indian in 1980. Yet, according to a survey made by *Wassaja,* a national Indian newspaper, income at the airport is provided by Pueblo administrators, and heads of projects and government agencies serving Indians, to the extent of forty percent of the total airport income for the operating airlines.

As a result of the long history of unemployment and underemployment, the United States Commission on Civil Rights held a public hearing in Albuquerque in 1972. The testimony and investigation revealed considerable neglect from federal and state agencies, as well as from the private sector. A few Pueblo Indians were hired by the Bureau of Indian Affairs and the Indian Health Service, but these jobs were mainly in the lower grade levels, and these individuals have had little opportunity for training or promotion. Other federal agencies hired very few Pueblo Indians, or none at all. The state and local governments have an even worse record, if that is possible. Another factor is that companies working on Indian reservation projects often bring their own men. The few Indians who are hired get lower pay, and menial and dead-end jobs.

Pueblo Indian unemployment may be attributed to such causes as bias on the part of the employers, negative stereotyping of Indians, poor preparation of Indians for the labor force, geographical isolation of reservation Indians, and failure of the federal government to enforce nondiscrimination laws. Yet, laws on equal employment opportunity for Indians have been on the records since 1821, with the Plan of Iguala, the 1834 Indian Trade and Intercourse Act, the Indian Reorganization Act, and the recent Indian Preference Act.

Recently, however, the image of the professional Indian work force has improved, especially the image of white-collar workers.

Nevertheless, the undereducated, semi-skilled, and unskilled Pueblos may continue to have problems with unemployment; and they often complicate their own problems by turning to drinking.

On the bright side, there is an increasing number of self-employed Pueblos who are building contractors, painting contractors, maintenance contractors, photographers, and architects. And more successful Pueblo Indian-owned businesses are emerging, such as gift shops, village grocery stores, feed stores, beauty parlors, optical shops, propane companies, and a computer software service company that also tests and evaluates armaments for the military. Of all the successful Pueblo businesses, Laguna Industries is perhaps the most prosperous, a prosperity reflected in its recent $1.5 million, 46,400-square-foot expansion. This company was awarded its first government contract in August 1985, which was a $10.8 million job to assemble mobile communications shelters for the United States Army. These shelters were used in Operation Desert Storm in the Persian Gulf. Laguna Industries has received a total of $72 million in federal contracts and in subcontracts from private companies. One factor contributing to the company's success may be its practice of keeping politics out of the firm's operations. The business is run by the company's operators and a seven-member board of directors, with tribal member Ronald Solimon as the president. Another important factor is the matching funds that the Laguna Pueblo tribe is able to generate. These matching funds come from the uranium mine that was located on their reservation for a number of years.

In an attempt to avoid welfare, many Pueblo people manufacture pottery, and some beadwork. But one cannot work with cold mud and pottery in the winter. Pottery is made at a few villages commercially, in Santa Clara, San Ildefonso, Jemez, Zia, Tesuque, and Acoma. A few families continue their home pottery making at San Juan, Cochiti, Santo Domingo, Taos, Picuris, Laguna, and Zuni. Isleta has only one or two families still producing Pueblo pottery. All the pueblos make distinctively different pottery that is easily identifiable. The greatest amount of silverwork comes from Zuni, and though there are many outstanding silversmiths at Santo Domingo, the latter is renowned for its shell and turquoise artistry. San Felipe is also producing beads known as *heshi.* In places where Zuni men have married mates from other pueblos, silverwork is to be found. Thus there are silversmiths at Laguna, Isleta, Jemez, Acoma, and Cochiti also.

Leandro Bernal gathering water from a stream running down from the sacred Blue Lake through the middle of Taos Pueblo. (Photograph by Marcia Keegan.)

Cochiti is the drum capital of pueblos, although Taos men also make drums; and some Indians are employed by non-Indians who make drums for mass sales.

Until approximately 1970 or 1971, the Pueblos had strong forest fire fighting organizations at nearly every village. For some reason, these organizations are no longer in existence. In their time, the Pueblo fire fighters were highly regarded and were flown all over the Rocky Mountain states to save valuable timberland. Although fire fighting is dangerous, these Pueblo men accepted this vocation and performed outstanding service. One can state that just as the Mohawks were great high steel workers, the Pueblos were outstanding fire fighters.

Water Rights: Life or Death

Any discussion of economy, development, preservation of the unique Pueblo culture, education, health, employment, and other aspects of Pueblo life must come to the heart of the question: Shall the Pueblo Indians, the oldest civilization in North America, live or die? The question is aptly put, and has been placed in this perspective by many scholars and environmental specialists. The struggle of the Pueblo Indians for their very lives is connected now, as it has been for an entire century, with the issue of their water rights.

The issue of the Indians' Winters Doctrine water rights has been treated in another chapter. Litigation continues, however, and at every turn the Pueblos are confronted with attempts to seize their waters, and by justifications of the illegal taking of Indian water by the state of New Mexico and non-Indian users, or through federal projects such as dams and river diversions.

The matter of Pueblo Indian water rights has been in and out of the courts for so long that one more case would appear to indicate nothing less than extreme harassment on the part of the state of New Mexico against the Pueblos. In a case currently in the courts, titled *New Mexico v. Aamodt,* the issue is again whether the state and the state engineer shall have jurisdiction over Indian water rights and usage, or the federal government, as it has since the Treaty of Guadalupe Hidalgo, and from the time New Mexico was accepted into statehood in 1912. Even before that, the ordinances and edicts of the Spanish Crown established Indian water rights as prior and paramount rights to the use of their waters in the present and future.

In the *Aamodt* case, the state asked the court to limit Indian water rights to their historical or present "beneficial use," and to place control of the watershed, both surface and ground water, under the state engineer. The Pueblos are right back where they started from in cases heard in the courts of the United States and in territorial courts before statehood. The Pueblo people say that if the decision goes against the four pueblos involved in this critical case, it will set precedents for all the Pueblos, and they will appeal all the way to the Supreme Court. A ruling made by District Judge H. Vearle Payne on July 6, 1973, declared that the "water rights in this situation go with the land to which they are appurtenant the same as they do in any of the other western states where the doctrine of prior appropriation applies, and that doctrine is in force in New Mexico. Considering the act and decrees of the court, it is my belief that the Indians are governed by that doctrine the same as whites." In a later ruling addressed to "all counsel of record," Judge Payne stated (August 28, 1973), "I do not believe that the decisions of the United States Supreme Court in the *Winters* case or in the case of *Arizona v. California* are exactly in point because in each of those cases the Court was talking about the reservation Indians, and for various reasons which I will not discuss, the situation of reservation Indians is not the same as Pueblo Indians. With regard to reservation Indians it is clear that the Supreme Court has held that 'enough water was reserved to irrigate all the practicable irrigation acreage on the reservation.' "

Judge Payne's ruling was opposed by the four pueblos involved in the litigation: Tesuque, Nambe, Pojoaque, and San Ildefonso. But he reiterated the position that the laws of the state must apply to water rights. The United States Department of Justice entered the case and ultimately confused the entire issue. After a time, the Justice Department assigned the case to an attorney. Meanwhile, the United States earned the bitter denunciation of the pueblos concerned, as did the All Indian Pueblo Council, for failure to prepare the case adequately, and for generally conducting the case so that it would be doomed to failure for Pueblos.

More recently, Judge Payne's 1973 ruling was reversed by the U.S. Tenth Circuit Court of Appeals in Denver. It ruled that Pueblo Indian water rights were to be determined solely by federal law, and that state law did not apply to these rights. And in 1985, Judge Edwin Mechem held that Pueblo Indian water rights were frozen in time between 1848 and 1924, 1924 being the date of the Pueblo Lands Act. In issuing this opinion, he stated that, according to the Federal Lands Act, the Pueblo Indians' irrigation rights were limited to the amount of land that had been irrigated during that time. In addition, Judge Mechem said that under the 1924 Pueblo Lands Act, amended in 1933, Pueblo Indians have certain replacement water rights. Currently, attorneys for the Indians and the United States are in the process of determining what those rights are. In 1986, pursuant to an oral motion in court by the United States, Judge Mechem further held that the Pueblo Indians were entitled to domestic, industrial, and stock water usages. Information about the various uses of water is still being gathered.

In March 1991, a major technical ruling quantifying Indian water rights was made by a special master in the twenty-five-year-old water rights battle. Harl D. Byrd, a special master in the *New Mexico v. Aamodt* case, drafted the report that sets the amount of water that the pueblos of Tesuque, Pojoaque, Nambe, and San Ildefonso are entitled to use. Byrd decided that these pueblos should be entitled annually to divert 4.65 acre-feet of water from streams in the basin for each acre of land irrigated. His calculations assumed that 1.84 acre-feet per acre does not flow back into the stream system but is absorbed by crops or evaporates. The remainder flows downstream for use by other holders of water rights. An acre-foot of water equals about 326,000 gallons.

The state had requested that the pueblos be allowed to divert 4.21 acre-feet of water per year per acre of land irrigated, with the assumption that 1.63 acre-feet per acre would not flow back into the stream system. The Department of Justice sought to allow pueblos annually to divert 6.84 acre-feet of water per acre irrigated, assuming that 2.37 acre-feet would be consumed. It was also reported that the Tesuque River has an annual flow of about 1,000 acre-feet, and Judge Mechem already has ruled that Tesuque Pueblo has first rights to irrigate about 270 acres of land. Thus, if Byrd's report is eventually adopted, Tesuque Pueblo in normal years could get all the water from the Tesuque River. Barring further appeals by any of the involved non-Indian parties, Byrd's report is a significant step forward in resolving the case.

In early October 1991, another court convened to determine if lands purchased by the pueblos since the 1930s were equally covered by the aboriginal water rights. This hearing was just beginning as we went to press, and it is uncertain when a decision will be reached.

As of April 1991 it will be twenty-five years since this case was initiated. If the case is ever officially concluded, surely many other regional water rights cases will be based on the final decision.

The state of New Mexico appears to have forgotten, or wishes to forget, that the act of Congress enabling New Mexico to become a state specifically required the state to disclaim all right and title to all lands held by Indians. But the state of New Mexico continues with every means possible to seize the water rights of the Pueblo Indians, on the basis that "Pueblo Indians are somehow different in a legal sense than other Indians in the United States" (Memorandum of United States, filed August 21, 1973, in United States District Court, in Civil Suit No. 6639).

Harassment by the state of New Mexico, in its attempt to seize Indian water rights for non-Indian users, has been common throughout the history of the state. But the Pueblo people persist, for they know that if they are forced to compete with the non-Indian users, who vastly outnumber them now, they will lose all rights, and their economy will be in shambles. No future economic development can possibly be planned or supported, if the situation continues. And without economic development the people will have no way to make their livelihood, the pueblos will lapse into ghost towns, and the oldest culture in North America will die.

Perhaps the most important ingredient for success in any undertaking is unity of purpose and action. This has been proven to the Pueblo people repeatedly. The All Indian Pueblo Council is of ancient heritage, an enduring confederacy of Pueblo Nations that has existed through the ages despite many defeats, small successes, and larger victories. This council has now grown in stature, taking on new responsibilities at every turn in events. The young people have shown increased interest, and many qualified Pueblo youth, men and women, are serving as directors of various projects.

The All Indian Pueblo Council

Of the many projects undertaken by the All Indian Pueblo Council, the oldest is the scholarship program, which funds Pueblo students' tuition at the baccalaureate level. A public employment program appears to be most apreciated by the adult Pueblos at the villages. In this program, the people are employed at the villages where they live, so that they do not have to pay transportation to a nearby town for work. A consumer education project employs Pueblo residents from each village. The employees meet regularly, and they in turn teach the Pueblo homemakers. A youth corps program was administered by the council for some time, but was phased out after a few years. The program included the two Apache tribes, the Jicarilla and the Mescalero. A mental health and alcoholics program is administered by the council. This project attempts to help those with drinking and drug problems in each village. A speech and hearing conservation program is also sponsored, jointly with the University of New Mexico. Another program under similar sponsorship is the on-site Pueblo educational training program. This program plans to develop a cadre of community personnel, from paraprofessionals to administrators, who will plan, design, manage, and operate their schools through on-site and in-service teacher education. The Indian community action program also serves the two Apache tribes in New Mexico and the Utes in southern Colorado. Another is the office of Indian child services, serving basically the same people as the community action program, but governed by its own board of directors. This program has a pilot project to videotape the sites of five languages: Apache, Keresan, Tewa, Ute, and Zuni.

Direct, close contact is maintained by the council with the Bureau of Indian Affairs and other federal agencies to see that these government services receive adequate information and funds to carry on the federal government's commitment to the Pueblo people. There are some who advocate termination of federal-Indian relationships, and the complete elimination of the Bureau of Indian Affairs or any other agency similar to it. This question has been a controversial subject since the beginning of the twentieth century. However, others with a different viewpoint point out that the bureau is an arm of the federal government, symbolizing the government's commitment to the Indians, its responsibilities for Indian development, and its protection of tribal rights.

The Pueblos hold the view that termination would mean the disappearance from tribal ownership of the land base. The nineteen pueblos comprising the All Indian Pueblo Council have thus far stood firmly against termination, insisting that the federal government has an obligation and a duty to the Indian people, which would be liquidated with termination. The council grows stronger with every year, and the young Pueblo people show their interest by subjecting themselves willingly to training for leadership.

A New Lifestyle?

Nearly all Indian tribes have experienced rapid changes in their cultural values. So, too, have the Pueblos seen changes in their traditional society. The American dominant society is very unlike that of Spain, with which the Pueblos were able to survive, their traditional values largely left intact. This dominant American society is, it can be said, more peremptory.

The traditional Pueblo framework still remains. However, judging from this writer's traditional upbringing, it is rapidly disintegrating in the face of a new order and a new lifestyle. The traditional structure is no longer as strong as it was even a generation ago, or in my own generation, or even in older generations forty or fifty years ago.

In the past, individuals and families who had lost faith in Pueblo religious values tended to leave the pueblo voluntarily, although there have been a few cases of resistance. This process of the dissidents leaving the pueblos resulted in keeping intact a population that values communal living and participation in a complex ceremonial life. Formerly, nonconformists consisted of individuals and families who had come under the influence of Spanish neighbors and the Catholic church. More recently, however, American culture and Protestant beliefs have produced their own nonconformists. The number of disaffected people alienated from their pueblos is still small. Even Pueblo people who could be considered "radicals" often choose to conform to the demands of the traditional life and its leaders, rather than leave their pueblo home.

A continuing concern is whether the knowledge of native languages is becoming diminished. When foreign visitors, especially visitors from Asia and Africa, come to the Indian Pueblo Cultural Center or attend Pueblo feast days in the villages, their most common question is, "How well do you retain your native language?"

Naturally, it varies from pueblo to pueblo, but in general people of the younger generation at all pueblos are more apt to speak English, especially if their parents speak several different tribal languages or dialects. Most young children now learn to speak English in Head

Start programs, and when they return home they turn on the ubiquitous television, which reinforces their use of English.

In the more traditional pueblos where the native religion is strong, religion dictates that the native language be used exclusively for ceremonial occasions, although some teenagers participate in the dances without understanding the orations of the leaders. This problem of retaining the native language is a new one. Most Pueblo parents, especially grandparents, did not speak English during early childhood; thus they may think that it is wonderful that their children speak English. But if new generations grow up without knowledge of the native language, there will be no one to assume the leadership of religious ceremonies, which require that only the native language be spoken in the kivas.

Other growing problems are law enforcement, environmental quality, and lack of social services. With the increase of Pueblo populations, bolstered by the return of some tribal members from urban areas and the increase of intertribal marriages, law enforcement has become extremely complex. Due to the complicated set of rules governing the respective pueblos, as well as those of the state and the federal governments, the question of jurisdiction has become a problem. The ambiguity of various rules has been compounded by a recent decision of the United States Supreme Court holding that tribes do not have criminal jurisdiction over Indians who are members of other tribes. Currently Congress is considering several proposals to address this problem, and hopefully some solution will be found. In the meantime, the pueblos, along with the state and counties, can resolve the problem at least partially through cross-deputization agreements. Such agreements would give tribal officers the ability to enforce state and county laws on the reservation.

Additional problems are being created by environmental issues and the lack of social services. The forthcoming expected changes in federal regulations concerning solid waste management and environmental quality will impose burdensome and expensive requirements on Pueblo communities for landfilling solid waste. These communities will be especially hard hit, since their current disposal techniques will not meet the new federal regulations, and most pueblos are too small to support expensive new facilities. This problem is compounded by the fact that the pueblos were not eligible for the federal funds available to the state and counties in the 1970s and 1980s for solid waste management planning. In addition, the Pueblos' role in waste management under federal law has not been precisely defined yet. It remains for the United States Congress to enact amendments to the Resource Conservation and Recovery Act, recognizing tribal authority and making tribes eligible for funding under the act. A joint memorial by the New Mexico State Legislature would hasten such an enactment.

Closely related to the problems connected with the Resource Conservation and Recovery Act are those related to the Clean Water and Air acts, as well as the Safe Drinking Water Act. The tribes have the opportunity to assume the same regulatory role on their lands as the state now has with regard to non-Indian lands. Some pueblos are beginning to develop their own environmental regulatory programs, and it may be that their standards will conflict with the state's standards concerning the same bodies of water or air-sheds. If so, it will be necessary for the Pueblos to communicate and cooperate with the state to find solutions to these problems.

Finally, there is at present a lack of social services to alleviate problems created by changing lifestyles. As intertribal and interracial marriages become more common, divorces are beginning to take place in the pueblos; and the practice of couples living together without being married is apparently becoming more acceptable. As a result of these changes in social patterns, there seem to be more Indian children from broken homes in need of foster care and temporary placement. This is becoming a critical issue for the pueblos. Unfortunately, there are few federal or tribal resources available to alleviate this problem, and the state has provided virtually no services in this critical area. This whole issue is an extremely sensitive matter to tribal leaders, since they fear that state involvement will result in children being placed in non-Indian homes, removed from the unique cultural atmosphere of the Pueblo people.

Many changes will certainly come. It is only to be hoped that a new lifestyle will emerge that incorporates the best of the two worlds—features of the Pueblo traditional world, and the best of the European world, with restrained technological development and a growing respect for the land as taught by the elders of the ancient Pueblos.

Perhaps the most significant change exists in the Pueblo disposition, or "nature," if one can express it that way. Their ancient history and culture were probably the most peaceful in all the world. With the kind of Spanish domination and repression the people were subjected to, economically as well as in religious matters, the Pueblos threw off the yoke in one of the most militant and revolutionary actions in American history. Today as well, the Pueblo people are long suffering and patient, but they will fight when conditions become unbearable. So it was, not too long ago, when a priest who attempted to continue his repressive activities at Isleta Pueblo felt the strong hand of Pueblo resistance. Father Stadtmueller, who served Isleta in those years, told the Indians, "Don't put pennies in the collection plate. I want to see some real money." He objected to the Indian traditional dances. His hobby was gun collecting. Generally, he was a most obnoxious individual. The time came when Isleta Governor Andy Abeita said, in the name of his people, "Enough!" Finding that the priest would not end his oppressive practices, Abeita led him out of the pueblo in handcuffs, and refused to accept his return, even though demanded by the bishop. Now, Stadtmueller has been made a monseignor, and one asks, "Is this a reward for past injustices?" However, priests such as this one are hardly ever in the pueblos anymore.

The people have developed weapons of peaceful warfare now. They know how to fight in the courts, with ideological weaponry, attempting to educate the public; and their patience will probably pay off. A broad group of non-Indians are very supportive of Pueblo issues. What is even more important is that the Pueblo people have the wholehearted, unstinting support of the Indian tribes of America.

Coronado mural, center panel, by Gerald Cassidy, 1921. (Courtesy Museum of New Mexico, Negative No. 20206.)

The Columbian Quincentenary
and the Pueblo Indians

THE YEAR 1992 will be the 500th anniversary of Columbus's arrival in America. Many people regard this as the date of first contact between Europeans and the indigenous inhabitants of America. But as an American in a free country, with freedom of speech, I do not believe that it was the first encounter between the people from these two continents.

I believe that the indigenous people of this hemisphere migrated thousands of years ago from the Old World, so long ago that the memory of it has been lost through the ages. I also believe that people from the Near East came across the Mediterranean, at a later date, before the Pillars of Hercules (Gibraltar) were closed by the Romans when they became the most powerful nation of the world at that time. It is said that the warning to people crossing read: *"Ne plus ultra"* ("No more beyond").

These former contacts with Carthaginians, Celts, Greeks, and Norsemen were never emphasized as Columbus's voyages were. What occurred in that fateful year of 1492 was a meeting of peoples— a mutual discovery—although effects of this contact have had an unequal impact on the peoples involved. European exploration and colonization meant the end of life as the indigenous people had known it. Their material wealth was forcibly taken, and existing economic balances were changed forever.

In some areas many natives were bound into slavery as mine workers. In the eastern United States thousands died in warfare with colonists, or as allies in warfare between the French and the English. Those Indian allies on the losing side were relocated to other areas and, later, even the rest of the tribes were moved, as a consequence of legislation after the new nation became powerful enough not to need native assistance. In the process, traditional tribal practices were changed or destroyed. In many instances, entire tribes vanished; it is estimated that millions died of European diseases such as smallpox, influenza, and bubonic plague.

In the Pueblo Indian world, the conquistadors thought that the discoveries of Columbus meant a perpetuation of traditions established during the medieval Crusades and during the reconquest of Spain from the Moors of North Africa. Such traditions included the practices of encomienda and repartimiento, which the Spaniards tried on the Pueblo Indians. These practices, along with the attempt to suppress native religious traditions, resulted in the Pueblo Revolt of 1680, when the Spaniards were evicted from Pueblo country for twelve years.

When the Spaniards returned, their attitude had changed; the Pueblos were able to retain a major part of their religion and language due to increased tolerance. The other tribes of New Mexico, the Apaches and the Navajos, also benefited—a fact revealed by census reports, which showed that the three tribes of New Mexico had retained their languages and their religion more completely than tribes from other states that had been settled by the English and French.

Another phenomenon that developed with the return of the Spaniards was the unity between the Pueblo Indians and the Spaniards; they formed an alliance to fight against other raiding Indian tribes. They now had a common enemy, and the Pueblos could repel the other raiding Indian tribes more efficiently allied to the Spaniards, who had guns and horses. Thus the Spanish military, meager as it was, assisted the Pueblos in withstanding the unrelenting raids by other Indian tribes. At the same time, considering the large numbers of auxiliary troops supplied by the Pueblos (Jones 1966), one could argue that the Pueblos should take credit for helping the fledgling Spanish culture survive in colonial New Mexico. Thus the Spanish eventually became compassionate *compadres;* and the shared culture of the Pueblos and Spanish ultimately became the basis for New Mexican culture as we know it today.

There are two men in particular who may be indirectly responsible for the change in the Spanish attitude toward the Indians in the New World. The first person is Padre Bartolome de las Casas, who as a young priest witnessed the atrocities of the Spanish soldiers in Mexico. After his retirement and return home, he began to write about his experiences, but no one believed his description of atrocities because people said that the Spanish soldiers were Christians and could not do such terrible deeds as de las Casas had described.

About the same time, if not earlier, a professor, Francisco de Vitoria, began to write about his ideas concerning who the New World natives were, and what rights they had. (See page 272.) The

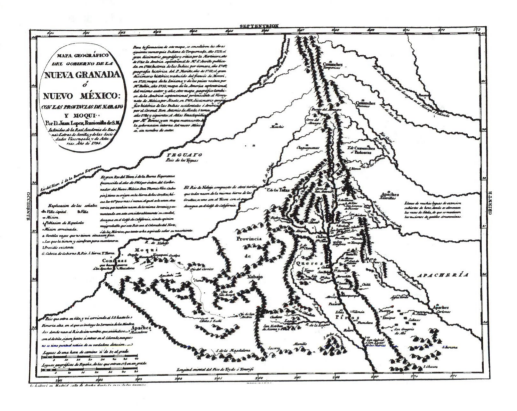

Nueva Granada of Nuevo Mexico by Juan Lopez, 1795. (Courtesy Museum of New Mexico, Negative No. 92061.)

Crown was convinced enough by these two men that a new policy was adopted toward the Indians, one that was more apostolic and less militant. Consequently, when the Spaniards began to arrive in Pueblo country there was always a padre for the military to reckon with before they attacked, if they had to. Of course, as we review history today, it is clear that this procedure was not always followed.

The Spanish culture is still highly visible among the Pueblo Indians today, and somewhat among the Apaches and the Navajos. Let us examine a few aspects of this culture adopted by the Pueblo Indians, focusing on the topics of religion, food, language, government, clothing, and social activities.

Religion

The majority of the Pueblo Indians were of the Roman Catholic faith until about the time of World War II. This religion was introduced by the Spanish Franciscan padres. It eventually became a major part of the Pueblo Indian culture. Each year began with the selection of a new group of officials, who were blessed and sanctioned by the church on Three Kings Day on January 6. Canes of authority were presented to all the pueblos sometime in 1620, and these were also blessed on January 6. (See page 243.) The secular government system that was introduced by the Spaniards still remains today at each of the nineteen pueblos. In addition, the Indian traditional system of war chief and war captains also still exists in most villages to handle religious and cultural activities.

Each pueblo was assigned a patron saint at the beginning of contact, and on the saint's name day the people celebrated. In fact, these saints' feast days, or fiestas, were the holidays from work, since the early New Mexicans did not have American holidays such as Memorial Day, the Fourth of July, or Labor Day.

The feast day started with a mass attended by the people of the pueblo and their Spanish *vecinos.* After mass the statue of the saint was carried in a procession to the plaza, where a shrine had been erected. During the procession Spanish church hymns were sung— and still are today. Two young men with rifles were in the procession and occasionally let loose a volley of gunfire, according to Spanish tradition.

At the end of the day the patron saint's statue was returned to its usual place in the village church, after being paraded between rows of hundreds of dancers and other participants.

Butterfly Dance, Acoma Pueblo, ca. 1946–1952. (Photograph by Ferenz Fedor, courtesy Museum of New Mexico, Negative No. 100402.)

During the day a dancing horse appeared at some pueblos, ridden by a man and attended by two or three masked men with whips called *abuelos*. The rider has been called "Santiago" by the Spanish, since Santiago was the patron saint of Spanish horsemen. To the Pueblo Indians the horse and rider are a reenactment of a scene witnessed by their ancestors, when Coronado and his men were first seen on horseback by the Pueblo Indians.

Likewise, at Jemez Pueblo on August 2 a bull, escorted by several young men disguised as soldiers of early times, appears in the village. This tradition began at Pecos Pueblo, which the Spanish called Cicuye. The remnant population of Pecos migrated to Jemez Pueblo in 1838, and the tradition continues there. Again, the people are reenacting a scene witnessed by their ancestors hundreds of years ago when the Spanish conquistadors appeared.

For Pueblo Indians, tradition was history; history was tradition. Through the art of ritual dance and mime, the Pueblo people related their traditional history, passing the stories down from generation to generation. That traditional history survives is shown in the many additions to the dances made through time, as events shaped and altered the lives of the people. Thus it is that the Spaniards appear in the ritual narratives of today at the pueblos on feast days.

The Spaniards also brought the Matachine Dance to the Pueblo Indians. Today, the Pueblos perform this dance as a traditional prayer-ritual. At Jemez Pueblo a very spirited and exciting dance is performed on December 12, which is the feast day of Our Lady of Guadalupe. Other pueblos perform the dance on Christmas Day or New Year's Day.

Food

The main food brought by the Spaniards was wheat. From wheat the Pueblos made what has become their staff of life, tortillas and oven bread. The oven bread is baked outdoors in a *horno* (Spanish for oven). A Pueblo home is not a home unless it has a horno in the yard next to the house. This bread is the pièce de résistance on feast day tables. Before wheat was introduced the Pueblos had corn tortillas, various kinds of cornbread, chakaway, wayave (paper bread), and atole to drink with their meal. The Pueblos also adopted sopa, or bread pudding, and panocha as dessert. Panocha fixed in various ways has become a special ceremonial food served as a

Picuris woman baking bread in her horno. (Photograph by Marcia Keegan.)

dessert or as a sweet drink, similar to atole in consistency. Other foods brought by the Spaniards did not come from Europe, but from Mexico and the Caribbean Islands.

The combination of Spanish colonial cooking and Pueblo Indian cooking established a cuisine that is found only in New Mexico, properly called "New Mexican food." The "Mexican food," served in other areas away from the Rio Grande corridor, hardly compares with true New Mexican food. New Mexican food differs also from Spanish food, since the Spanish do not eat chile.

Language

As the two cultures merged, Spanish very quickly became the language used for trading, and thus the official language of New Mexico. Even today the New Mexico Indians (Apaches, Navajos, and Pueblos) use Spanish monetary terms such as peso, reales, and centavos in their native languages; they also use Spanish terms for the months of the year and the days of the week. Likewise, many animals, tools, and other objects brought by the Spaniards have Spanish names, adapted slightly differently in each dialect.

Government

According to historical accounts, the Spaniards supposedly introduced their form of government to the Pueblos in 1620. Thus the secular head of each village is the governor, who has a lieutenant; a fiscale and his lieutenant, with five aides each; and an alguacil (sheriff). (See pages 14–15.)

This form of government was to supplement the traditional form of government rather than replace it. The Pueblos still also retained their traditional form of government—the cacique, the war chiefs, and the war captains. The Spaniards called the war captain "capitan de la guerra" in their reports. Most of the Pueblo Indian court systems are patterned after the Spanish system. And most water rights laws are still based on decisions made in the Spanish courts, much to the consternation of modern American lawyers.

Clothing

The Pueblo Indian women adopted several clothing styles from the Spanish: the omnipresent shawl, the lace-covered dress worn under the manta, the apron, and a piece of cloth worn in the back like a cape, the edges of which are lined with two-inch lace or ribbons.

Pueblo men's shirts fashioned after Spanish men's shirts were worn until World War II; and at Isleta Pueblo men still wear the shirts on feast days and ceremonial occasions.

Social Activities

The social activities of the Pueblo Indian people have been influenced by the Spanish ways of celebrating weddings, christenings, funerals, Easter, All Souls Day, and All Saints Day. Hoeing bees and communal wheat cutting of the past were patterned after Spanish traditions. A Spanish governor of New Mexico also decreed that all Pueblo Indians should keep their irrigation ditches and public roads in repair. Today, most Pueblos still work on their community ditches as a civic project.

Thus early New Mexican culture was a union of two cultures. The Pueblo Indians of New Mexico inherited a considerable part of Spanish culture, and the citizens of New Mexico are benefiting from this early encounter.

Paradoxically, the Indians' acceptance of the new Catholic religion and some other aspects of Spanish culture actually allowed them to continue practicing their own religion simultaneously. This has helped the Pueblos to sustain a greater part of their own culture than other Native Americans.

That the Pueblos have preserved so many aspects of their own culture is quite unusual considering the fact that they have been under the rule of three different governments—Spanish, Mexican, and American. Although Anglo-American influence on Pueblo culture was not immediately apparent, after many years some changes in culture are visible. Let us review them in the same order as before.

Religion

Since World War II, some families have gone to Protestant churches. The negative influence of this on the Indian communities was the reluctance of these Protestants to participate in tribal dances at first. This is because the Protestant credo has always been to be a Christian and not an Indian. Recently, however, some of them have been participating again, especially on feast days.

Food

The food originally established in conjunction with the New World Spanish diet remains the core of Pueblo food. However, other foods that have been introduced are Jell-O desserts, cakes, salads, fried chicken, roast turkey, and even various dips and chips.

Language

To the chagrin of many Pueblo elders, many Pueblos of the younger generation prefer to speak English. This may be attributable to the Head Start programs that exist in every Pueblo village. The use of English is also reinforced by television. Another factor is the growing number of interracial or intertribal marriages, where the parents speak different languages or dialects. Very few Pueblos younger than middle age speak Spanish anymore in addition to their native language.

Government

There have been a few changes in the style of government. In 1934, during the Indian Reorganization Act heyday, three Pueblo tribes accepted the ballot system of selecting their officials for the year. Since then four more tribes have opted for the ballot system. The other twelve villages continue the traditional system of relying on the cacique society to select the officials for the year. Court judges are also appointed by the officials selected under the ballot system. They are usually appointed after advertising in the local papers.

Clothing

Clothing, including three-piece suits for young people and men, now comes from stores in town. However, many women continue to dress as traditional Pueblo women. Many more Pueblo men and women appear to have long hair than before; they take pride in their long hair, which is tied behind their heads in a bun called a *chongo*. When taking part in dances, the hair hangs toward the back and adds to the authenticity of the veritable Pueblo Indian.

Social Activities

Additions to Pueblo social activities include Bingo, and high school and university athletic events. Five Pueblo communities now operate Bingo parlors.

A final consideration is the question of whether the Pueblo Indians are entirely satisfied with their destiny as dictated by the encounter with another culture. It is probable that those who have attained a good education and salable skills are contented. But unfortunately, the majority of the Pueblo people do not fall into this category. The Pueblo people have been tilling the soil for countless years, and for many, the land is the focal point of existence. Prior to the encounter, 1539 for the Pueblos of New Mexico, the people offered their prayer feathers and corn pollen each morning, thanking the Creator for all the surrounding land, over which they were the sole masters.

Since that initial encounter, beginning with the Mexican administration, possession and ownership of Pueblo Indian lands in New Mexico began to be contested, and often illegal encroachment occurred. By 1848, another breed of people arrived. These new people did not fight the Indians for their lands, but relied instead on a treaty with the government that governed the Pueblos.

These new people used such terms as "manifest destiny" and "the doctrine of discovery" as passwords to gain control of a continent, and finally reached our land. Thus they gained control despite the fact that they did not discover the New World. And although they professed to bring civilization to the wilderness, New Mexico has never been a wilderness; civilized people with a peaceful culture have lived here long before the Old World enjoyed peace.

Thus in reality, who really benefited by the encounter that began in 1492? Who destroyed the so-called wilderness and feasted on the natural resources of the New World? Who became the millionaires, while the original owners of the land became dependent nations, if they survived at all? If there is to be any celebration in 1992, let those who profited from the New World do the commemorating, and the rest of us will watch.

In conclusion, to paraphrase other natives who have spoken out, if the First Americans choose to be ambivalent about the celebration, it is because they have justifiable cause.

Maria Martinez (1886–1980), from San Ildefonso Pueblo, is internationally recognized for reviving the ancient technique of black-on-black and black-on-red pottery, and, along with her husband, Julian, for helping to create a renaissance of Indian arts and crafts in the first half of the twentieth century. (Photograph by Marcia Keegan.)

❖ 8 ❖

Some Who Shaped
Pueblo History

AT AN EARLY AGE, Indian school children are taught that George Washington was the "father of our country." There is nothing in Pueblo history or legend to justify this honor. The Pueblo Indian "father" of their country was the original cacique, whose successors serve each of the nineteen pueblos today. The American educational system fails the Indian students therefore, in not teaching the history of their own native leaders.

A Pueblo name that is occasionally mentioned, however, is the person whom the seventeenth-century Spaniards called Popé, or El Popé. The Tewas from Popé's home village of San Juan Pueblo may identify this person as Po-'png (pumpkin mountain, pile of pumpkin). Popé has been singled out as the lone planner and leader of the very first American revolution, a revolution made by Native Americans against foreign oppressors. The "Americans" in this case were the indigenous natives of New Mexico, whose descendants and heirs today are the Pueblo Indians. The foreign oppressors were the Spaniards.

There is no desire here to belittle the role of Po-'png as a participant in the Pueblo Revolt. But he was only one of a corps of leaders, probably one of the war captains who met secretly to plan the Pueblo Revolt of 1680. There were many others whom history has all but forgotten. In this way, the heritage of all the people of this nation is diminished, and the story of this country is left incomplete.

Two outstanding Pueblo leaders, recognized and reared by the Spaniards, were Luis Tupatu of Picuris, leader of the northern pueblos (Rio Arriba); and Antonio Malacate of La Cienega de Cochiti (or Cieneguilla), and of the Keresans (Rio Abajo).

General Diego de Vargas, following his entry into Santa Fe on September 13, 1692, reported to the Viceroy Count de Galvez that it had become necessary to choose a governor of the Pueblos who would be obeyed by the "reduced and conquered" tribes. He chose Don Luis Tupatu, who received his cane of office in the presence of the northern pueblo leaders. Tupatu took the oath "in the name of our Lord and by the sign of the cross," to fulfill his civil and religious duties faithfully. Following the ceremony, he was given a horse and saddle. Spanish officials and chroniclers often called him "El Picuris" in their reports. He was well known for his influence with the northern pueblos, and had a large part in the planning and execution of the Pueblo Revolt twelve years before this ceremony.

Luis Tupatu is not to be confused with his brother, Lorenzo Tupatu, who led the flight of the Picuris in 1696 to the homeland of the Cartelejo Apaches (the Jicarilla Apaches today), near Pueblo, Colorado. Like most of the other Pueblos, some of whom fled to the Hopi country and some to the Navajos, the Picuris were returned to their own land in New Mexico, from then on to live in peaceful "detente" with the foreigners and their culture.

Antonio Malacate, the Keresan, was sufficiently feared by de Vargas so that upon his arrival in Albuquerque on September 10, 1692, he made plans to attack Malacate's home. From Albuquerque, the party of conquistadors went to Cieneguilla. However, there was no resistance from the Keresans. Following his successful entry at Santa Fe, de Vargas visited the northern pueblos and Pecos to obtain their allegiance to the Spanish government. On September 26, while at Pecos Pueblo, de Vargas sent a messenger to Malacate, carrying a small cross and a rosary for the "captain and chief of the Queres tribes," including Cieneguilla, Cochiti, San Felipe, Santo Domingo, Santa Ana, and Zia. The messenger found Malacate in ill health, but he agreed to see de Vargas. Later, when de Vargas visited the Keresan Pueblos, offering to pardon them for the revolt if they would swear allegiance to Spain, Malacate accompanied him.

On October 24, at the last Keresan haven, called Cerro Colorado, two miles west of Jemez Pueblo today, Malacate requested that he be relieved of his position as capitan de la guerra of the Keresan tribes, giving his reason as age and illness.

Among other leaders known to the Indians and mentioned by the Spaniards are Francisco El Ollita and Nicolas Jonva of San Ildefonso; Domingo Naranjo, a half-black man from Santa Clara (father of Joseph Naranjo); Domingo Romero from Tesuque; Antonio Bolsas, a Tano; Cristobal Yope of San Lazaro; Felipe de Ye of Pecos; Juan El Tano of Galisteo; Alonzo Catiti of Santo Domingo; and Luis Conizu (or Coniju) of Jemez. There were many planners and leaders of the Pueblo Revolt of 1680. The modern world, however, knows only Popé, who is given sole credit for the first American revolution. He is, moreover, inaccurately described, by accounts that have been handed down in story and legend from generation to generation. Among some Pueblo elders, Popé is believed to have been a cruel despot, a medicine man, and a sorcerer all at once, although he is credited with participating as one of the revolt leaders.

In the following pages, some of the people who shaped Pueblo history are described. Many others are known mainly in family and clan history. Those heroes and heroines of the distant past must be left for another study, an arduous one; it is now difficult to recover all the facts because in the past it was considered discourteous and improper to assume or accept credit. One did not wish to place oneself above all others. This is not to say that the Pueblo Indian was not competitive. The idea of a noncompetitive Pueblo individual is a fantasy of some novelists and a few anthropologists. Competition was keen, but on a different level and in a different way than we know today. Contests were strong in such areas as sports, for excellence of performance and stamina; in planting or harvesting, for producing the best; in the arts, for distinguished workmanship and creative ideas.

Those whose lives are narrated here have influenced Pueblo history in one way or another. They are only examples. I have restricted the biographies to those who have died, since the prominent living Pueblos can be expected to add to their contributions. Such people as Maria Martinez, the distinguished potter; Pablita Velarde, the outstanding artist; Alfonso Ortiz, our great anthropologist and scholar, are not treated, therefore, in this section. (Maria Martinez has died since the first edition of this book, but she deserves a comprehensive book of her own.)

The example of the people whose lives are presented here will, I hope, prove an inducement to the Pueblo youth to match their own efforts to those of some of the Pueblos of the past and help guide the people in fulfilling a great and distinguished destiny. In times to come, the Pueblo people, and indeed all of America, will sing the praises of those Pueblo men and women who made important contributions, leading the people in one area or another, showing the way by example, and carving a road to future progress.

In each of the following biographies, a small part of the people's history may be traced. In fact, the historical events and issues come into better focus when viewed through the lives of such persons.

Pablo Abeita, Isleta Pueblo. (Photograph courtesy of the family.)

Complex situations and problems are revealed more clearly as we note the role of these men and women in their efforts to resolve the affairs of their times.

Pablo Abeita

Pablo Abeita was a man who might well have become a governor of the state of New Mexico. He spoke Spanish, English, and his own mother tongue of Tiwa fluently. His experience and abilities, in another era, could have earned him the highest place in the leadership of the state. Abeita was the product of three civilizations and was perfectly at home in each of them.

He was born February 10, 1871. His parents were Jose P. Abeita and Marcelina Lucero. The day before his eighteenth birthday, he married Maria Dolores Abeita. They had five sons: Juan Rey, Jose Simon (the author's godfather), Remijio, Ambrosio, and Andrew. In 1889, he was appointed by the governor of his tribe to serve on the All Indian Pueblo Council. From that time on he remained a member of the Isleta Council and served in many offices of the village government.

The local Catholic priest enrolled Abeita in a Jesuit school at Old Albuquerque. From there he was transferred to St. Michael's College in Santa Fe. Altogether, he had ten years of formal education, a rare scholarly achievement in Territorial New Mexico. After completing his education at Santa Fe, he returned to Isleta Pueblo.

During his youth, Pablo Abeita worked as a typesetter on the *Albuquerque Morning Democrat,* now the *Albuquerque Journal.* He was a commercial clerk for three years, before entering the Indian Service. Here he served as a resident farmer, as they were called in those days, a post equivalent to an extension agent today. In 1905, Pablo Abeita began to operate the family general store at Isleta, his family having been in the trading business for many years. It is said that his grandfather, Ambrosio Abeita, advanced some fifty thousand dollars to the United States Government through military officials, in the early 1860s, to pay federal troops when the New Mexico Territory was invaded by the Confederates. The money was raised locally by Colonel Canby. It is also said that this financial advance was in the nature of subsistence and forage for the troops and their animals. In 1863, while Ambrosio was in Washington, President Abraham Lincoln presented him with field glasses that Pablo later owned. For his assistance to the government, Ambrosio's estate was reimbursed during the administration of President James A. Garfield. Ambrosio Abeita died in 1879.

In 1912, Isleta Pueblo organized a business council, and Pablo Abeita was chosen as its first president. This council was the closest thing to a compromise between the two factions of the pueblo leaders, the so-called conservatives and the progressives. This type of organization was part of a movement largely of progressive Pueblo conception, supported by the Indian agent. Through the business council, the pueblo was able to restore large areas of land, as well as to triple pueblo funds, in less than three years. In comparison, according to the Indian agent, the conservative Isleta Pueblo Council had no financial showing. They were more interested "in old tribal ways, ceremonies, and graft," said the agent.

As a member and president of the Isleta Pueblo Council, Abeita attended the All Indian Pueblo Council meetings. Since he was one of the most articulate and efficient leaders of that time, the council appointed him to conduct the meetings, record the proceedings, write the resolutions, and generally do the clerical work.

In 1913, Abeita was appointed a judge in the Indian court system by the Indian Service, and served in that capacity until 1923. By this time he had become the secretary of the All Indian Pueblo Council, which fought the Indian Service in favor of self-government within the pueblos. The Indian courts had been abolished, and judges were now being appointed by the federal government's Indian Service.

Any strife between the factions of Isleta always culminated in the Court of Indian Offenses, which had jurisdiction over all Indian misdemeanor offenses. Abeita held the post of judge for ten years. Naturally, he was open to the charge of advancing his minority party and his own personal interests. One case in which Abeita had to act against the rival governing party took place when the Isletas were still making their own wines, and the United States Liquor Service had not succeeded in discouraging the circulation of such beverages. One night, when many of the conservative Indians were engaged in a dance, and the jugs were flowing, Indian agent Lonergan attempted to disperse the group. The agent seized the ceremonial drum. As a result, his life was threatened by the Tiwas. Lonergan arrested and charged their leader with inciting a riot. The arrested leader demanded counsel at his trial, and a man from Bernalillo appeared to defend him. The trial was conducted in accordance with authorized Indian Service legal procedures, Judge Pablo Abeita presiding. The defendant received a sentence of forty days in jail. It was useless for the defendant to appeal to the Indian agent, a course next open to him, since the agent himself had prosecuted him. Instead, he appealed to the commissioner of Indian affairs, then to the secretary of the interior. Receiving no word of sympathy, he was preparing a petition to the president of the United States when his sentence expired. He served the entire period in jail writing letters to various officials.

Albert, king of Belgium, and his queen visited Isleta in 1919. The celebration at the pueblo to honor the visiting royalty was an affair stimulated by the citizens of neighboring Albuquerque. The American city had little to show the royal guests that they had not seen in other southwestern towns. But here was an ancient pueblo, only thirteen miles away. The secretary of the Albuquerque Chamber of Commerce enlisted the help of the Indian agent, who pledged that the plaza of Isleta would provide a historic stage. The Franciscan cathedral, built by Fray Juan de Salas before July 1629, would be a backdrop, and the entire Indian population would be present.

On the appointed day, the scene was later described in this way: Over one bell tower floated the flag of Belgium. Over its companion waved the flag of France, and high above them both and in the center, with its staff supported by the cross, was the United States flag with its red, white, and blue. The mission bells, gift of the Spanish king three hundred years earlier, vigorously announced the approach of the king and queen, who were virtually mobbed by their hosts, the Isleta Pueblo Indians. They were received by the pueblo governor, J. Felipe Albeita, with a speech in his native tongue. The official interpreter was Pablo Abeita. This event was the talk of the state and the countries involved for many months.

Pablo Abeita was elected secretary of the All Indian Pueblo Council on November 5, 1922. In this capacity he traveled many times to Washington on behalf of his Isleta people and the nineteen pueblos of New Mexico. Pablo used to say that he had met and shaken hands with every United States president from Grover Cleveland to Franklin D. Roosevelt, the one exception being President Calvin Coolidge.

Through all of his life, Pablo Abeita dressed in typical Isleta fashion. He wore a tall, white Stetson hat with no crease and a straight brim. His red undershirt, showing around the sleeves and collar, was covered by a lace-front white shirt. He always wore a handwoven Pueblo red sash as a belt, the fringes hanging at his right side. Pablo had a wry sense of humor. And as Marc Simmons wrote in an article about Abeita entitled "Pablo and the President," "Even when criticizing his political foes he made his points with quaint sarcasm rather than malicious barbs. And he loved a joke, especially if he could put one over on the Anglos" (Weigle and White 1988, 156).

Abeita was an able spokesman of the Pueblo people and an avid writer to the newspapers, presenting his views on problems of the day. During the difficult days of the Bursum Bill, Senator Bursum sought to demonstrate that the Indians were to blame for their problems. To this, Abeita said, "My grandfather used to tell me that his grandfather was half Spanish." When friends asked him why he always wore a blanket, he would reply, "I can drop this blanket quicker than I can an overcoat should a bear get after me." In a speech before a congressional committee, when he referred to Columbus discovering America, Pablo said:

> *Columbus goes back to Europe and claims that he found a New World. What right did Columbus have to make such a claim, or what proofs did he have that it was a New World that he found? This world was not "lost," and may be as old if not older than the one Columbus came from. . . . Imagine what Europe would have been if some Indian sailed eastward in search of the rising sun, and had come into the port of Palos, to claim and proclaim that he had found a New World. . . .*
>
> *The white people may say that they did not take all of this country by force, but in some cases had bought it off the Indians. We will not deny that, but look at the bargains they used to get, and remember that Manhattan Island was sold about three hundred and eight years ago for $24 worth of glass beads. . . . Had it been the other way, and some foolish Irishman had sold the British Isles for $2 worth of tobacco, would that have been a good bargain?*
>
> *Our principal needs today are that you eject all non-Indian trespassers off our lands. Instead of reimbursing*

the Indian for what land the non-Indian holds, why not
reimburse the non-Indian trespasser and make him get
off? He knows that he is holding the land illegally, only
you know that he won't vote for you if you don't kick us
into submission.

In November 1926, the Pueblo leaders were called to Santa Fe
for a three-day meeting, when representatives of the federal government led by New Mexico Governor Hagerman attempted to form
a council that would work under the dictatorship of the United
States Government. Many Pueblo leaders refused to attend that
meeting, but a few stalwarts were present. The conversations in the
business sessions went this way:

> Pablo Abeita: *I said last night that if we were to form*
> *a new organization, the new organization would not*
> *interfere with the All Indian Pueblo Council. I do not*
> *want to give that name to the new organization, the*
> *name must remain in the old organization. You can call*
> *the new organization anything you please.*
> Gov. Hagerman: *I suggest that the name of this*
> *organization be "The United States Pueblo Council."*
> Dr. Charles Lummis: *Why not call it something that*
> *will let the people know that we are still Indian. I*
> *suggest "The United States Junta."*
> Pablo Abeita: *The people in Washington would not*
> *know what* junta *means. We are talking in the American*
> *language now and in terms that will be accepted by the*
> *authorities in Washington. I think* junta *is a good word,*
> *but the Americans will not know what it is. But I*
> *suggest that we put in the word* Indian. *The "United*
> *States Pueblo Indian Council."*
> Gov. Hagerman: *I believe the suggestion is a very*
> *good one.*
> Pablo Abeita: *My friends, may I have a few moments.*
> *Of course, this is the third day of the meeting, and in my*
> *opinion we have just about started. I think there should*
> *be another day if we have the assurance that the sessions*
> *will be continued until the business is finished.*

I do not want to take too much of your valuable time telling about the traditional history of the Pueblo government of today. I cannot, as I did in 1905, talk for an hour and a half to President Teddy Roosevelt on this interesting subject, but I will try to say a few words explaining our government. This form was given to us, not by the king of Spain, but by the Christian missionaries who were more orderly than the king himself. This is Christian law that we have.

It is from the Spanish that we get the name "governor." We were put on this part of the earth by the Great Spirit, and in the early days we always had among us "a man who leads," or what is now called the government, very much like our own. Where your president takes the place of our governor, and your councilmen take the place of ours, or rather your Congress. We do not want our governors to be merely scarecrows; we want them to have some authority among their people.

Other tribal governments throughout Indian country had been shaken up, replaced by the European or American system of government, and even forcibly transplanted to the Indian territory. But the Pueblos were fighting to keep their form of government as they knew that it served them best. At this meeting, men like Abeita had to talk fast and negotiate carefully to maintain their government and avoid confrontation. Pablo continued:

This seems to be one of the great steps we are able to undertake to serve our people. Consequently, we cannot sign our names to a paper of this sort. This is a very good thing that has just been mentioned. We will have to make our people understand. I understand that I can write a paper like that, but I would ask if you grant time enough, that we go back home and present this matter before our people. We write up some sort of a resolution and then call on our old Pueblo Council, and each pueblo has their own resolutions read and out of them all then make one, in that way it can be more satisfactory. If it was only me they could finish the business in fifteen minutes, but I have to consider one thousand people at home. . . .

186

The fox had circled the snake. Both were wary, but the fox had avoided being bitten. The new group was indeed formed at the meeting, and it was Pablo Abeita who then said:

> *Mr. President, since I have agreed with you in all of your talks, I agree that a president be elected, and I present the name of Frank Paisano, who is from Laguna Pueblo.*
>
> Gov. Hagerman (quickly): *Friends, you have heard the nomination. The motion has been seconded. All in favor of this motion will signify by rising.*

There was not one negative vote. Paisano was elected president of the "United States Pueblo Indian Council." Following this piece of railroading by the representatives of the federal government, Abeita rose and said:

> *I want to say a few words, since Mr. Hagerman made a remark about the council. We have an organization that we call the All Indian Pueblo Council, and we want to know if this is going to be abolished. I know my people would refuse to discontinue it. We would like to keep the All Indian Pueblo Council. During our Indian meeting last night I tried my best to make them understand. I told them to think very carefully, and here is another thing: I told them in the Santo Domingo meeting that we don't want outsiders to settle our matters, so what can we do? We cannot let go of our hold on the Indians. Is it not best that we get together?*
>
> *After the fight between Santo Domingo and San Felipe in 1905, we made a solemn pledge, followed by a solemn pledge by all the pueblos in 1922; we agreed that in the future, if any disagreements should come up between any one of the pueblos, these things should be settled in the council. Also, if there is any trouble, we would all join in and help them. If there should be a plague of grasshoppers, epidemics, or floods, they would help them until they could get along.*
>
> *If the present council has been called here to do away with this solemn pledge, I might as well go home. I have nothing against John Collier, Mr. Hagerman [governor], or Charley Burke [commissioner of Indian affairs]. I*

have no doubt that the United States Government
means well, but actual facts make us feel the need of
conferring with our friends outside the government. We
do not want to be deprived of our right to appeal to our
friends.

The new organization was formed as a rival of the All Indian Pueblo Council. A budget was established by the federal government. However, during the year, none of the Pueblo leaders ever attended a meeting called by the president. And so, after a year, the new organization was discontinued for lack of Indians to attend the meetings. But the All Indian Pueblo Council continued, and Pablo Abeita remained as its secretary.

On April 6, 1936, the All Indian Pueblo Council was meeting at Santo Domingo Pueblo. A discussion took place as to the appointment of John Collier as commissioner of Indian affairs. Abeita said at this time, "I for one, did not pull for him because he had been a friend of the Pueblo Indians for such a long time that I thought if the doings in the office were going to continue in the same shape and form that they had been for years past, I would probably be the one who would go to Washington and fight Mr. Collier face to face, and in all our fights since the time we have known Mr. Collier, he has fought our battles. After Mr. Collier is appointed commissioner, who is going to fight for us? I thought instead, we are going to fight him. That is one of the reasons why I did not pull for him. When he was appointed commissioner, I think I was the first one who wrote a letter of congratulations to Mr. Collier. I did the same thing when he announced that he was going to appoint Dr. Sophie Aberle to be our superintendent of the United Pueblos Agency."

On the subject of the United States national elections of that time, Pablo said:

I don't care about politics, but I hope that I will
be seven feet under the ground when my people start
voting. But I hope that Mr. Roosevelt will be re-elected
so that Mr. Harold Ickes will remain as secretary and
Mr. Collier as commissioner. I wrote a little article
in the paper the other day about somebody trying to
introduce a bill in Congress so that all the federal
land would be given back to the states. I said, "Why

*not do a little better than that—give it back to the
original owners? The government never bought it,
and the states never bought it. What land we hold
today is land that the white people didn't take away
from us.*

*We have a patent, saying the United States gave us a
piece of ground. I don't like to say that that statement
made in the patent lies, but it looks that way, because I
see no reason why the government gave us a piece of
land. Where did they get that right? The land was
always ours, so I consider the patent doesn't read right;
but we were always a peaceable people. We probably
had the same sort of government that we have today
long before Christopher Columbus had any grandparents.
We were civilized, more or less, in the same form of
civilization that we are today, when the Europeans were
murdering, pillaging, and everything else when they
came here and tried to civilize us.*

*What is civilization? To my way of thinking, civiliza-
tion is nothing but happiness and contentment. The
white person doesn't seem to feel civilized unless he has
a million dollars, and then he is not satisfied because the
million isn't ten million, and after the ten million, the
whole world."*

In recognition of his renown, the 1937 issue of *Who's Who in
New Mexico* contained a half page devoted to Pablo Abeita.

In 1940, the state of New Mexico observed the Coronado Quatrocentennial. On May 29, one celebration was held at the old Pueblo
ruins in Kuaua, the present site of the Coronado Monument across
the river from Bernalillo, where Coronado supposedly visited. Pablo
was invited by the centennial committee to speak. Among the members of the committee was Senator Clinton Anderson. Pablo's ver-
batim speech could not be located. However, this writer's grandfather, Jose Manuel Yepa, of Jemez Pueblo, was present at the
celebration. (Grandfather Yepa was a leader of his pueblo.) Upon
his return home, he told his family about the speech given by his
good friend Pablo Abeita.

As I recall Grandfather's interpretation, the gist of Pablo's speech
was this:

189

*I don't know why you invited me here, because I
am not particularly proud to be here to observe this
quatrocentennial. After all, you people are honoring
those who brought diseases to my country and my
people, thereby reducing the Indian population. We have
very little land left, but you continue to encroach upon
our villages. You strip our trees from the watersheds to
produce lumber and floods; you plow up the earth to
raise grain crops and sandstorms; and you have turned a
large section of land that used to be fertile enough for at
least a subsistence economy for Indians, into outright
desert.*

*You call us savages for dancing without street clothes
on, although our costumes are very pretty, and then you
show up at our dances with so little clothing on that we
wonder who the real savages are.*

According to another report of the event by Marc Simmons,
Pablo also remarked, "I am afraid I will have to contradict some
of the things you gentlemen have said. Coronado came by Isleta,
and as you who have read his chronicles know, was given food and
royally received. He came up the valley, and what did he do? Well,
we had better say no more about it, for his record isn't good and
you know it" (Weigle and White 1988, 429).

And still another account of the celebration reported later by
Marta Weigle and Peter White in their book *The Lore of New
Mexico* noted that the crowd broke into the heartiest applause of
the afternoon, and did so again at every pause, as the respected
Isletan continued a short and cutting debunking of white man's
history, which he said is ninety percent wrong (Weigle and White
1988, 429).

Seldom mentioned is the fact that Pablo Abeita was also an
important figure in the native religious life of his pueblo. Through
all the changes in the civil life of the pueblo, and all the changes
in the world outside, the one thing that did not change was Pablo's
feeling for his native religion. Every morning, with his corn pollen
sack in hand, he would address the Great Spirit and thank Him
for the blessings, and beseech Him for peace and prosperity for
all mankind in the world.

Sotero Ortiz, San Juan Pueblo. (Photograph courtesy Smithsonian Institution National Anthropological Archives, Bureau of American Ethnology Collection, Negative No. 2035-A.)

Those who knew Pablo Abeita knew that he was important for being himself, and not for the many offices he held in his lifetime. The Grand Old Man of Isleta Pueblo, Pablo Abeita, was truly an important and great Pueblo Indian leader. He stood between the people of the pueblos and the people outside, since he was erudite and multilingual. He could communicate with legislators in Washington, as well as with businessmen in Albuquerque and Santa Fe. For all these qualities his Pueblo people recognized him, trusted him, and had faith in him.

Pablo Abeita died December 17, 1940.

Sotero Ortiz

The period of 1870 to 1920 was an era of unprecedented persecution of the American Indians. Military reprisals, fraud, deceit, and attempted annihilation by the United States Government were the order of the day. But the Indians endured. Soon the United States found that some sort of action would be necessary to consider the many problems that persisted, despite efforts to eliminate the Indians through genocide, quiet them by removal, or starve them into submission.

The federal government was compelled to recognize the American Indians as natives with inalienable rights, as a result of the *Sandoval* case of 1913. To "recognize" or "not to recognize" was always a question of ponderous importance to the government. Also, the Pueblos could not be considered in the same way as the Mohawks, or the Indians of California, or the Choctaws who had been removed to Oklahoma. The complexity of Pueblo-United States relations has been the cause of litigation, congressional legislation, and congressional hearings ever since this country acquired the territory of the Southwest. For the Indians, this was now a way of life. As a result of the *Sandoval* case, the Pueblo Indians became entitled to benefits under the Indian legislation of 1834. One such law was the Indian Trade and Intercourse Act. The other was the Indian Service Act. The first act required that traders with Indians be licensed by the government. The second established the Department of Indian Affairs as a government bureau.

The Pueblo leadership had faced these stubborn problems under a traditional system of government since 1912, when New Mexico had attained statehood. To deal with these problems under a form of government understood by the non-Indians, the Pueblo leaders had reorganized their council of governments, and included a statement of purpose.

Into this beleaguered leadership was thrust a descendant of that tribal group that had suffered most from the ambitions of the conquistadors who caused the Pueblo Revolt of 1680. He was Sotero Ortiz of San Juan Pueblo.

Sotero Ortiz was the first elected leader of the modern Nineteen Pueblos, chosen by vote on November 5, 1922, at Santo Domingo Pueblo during the reorganization meeting resulting from the threat of the Bursum Bill.

Ortiz was born at San Juan Pueblo in 1877. His mother was Maria Reyes Atencio of the Summer moiety. His father was Jose Dolores Ortiz, a Spanish man from a neighboring community. Although his first language was Tewa, his mother's tongue, he also learned Spanish from his father. He attended the government day school at San Juan Pueblo through the fourth grade. After this, he helped his family with farming. Often he and his father would help other non-Indian farmers, for which they were paid in cash. With this they purchased shoes for the family, sugar, and beans. They grew their own wheat for flour, and corn that was prepared for food in a variety of ways.

Sotero's fourth grade education did not prepare him for life in frontier Anglo New Mexico. Nor did he have a knowledge of the English language sufficient to make a place for himself in that society. One year there was a good piñon crop in the hills southeast of Santa Fe. Many San Juan Pueblo people and others gathered to harvest the nuts. Sotero was one of these piñon pickers. Soon he found himself inside an enclosure, where a no trespass sign had been posted. As Ortiz was gathering the piñons, the owner of the posted area appeared.

"Didn't you read the sign?" the man asked. Sotero said, "Maybe I saw the sign, but I am looking for piñons, and I have no time to read signs."

"Young man," the stranger said, "this is my land, and any piñons within my land I will pick. I'll have to ask you to leave."

"I am not going to leave until I have picked all I can carry," Sotero responded. "These piñons are for all of God's children, and we have a right to pick them wherever we find them. This is the way of my people, and they have been doing this long before you white men came." The stranger was interested. He was aroused by the piñon picker's spirit.

"What is your name and where is your home?" he asked. Ortiz replied, giving the information, and the man then asked if he would like to work for him occasionally. "I'll have to ask my father," said Sotero. The man who had challenged Sotero's right to pick the piñons was Thomas B. Catron, a lawyer. He was the greatest land baron in the history of New Mexico. Later that fall, Catron came to San Juan Pueblo and brought Sotero back to Santa Fe, where the boy did such work as chopping wood and laying adobes for constructing a wall around the Catron residence. Since it was a long way back to San Juan, the youth remained at the Catron home for several days at a time.

Evenings in the Catron home were especially interesting for Sotero. The lawyer had a good library, and the young man began to read the law books, "skipping over the big words," as he later explained. He became particularly interested in the land problems of the state. Available in the library were also the letters and papers of attorneys from other parts of the state, brought home by Catron. Sotero had an opportunity to examine some of these.

Whenever Sotero Ortiz was at work in Santa Fe, he took special pleasure in reading. Often he would just talk with the lawyer. Soon he had improved his English, both in reading and speech. As a result, he was appointed by the Indian Service as a policeman in his village. Later, Ortiz served as an interpreter when the governor was selected from the Summer moiety, his own group. As interpreter for his governor he attended the All Indian Pueblo Council meetings. It was a long wagon ride to Santo Domingo. Delegates from San Juan started their journey at the break of dawn; the sun would be well up in the sky by the time they reached Pojoaque. Sometimes they met delegates from other Tewa villages as they traveled towards Santa Fe. There were occasions when the delegates went to Lamy, boarding a train that took them more quickly to Santo Domingo. When this occurred, a young lieutenant drove them to Lamy, and after they had boarded the train, the youth drove the wagon back to San Juan. He returned to Lamy to pick them up three or four days later, when the council meeting ended.

Sotero was quick to learn the procedures of the meetings. Pablo Abeita of Isleta usually chaired the meetings. Sotero, with Charlie Kie of Laguna and Alcario Montoya of Cochiti, contributed to most of the discussions, interpreting to their fellow delegates throughout the meeting. Later, other young men, such as Porfirio Montoya of

Santa Ana, Martin Vigil of Tesuque, Jesus Baca of Jemez, and Abel Sanchez of San Ildefonso, began to take part in the discussions. These men tried to explain the problems confronting the Pueblos to the older delegates and the councilmen.

When the Bursum Bill was introduced, John Collier came to the council meeting to ask the Pueblos to organize their council on an official basis, so that the "people in Washington" would understand, and recognize them as official spokesmen for the Pueblos. A special meeting was called for this reason, on November 5, 1922. A "statement of purpose" was drawn up, and an election of officers was held. On this occasion Sotero Ortiz was elected to be the first chairman of the All Indian Pueblo Council.

It was also decided at this time that a few of the Pueblo leaders should appeal directly to the American people in the East and West, to explain the situation threatening the Indians in New Mexico, and to raise money to fight their case in the courts. Collier was their guide on their trip to the East. When they arrived in New York, Collier said, "Now it is up to you. Speak up and talk like you never have done before." As chairman, Ortiz knew he would be required to speak, and he protested, "I don't know what to say, I can't even speak good English. I have never talked to so many white men in my life. What shall I say?"

"You know the history of your people. Tell them how you lost most of your land. Tell them what this Bursum Bill will do to your people," Collier advised.

Pablo Abeita volunteered, "Don't be afraid. Just look over their heads, and you won't even know they are looking at you. What you don't cover, I'll tell them."

Later that evening, in a large auditorium, with the biggest crowd the Pueblo men had ever seen, Sotero spoke.

"Ladies and gentlemen," he began. "My name is Sotero Ortiz. I am a Tewa Indian from San Juan Pueblo, New Mexico. We are here tonight to tell you we are in deep trouble. We want to ask for your help. We need money. We need your letters to your congressmen about our problems. We are here to tell you the truth about ourselves, and you should not listen to what someone else says about us."

He was referring to a statement made by the sponsor of the bill, Senator Bursum of New Mexico, who claimed the Pueblo Indians supported the bill.

Ortiz continued, "We do not want this bill. We were never consulted about this bill. Once already our ancestors were overcome by the forces of the kingdom of Spain, in the year 1680. They then gave up their rights to the central part of what is now the state of New Mexico. They were forced to do this. In return, the Spanish government gave us small grants of land. We have become, in time, used to these small confines of land. But, in all the years from that time till now, we have been the victims of continued trespass and intrigue, until there is little left to us of the original grants of land even. Many among us are very poor. The population, mostly descendants of the soldiers of Spain who fought against our people, and Mexicans from Old Mexico who drifted into our country, have now become so numerous that we feel the time has come when we must stand in our own defense. Otherwise we will lose everything, even the little that remains from the great land that once was ours."

He was speaking freely now, recovered from his stage fright, and was discussing his favorite subject. Sotero Ortiz made a lasting impression upon his New York audience. He exposed the fact that the Pueblos were opposed to the legislation, and that Senator Bursum was practicing fraud in claiming the bill had the Indians' support.

After protests such as these, the Senate took another look, had another vote, and recalled the bill.

The "first team" returned home from the East, and made plans for another tour, this time to the West Coast. Collier took the Pueblo leaders to San Francisco, and one evening the Ladies' Club planned a special social event for the traveling Indians. Collier told them they were invited to a cocktail party at the hotel before dinner. They had never been to such a function, and did not know what to expect. Alcario Montoya of Cochiti Pueblo said, "I am glad we are going to this cocktail party. I think I am going to get some parrot feathers. I hear the people in California have many kinds of birds and the feathers are pretty. We need the long ones for our Buffalo Dance." Ortiz thought he, too, would like to get some peacock feathers. "They will look good on my sons when they do the Comanche Dance at Christmas time," he remarked.

The crowds were large in the West. A considerable amount of support was generated, and information finally became available to the American public about the true state of Pueblo Indian affairs.

Although Sotero Ortiz served as an official of the All Indian Pueblo Council for a quarter century, he was never elected to any office in his home village, other than serving as an interpreter. But he was a willing servant of his people. On March 7, 1921, he composed a petition to the secretary of the interior for his pueblo. They were fighting for their diminishing land base. He lived at San Juan Pueblo most of his life, farming and doing odd jobs in the off-season for his old friend Thomas Catron. He was married to Maria Reyes Abeita of San Juan, and they had four children: Jose Manuel, Pasqualita, Rafaelita, and Joe Dolores.

During his many years of service to the All Indian Pueblo Council, Ortiz often attempted to persuade the council to replace him as chairman. At the meeting held April 6, 1916, he said:

> *The chairman and secretary and interpreter were not to be appointed for life. When we believed that our term had expired, then I stood up, just as I am now standing, and spoke to you that the time has been terminated, and it was our duty to appoint another chairman here, say a new board. Well, then you reelected us again and every time we try to bring up the question to retire us, you have been reelecting us, and you know very well for how many years I have been your chairman. I don't know if you have been reelecting us because we have been giving you good service here.*
>
> *You know very well I am not taking this seat because I want it or am asking for it. Because you have asked me to take it, I am still your chairman, and also the two gentlemen on my sides, one of them is your secretary and the other is the interpreter.*

On May 31, 1940, during their regular meeting, Ortiz finally got his wish to step down as chairman. But instead of retiring from office, he was elected to serve as interpreter by the council of governors, the All Indian Pueblo Council. He served in this position until October 12, 1946, another six and a half years, for a total of twenty-four years of public service to the Pueblo Indians.

During the early years of Ortiz's chairmanship, the council had a running battle with the Indian Service. The service denounced the All Indian Pueblo Council as an unauthorized and outlawed governing body. Attempts were continually made to undermine the council. At one time the superintendent of the Eight Northern Pueblos, a Mr. Crandall, sent out an announcement ordering that the Pueblos give up their old government and adopt a new system of electing their officials at a European-type election, once each year. Crandall said that the old pueblo governments were contrary to American ideals and would have to go. He reminded the people how, in Taos Pueblo, the governor and all his officers were arrested and brought to Santa Fe and locked up for having administered a mild punishment to an offending pueblo member, exercising their old-time traditional governing ways.

The Indian Service attempted to prohibit the Pueblos from practicing their religion. In 1923, they were given one year in which to give up their religion. If they refused, the service would use compulsion, they declared. During that time few Indians were able to go to Washington, even though they would be using their own funds, held for them by the United States. The Indian Service controlled the tribal monies, as well as the funds belonging to the individual "restricted" Indians. In this manner the service was able to dictate which Indians should go to Washington, when they should go, and, of course, what they should say.

Many and grave were the problems that Sotero Ortiz and his colleagues had to deal with during those years. Some of these problems were related to stock reduction on certain Pueblo reservations, land purchases under the Pueblo Lands Board Act, and the organization of individual pueblo governments under the Wheeler-Howard (Indian Reorganization Act) legislation. His village of San Juan was hardest hit by squatters, and much of their land was lost in this way. He had always maintained that their southern boundary extended from Tschicoma Peak in the Jemez Mountains on the west to Truchas Peak in the Sangre de Cristo Mountains in the east. He was able to hold on to what his people had, mainly by physically removing squatters from the reservation.

Sotero Ortiz lived to the age of eighty-six, and died July 28, 1963. He was a fighter for his people to the very end, a hard working, gentle Pueblo man who strove mightily to improve his knowledge. Like most other Indians who are forced into the position of leadership by the needs of their times, his entire life was spent defending the rights of his people. In the face of such longtime struggles, it is difficult to see a man "in the round," as his children and grandchildren knew him. Instead of the old times of pleasure and contentment of traditional ways, with the regular ritual and

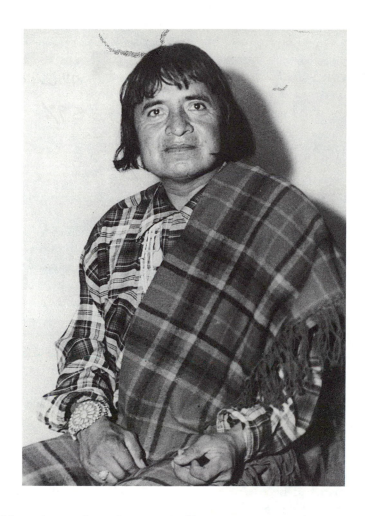

Mateo Aragon, Santo Domingo Pueblo. (Courtesy of the All Indian Pueblo Council.)

religious observances, the story of birth, growth, and death, life had become one round of litigation, legislation, pouring over law books and legal documents, travel to let the people know what was happening, and conferences for devising strategies for self-protection. Ortiz was a great man, a dedicated Pueblo leader.

Mateo Aragon

The boy was up early with the morning star. As usual, after he had washed, he went outdoors to sprinkle sacred corn pollen to the cardinal directions, giving thanks to the deity. There was an air of anticipation this morning, and in a fever of excitement he sang one song after another, from Buffalo Dance songs to Butterfly Dance songs, before his mother called him to breakfast. He was too excited to eat, for this was the day when he, together with hundreds of other young boys and girls from Santo Domingo Pueblo and other pueblos, all the way from Acoma and Laguna, would be boarding a train to take them to Santa Fe Indian School.

After breakfast, Mateo was at the corral catching the horses, so they could be harnessed and hitched to a wagon to take him to the Santa Fe Railroad depot at Santo Domingo, about six miles northeast of the village. When the prospective student, with his grandfather and mother, arrived at Santo Domingo, the train stop was bustling with wagons, horses, and people. The students from Cochiti Pueblo had also been brought in by horse and wagon, and the wagons were parked all over the area. Students and their parents were roaming about the trading post, which also served as the railroad depot.

A man had been sent down from the school to supervise the departure. A few minutes before the train was scheduled to arrive from the south, the stranger began to order the girls and boys to line up. Eventually, young Mateo reached a place in the lineup for inspection. After one quick look at the boy, the man said, "I'm sorry, son. You are too small; come back next year." Mateo did not understand, but someone told him that he must return home with his mother. With his extra denim trousers and one shirt rolled in a paper wrapper, Mateo returned home to his village, to wait still another year before he could begin his education.

The year of waiting went by quickly enough, and by the fall of 1916 Mateo was a first-grader at Santa Fe Indian School. He did well, and was especially noted for his grasp of problems in arithmetic.

At that time, the school took the students only through the eighth grade. To continue his education, he would have to go either to Albuquerque Indian School or to the Haskell Institute at Lawrence, Kansas. However, because of an aging grandfather and a young brother Mateo returned home in 1923 at the end of his eighth grade school year. Seventeen-year-old Mateo took over the family farm. Thereafter he remained at the pueblo, not even accepting employment in a job that would take him away from his village.

According to his mother, Domingita Carmelita, Mateo was born on the feast day of the Jicarilla Apaches at Dulce, New Mexico. The annual Apache feast day is September 15; Mateo was born in 1906. He was raised by his mother and grandfather, Cruz Aragon. Mateo and his mother were of the Fire Clan.

Since he was supporting a family, Mateo did not marry for many years. Finally, he met and married Mrs. Petra Chama; the Aragons had three daughters—Mrs. Marie C. Pajarito, Mrs. Rebecca C. Chavez, and Irene. To supplement his income, Aragon learned to make white shell beads that he traded and sold.

When Mateo's younger brother, Vidal, returned from the armed forces, he learned the silversmith trade. Today, Vidal Aragon is known throughout the world as a gifted craftsman. The two brothers formed a business, whereby Vidal made all the silver and turquoise jewelry, and Mateo took it to the cities to sell and trade.

Mateo Aragon was a popular figure in the state capitol building in Santa Fe, where he offered his jewelry for sale among the employees. He took the opportunity also to inform the governor and other state officials on the state of affairs in Indian country. This was his way: unofficial contacts, friendly persuasion, a very personal system of communications.

In Albuquerque, Aragon was just as well known in the Bureau of Indian Affairs offices. People would say that he knew all the paydays of federal and state employees, since those were the days when he showed up at their offices to sell, or to collect from a previous sale.

As a member of the Santo Domingo community, Mateo served in several minor posts in his younger days, but as he mastered the English and Spanish languages, through his trading and travels, he earned the respect of all for his ability and friendliness. He learned to speak Navajo as well as some of the Jemez and the Tewa languages. He even ordered his meals in Greek from his Greek friend in Santa Fe. In 1949, he was appointed to serve as a lieutenant fiscale of his village, and the following year he was advanced to the position of lieutenant governor of his tribe. Between 1950 and 1963, he served five times in that capacity. He was a member of the education committee of his village. Later he was elected chairman of that committee. As chairman, he served on the Advisory School Board of the Bernalillo School District. This interest, and his experience in Indian education, led to his appointment to the education committee of the All Indian Pueblo Council.

Mateo Aragon used to say, "Circumstances beyond my control kept me from obtaining more education beyond the eighth grade. Therefore I want all the Indian children to take advantage of the benefits and special assistance available to them now." He visited the Santo Domingo Elementary School, unannounced, to obtain a list of absentees for the day, and then he would visit the homes of the absentees and talk to the parents of those children. He followed the same pattern at the high school in Bernalillo.

Whenever there was a conference, Aragon was there. He loved to challenge non-Indians on historical and related matters. At a meeting in Bernalillo, where many school officials of Spanish-American descent were present, he said, "Our children are absent from school often because they are honoring a saint on the saint's name day. Your ancestors gave us those saints, and they told us to honor them. We still honor them, but it seems like you have forgotten them."

At another education conference, where curricula and other subjects relative to interests of Indian students were being discussed, a review of Southwest history was held. Aragon remarked, "You teach our Indian students history, but everything is about the white man."

Besides serving on the education committee, Aragon acted on behalf of his tribe on the irrigation committee, and was also a one-man water utility authority. In this last position he maintained records and collected water fees from families in Santo Domingo Pueblo. After his death, he was replaced by a committee of four or five persons to do the many things he had done alone.

Mateo Aragon was the All Indian Pueblo Council's representative on the state committee on tourism. He also served as spokesman for the Council of Santo Domingo, and he was the bonded treasurer for his pueblo. At all meetings he attended, Aragon took copious notes and wrote them in a stenographic notebook. These are now in the possession of his family.

Whenever the various governors received notices of meetings over the years, they notified Aragon, knowing that he would find the time to attend. On days of the meetings, Aragon would notify the governor first, before he left the village. He then hitchhiked to Albuquerque, Bernalillo, Santa Fe, or wherever the meeting was to be held; he never owned a motor vehicle. On these trips he took trade items along, so he could obtain money with which he could buy his meals. Conference sponsors in those days did not pay per diem and mileage.

Aragon served his people for fifteen years before his untimely death. During those years he never received any kind of salary. He made several trips to Washington, using tribal funds. Upon his return he gave meticulous accountings for every penny spent. It is said that Mateo Aragon probably missed only two meetings where he was supposed to be present. Both were held during the week of his death. He was buried September 15, 1968. The day would have been his sixty-second birthday. Three days later, on September 18, a day of mourning was set aside, and the American flag was flown at half mast at the Indian Village of the New Mexico State Fair.

Among his many qualities, Mateo Aragon had a way of communicating with the older Pueblo leaders, and for this he had the respect of the younger, formally educated leaders.

Close to the fireplace in his old home are two certificates. One reads: "To Mateo Aragon, an Award of Merit, for Outstanding Contributions to Public Education in New Mexico." This honor was given by the New Mexico School Board Association on October 18, 1960. The other is from the United States Department of Labor, given at the 1967 National Conference on Employment, in Kansas City, Missouri, February 16, 1967, and signed by William Wirtz, secretary of labor.

Driving away from Santo Domingo Pueblo, one travels under an overpass before turning on to State Road 22. Arriving at the blacktopped road, a sign is clearly visible against the blue sky and open country, proclaiming in memory of a simple man who did his best for his people, "Mateo Aragon Overpass."

Martin Vigil

In 1921, when the state of New Mexico was barely nine years old, a white man fraudulently purchased sixty-five acres of Tesuque Pueblo land and fenced it. The Pueblo Indians were not even consulted. Learning of this deceit, a young leader of the pueblo led a party of his men to tear down the fence that had been built on their land a few miles south of their village. A few days later, a horde of law officers from Santa Fe descended on tiny Tesuque Pueblo.

The twenty-five-year-old leader was singled out as the instigator of this defiant deed. He was Martin Vigil, and one of the lawmen invited him to look at a government survey marker. "Can you read?" asked the man in a gruff voice. "No," answered Vigil. "Well," the lawman said, speaking in Spanish, "this marker says anyone who removes it will be fined $200 and may also be sent to the penitentiary." "We don't care about that," Vigil retorted. "This is still Indian land, and nobody asked us if they can put the marker there, or the fence."

The land in question had been surveyed two years after statehood by government men, but it had not been explained to the Indians, nor had they been consulted about the boundaries that had been set. "You can repair the fence, but we'll give you ten days to remove it," Martin continued. An English-speaking man tried to challenge Vigil, but Martin realized he did not stand a chance, since he knew little English. "We know this is our land, so we'll use your court system to prove it," Vigil said in Spanish.

Issues of the *Santa Fe New Mexican* were full of articles about defiant Tesuque Indians. San Juan Pueblo officials came to offer their help. A women's club in San Francisco sent a "do-gooder" to assist them in their plight. As a result, a four-day court was eventually held in Santa Fe. One month after the hearing, the intruder removed his fence from the Tesuque Pueblo land. The "do-gooder" from San Francisco came to Tesuque to see the governor. The governor called his nephew, Martin, to come and give his opinion of this strange-looking man, who wore a hat, a tightly-buttoned high-collared shirt, and a jacket with at least four buttons in front. "He looks like a tramp, let's not pay any attention to him," said Vigil to the governor. This man with the strange-looking clothes was John Collier, later to become commissioner of Indian affairs.

Martin Vigil, one of the leaders who fought against the Bursum Bill, 1923. (Photograph by a member of the Bureau of American Ethnology, courtesy Smithsonian Institution National Anthropological Archives, Bureau of American Ethnology Collection, Negative No. 2062.)

Thereafter, the two men, Martin Vigil and John Collier, worked together on Indian causes for twenty-four years.

The fight for his people became the life work of Martin Vigil. Known in later years as the grand old man of Tesuque Pueblo, he was chairman of the All Indian Pueblo Council for nine years, and a spokesman for his people for thirty-eight years.

Martin Vigil was born at Tesuque Pueblo in 1896. His parents were Ignacio Vigil and Candelaria Romero. His father was fluent in Spanish and could read and write. Martin began school as an eight year old in his village in 1904. But the school closed in 1905. Consequently, for the next two years of his education, he had to attend St. Catherine's in Santa Fe. However, he did not learn to speak English at this school. He learned Spanish and became a fluent speaker in that language, since his classmates and dormitory companions were Spanish-speaking students attending St. Catherine's with the Indian students.

After the death of his parents, Martin lived with an uncle, who would not allow him to attend school. Instead, the boy was put to work herding the uncle's cattle. He longed to go to school, or work elsewhere, out of the village. But the uncle said that if Martin became educated he might leave the village for good and forget his Indian culture.

When Martin was about nineteen years old, he married Catherine Swazo of Tesuque. He recalls telling his bride, "Now I am free, and I can go to work anywhere I please." He found a job in 1914 in Cerrillos, New Mexico, at a smelter, and was soon advanced to the position of foreman with twelve other men from Santo Domingo working under his supervision.

He also found lodging at Santo Domingo Pueblo, where he returned with his men every evening. Martin remembered that as they approached the pueblo they all changed to moccasins and put on their headbands. Many years later, he often returned to Santo Domingo to watch the ceremonial dances. On one occasion some young men stopped him at the outskirts of the village and asked who he was. He answered the young men in the remembered Keresan tongue, and gave them his Santo Domingo name, as his men had called him back in 1914.

Martin also recollected going to Delta, Colorado, one summer to work on the railroad for two months. He was with the track repair gang for five days before he was put to work in the ice house.

But always he had to return home to harvest his own crops at Tesuque. One year Martin worked with a movie-making company in Hollywood, California, where he served as a messenger boy around the set. He remembered going to his first All Indian Pueblo Council meeting in 1912 at Santo Domingo Pueblo. He said the acting chairman of the meeting was also the recording secretary, and was from Isleta Pueblo. The man was Pablo Abeita. Martin said Abeita was the first Pueblo man to drive a Ford to Santo Domingo. He brought his Isleta council members to the meetings in this Ford.

The Tesuque delegates, Martin said, hitched their horses to a wagon early in the morning and proceeded by way of Santa Fe. They stopped for lunch at La Bajada Hill, twenty miles south of Santa Fe, and after lunch resumed the journey, arriving at their destination around four o'clock. The wagon ride generally took about eight hours from Tesuque to Santo Domingo. The Santo Domingo officers met their wagon and took care of the horses while the delegates walked to the meeting hall. The meetings began as soon as a majority of the Pueblo leaders arrived. Often the meetings started after supper, which was around six o'clock, lasting until midnight. The next morning they would resume around eight o'clock. These meetings were seldom one-day affairs. Transportation was too tedious and too precious to waste on a one-day meeting. Usually it was two to three days and nights before the delegates returned home.

As Martin began to participate in All Indian Pueblo Council affairs, he improved his English. He said, though, that he was never able to speak English as he did his own Tewa language and the Spanish that he had learned as a young boy.

In his many struggles for Indian rights, Martin felt the greatest challenge was the fight against the Bursum Bill in the early twenties. Many Pueblo leaders toured the country in 1923, explaining Pueblo life and their fight for their rights. "I was elected to go to the East, although I did not know hardly anything. I could not even speak in English. That is where I got my education, by travel," he said.

At many places the Pueblo Indians spoke to huge crowds. In New York City, Martin remembered, the crowd was the largest. Some of the leaders could not speak English at all, so they spoke a few words in their language and in Spanish, amid much hand-clapping by the curious audience. Martin, in his fragmented English, explained the hard life of the Pueblo people. He told the New Yorkers how a Pueblo man would go after wood on a donkey one day, and spend another day chopping it to fireplace size, before he took it to the city to sell, on the third day. The three days of labor often netted only $1.00, when a sack of flour cost $1.50. Martin said that an archbishop came to the stage after his talk and hugged him and congratulated him for his speech. At this meeting, the Pueblos collected $1,600, which was later used to pay their tribal attorneys who were representing them in the fight against the Bursum Bill.

Although Martin began attending the All Indian Pueblo Council in 1912, he did not hold office until forty years later. In 1952, he was drafted to serve as chairman for the first time. He said, on that day he also learned another new English word, *drafted*. He thought he had a "bigger voice" and was more at liberty to voice his opinion as an ordinary delegate. During his first term as chairman he served from November 15, 1952, until February 12, 1955. He was out of office for two years before he was voted into office again in March 1957. After this election he served until February 1964. It was during these years that he was also elected by his own Tesuque people to be governor in 1958, and again in 1962. He had always been an interpreter and assisted the various governors.

During his tenure, he continuously demanded assistance for building community centers, where pueblo officials could maintain their offices and hold meetings. After many years in the discussion and planning stage, the majority of pueblos today do have modern meeting halls. He had always been an advocate of land leveling for the Pueblo farmer. Some of this had been done, but it was not enough to satisfy Chairman Vigil. Another project of Martin's was to build a Pueblo Indian capitol building at Santo Domingo, where he envisioned the chairman could have his office.

Martin had always believed in cooperation for progress. When he became chairman, he began to invite state officials to All Indian Pueblo Council meetings so they could learn about the problems of the Pueblo people. As a result, Governor Edwin Mechem of New Mexico became a good friend of the Pueblos. As Indians began to take an active part in state elections, they generally voted for Mr. Mechem, who was perhaps New Mexico's only Republican governor to be elected for three terms. As a result of cooperation with the state government, the New Mexico Commission of Indian Affairs was established in 1955. Martin's very good friend, Charles Minton of Santa Fe, was the first executive secretary of the commission. Martin Vigil was also named to the State Commission on Indian Affairs.

Vigil had been a "watchdog" for his Tesuque people for many years. He was aware of their resources, their plans to improve their economy, their reservation boundaries, and the history of their land.

There was a sparkle in Martin's eyes as we sat in his spacious living room in front of the fireplace on a cold spring day. Looking out of the picture window, snow was visible half way down the side of the Sangre de Cristo Mountains a few miles to the east. Every now and then a grandchild or two came in to interrupt "Tahtah" with some question.

Obviously, Mr. Vigil was very pleased to have an audience while he reminisced. He talked about old acquaintances and friends, about conversations with various persons, as if they had occurred only yesterday. He showed pictures taken with senators in Washington and with other friends in the eastern cities. Martin was happy as he talked about his experiences in the past, knowing that he had worked many years for the benefit of Indian people, generally without compensation.

Martin and his wife, Catherine, who died many years ago, had five children. They all have their own families. Three of them live in Tesuque while one lives in Albuquerque and another in Farmington, New Mexico. There are many grandchildren.

In his old age, Martin was still able to do the things he had done fifty years before. He maintained his farm, where he grew corn, beans, and other crops; he even experimented with an evergreen nursery, with the young trees coming from the mountains east of the village. He attended an occasional All Indian Pueblo Council meeting to renew acquaintances and advise some of the young leaders. The young men were always glad to shake hands with the elder statesman of the All Indian Pueblo Council. In fact, he was the epitome of the Pueblo elder.

Martin Vigil was also a familiar figure in neighboring Santa Fe. State officials continued to consult with Chairman Vigil on many problems concerning Indian people and sought his recommendations for appointees for board and commission membership on the state level.

Edward Pasqual Dozier, Ph.D., Santa Clara Pueblo. (Photograph courtesy of the family.)

He is remembered, even now, as a man easy to talk to. He enjoyed telling stories, relating his many experiences, and expounding on Pueblo history. He was an engaging and friendly personality. There are many among us today who wish they had spent more time at the side of Martin Vigil, listening to the history and the tales of the public career that filled his life.

On September 24, 1973, as he was tending his farm a few miles from the village, he had a heart attack. Word of this tragedy reached his daughter in time so an ambulance was called from Santa Fe. The ambulance took him to Santa Fe, but Martin Vigil was dead. He was buried at Tesuque Pueblo, where many of his friends from far and near came to see Chairman Martin Vigil for the last time.

Edward Pasqual Dozier

Edward Pasqual Dozier was the first of his people to receive the doctoral degree from a university, at a time when the average educational level for Pueblo people was the sixth or seventh grade.

Dr. Dozier was born at Santa Clara Pueblo on April 23, 1916. He was certainly not an ordinary looking boy. His hair was not as dark as most, though his eyes were brown like those of his childhood playmates. His mother was Leocadia Gutierrez of the Badger Clan. His father was Thomas Dozier, a white man who had come to the pueblo to teach, and later married one of his former students.

Dozier did not feel any different from his all-Indian playmates. He spoke the same language; he enjoyed the same games, dances, and other Indian activities. Although he did not start school until he was ten years old, he had listened carefully as his father discussed the value of education. Early in life he realized that he must try to get the best education possible.

After completing his early schooling to the sixth grade in less than six years, at the pueblo day school, he was enrolled at the Santa Fe Indian School, where he completed the seventh and eighth grades. He attended St. Michael's College as it was known from territorial days, although it was in fact a high school, graduating in May 1935. That fall, he matriculated at the University of New Mexico in Albuquerque. He lived on the campus of the Albuquerque Indian School, and traveled daily by bus to the university. For his room and board at the Indian School, he did a variety of jobs, from helping in the kitchen to making bed checks in the boys' dormitory.

During the school year of 1937–1938, when he would have been a junior at the university, Dozier did not return to class. He was hired by the Indian School as a general clerk in the school superintendent's office, and as a substitute teacher. The following year, he went to Washington, D.C., to work in the Department of the Interior as a mail and file clerk. After one year in that position, he returned to Albuquerque to resume his university studies, and completed his junior year; but World War II soon intervened.

Dozier was drafted into the air force in 1941. He took his basic training at Jefferson Barracks, Missouri, before he was assigned to a B-17 crew in Chico, California. A few months later he was sent to an intelligence school in Salt Lake City, Utah. After this period of training, he was assigned to a B-29 crew in Nebraska. In time, his squadron arrived in Saipan in the Pacific Mariana Islands. From there, Dozier flew as an observer, inspecting the amount of damage inflicted by bombing raids. He briefed other bombing crews on enemy facilities, or target areas missed; and he also interpreted areas to be bombed, by means of photographs.

In October 1945, Dozier returned to the United States and was discharged from service in California in November 1945. He then returned to Santa Clara to his family. Once at home, he renewed his acquaintance with his early love, the mountains and the Santa Clara Canyon on the reservation west of the pueblo. He helped his family with the farm and garden work; and on weekends he fished and camped.

In the fall of 1946, Dozier returned to the University of New Mexico for his senior year, majoring in history and anthropology. He graduated in June 1947, with a bachelor's degree. That summer he began a series of field research projects with the university's School of Anthropology. Two years later he received his master of arts degree in anthropology.

That fall, Dozier accepted a job as a teaching fellow at the University of California, Los Angeles, where he taught for the next two years. Simultaneously, he received a Social Science Research Council Predoctoral Fellowship, to do field studies of the Hopi and Hano in Arizona. The following year, he was able to continue his studies and research, through a John Hay Whitney Fellowship. As a result of this work he published a monograph in 1954 on the Hanos (the Tewas) in the Hopi country.

With the two years of experience he had gained at UCLA, Dozier then moved to the University of Oregon as an instructor in anthropology and linguistics. While there, he completed his requirements for the doctor of philosophy degree, gaining this academic honor from UCLA in 1952. At this time he was the subject of a feature article in *Time* magazine, as the first American Indian to earn a university doctoral degree in the humanities.

Soon after, Dozier was awarded a Wenner-Gren Foundation Grant for postdoctoral field study of his people, the Rio Grande Pueblos, during the academic year 1952–1953. After this year of study and research, he was appointed an instructor by Northwestern University, where he remained for the next five years. During this time, he was elevated from instructor to associate professor. The following year, he was appointed a fellow at the Center for the Advanced Studies of the Behavioral Sciences at Stanford University, California, for the academic year 1958–1959. Soon he received another senior postdoctoral fellowship from the National Science Foundation, for field study in northern Luzon, the Philippines, during 1959–1960.

Having married Marianne Fink of Los Angeles, Dozier now had a family to transport across the Pacific. Their plans took the family to Alaska before arrival in the Philippines. Dozier often spoke of his many happy experiences with the Kalingas of northern Luzon, whom he studied at this time. "Like the American Indians in our country, the Kalingas are not well known in the Philippines by the Filipinos," he said, "and a number of times when I was a guest speaker in a city, I was asked questions about the Kalingas by the city-dwelling Filipinos, as do the Americans about the American Indians."

After completing this year of study, the Dozier family flew to Hong Kong from the Philippines and then on to Calcutta, Beirut, Paris, and London, before returning home. Dozier obtained a post as professor of anthropology at the University of Arizona in Tucson, and he remained there as a member of the faculty until his death in 1971. During a sabbatical year in 1967–1968, as a John Simon Guggenheim Fellow, he returned to his first love, New Mexico, his home, and his people to do additional research. As a result of his research on the Pueblos at various times, Dozier had written *The Pueblo Indians of North America*. In this book, Dr. Dozier explains the prehistoric and historic background of the Pueblos.

In the summer of 1969, Dozier received another research grant, from the Rockefeller Foundation, to investigate future research on Mindanao Island in the Philippines. On this trip the Dozier family was smaller by one, since the daughter, Wanda, had become Mrs. Michael Kabotie and was living at Santa Clara Pueblo with her Hopi husband. The Dozier family returned to the United States via Hong Kong, Moscow, London, and New York City.

Shortly thereafter, Edward Dozier became a member of a team of Indian scholars with a double task. Sponsored by the American Indian Historical Society, the First Convocation of American Indian Scholars was being arranged and was to convene at Princeton University in March 1970. Although he assisted in the preparatory work, he was unable himself to attend the convocation; the illness that soon took his life had begun. In another project of this all-Indian society, Dozier helped prepare curricula on the college level in his special subject, linguistics and the American Indian. During conferences preceding preparation of curricula guides, Dr. Dozier made several outstanding contributions, and one of his proposals is still being considered by Indian scholars. He proposed that a language common to many Indians be adopted as a universal native tongue, that of Nahuatl.

In 1969, Dozier began a second term as a fellow of the Center for the Advanced Studies of the Behavioral Sciences at Stanford. This time he was preparing a research study on the urban Indians in the Bay Area. His work was interrupted by a fire said to have been started by activists of the Third World, in which most of the center was gutted; as a result, the work of the scholars was ended for a time.

Edward Dozier was active in many professional associations. He was a fellow in the American Association for the Advancement of Science, the American Anthropological Association, and the American Sociological Association. He was a member of the executive committee of the Society for Applied Anthropology, a member of the Linguistic Society of America, and of the American Folklore Society. He was also a member and a vice-president of the Association on American Indian Affairs, New York. He served as a member of the editorial board of *The Indian Historian,* official publication of the American Indian Historical Society, and before his death was named "Honored Indian Historian" by the society. Dozier's

Popovi Da, ca. 1952. (Photograph courtesy of the family.)

article, appearing in the spring 1969 edition of *The Indian Historian* ("The Teacher and the Indian Student"), has been reprinted in scholarly journals many times since its publication. More than fifty articles in the areas of social anthropology and linguistics were written by Dozier and published in various scholarly journals.

Besides the books and articles mentioned above, Dr. Dozier has written: "The Hopi-Tewa of Arizona" (*University of California Publications in American Archaeology and Ethnology*, 44, no. 3, 1954); and *Mountain Arbiters: The Changing Life of a Philippine Hill People* (University of Arizona Press, 1966).

Despite many years away from his childhood home, Edward Dozier continued to speak the Tewa language fluently, returning with his family again and again to his home at Santa Clara Pueblo.

Above all else, however, Dr. Edward Dozier was a superb teacher, and he leaves many students who remember him as their "beloved professor" who understood, and made the story of his people come alive. His heart "was big," one student said upon learning of his death. "This was the most gentle soul and the kindest heart ever to be met in a classroom," another said. The man with a gentle soul and a big heart ended his journey upon this earth on May 2, 1971. As the family gathered for Sunday dinner, he suffered a heart attack, was rushed to a hospital in Tucson, and died on the way. He was brought back to his ancestral home on May 5, and lies buried there, an unforgettable Pueblo man who suffered all the hardships of those days in America in order to obtain the highest education offered in this country.

Popovi Da

Popovi Da, artist, craftsman, businessman, and Pueblo Indian leader, was the son of internationally famous craftsmen. His home was Po-sogeh, the tribal Tewa name for San Ildefonso Pueblo. "Po," as he liked to be called, was the son of Maria and Julian Martinez, both legends in the Indian art world who specialized in pottery. His parents were recognized for the most remarkable renaissance in the arts during the first half of the twentieth century. Through the encouragement of Dr. Kenneth M. Chapman, of the School of American Research, the team of Maria and Julian began to experiment with the nearly lost technique for making traditional black-on-black and black-on-red pottery.

Po developed his own individual method of producing the

beautiful pottery glazes, and he is principally responsible for the revival of polychrome. He developed the use of sienna with black, and the striking steel-like new glaze now used for Pueblo blackware.

This son of distinguished Pueblo artists had an important message in the arts, and in one of his many talks before public audiences, he said:

> *I stand before you, ladies and gentlemen, as an Indian, to speak about our pottery, our traditions, and our culture. Our culture and our creative arts are interwoven and inseparable. Everything in our lives is all-inclusive. We must preserve what has been created and what can be created.*
>
> *Time is the limiting factor in the endless spirit of our people that shortens what I have to say. Indeed, the clockwork time which you have invented can be disastrous. And there is another matter which disturbs me: the way that we are often treated as academic curiosities. This indeed is sad. You have written too many books and papers about us without having the experience of the feeling with us.*
>
> *We believe we are the first conservationists. We do not destroy or disturb the harmony of nature. To us this is beauty; it is our sense of esthetics. We care for and husband our environment. We feel ourselves trustees of our environment and of our creative values. And this gives us a union with all existence.*
>
> *We have multitudes of symbols—corn blossom, squash blossom, eagle and deer, rainbow and fire, and storm clouds; the design of plants, of all living things; the underworld which gave forth man and all the creatures—symbols whose secret meanings are only secret because they are within and cannot be easily expressed. This symbolism is perpetuated through memory alone, because we have no written language. But to be able to use our symbols and keep in harmony with our world we must work by fasting, continence, solitary vigil, and symbolic discipline. Out of the silences of meditation come purity and power which eventually become apparent in our art: the many spirits which enter about us, in*

*us, are transformed within us, moving from an endless
past not gone, not dead, but with a threshold that is the
present. From this time sense, from this experience deep
within, our forms are created. Even our smaller children
sense this, and consequently create beautiful designs.
Our simple lines have meaning.*

*We do what comes from thinking, and sometimes
hours and even days are spent to create an esthetic scroll
in a design. Our symbols and our ceremonial representa-
tions are all expressed as an endless cadence, and beauti-
fully organized in our art as well as in our dance. . . .*

Born in a fishbowl, so to speak, due to the fame of his parents,
Popovi Da learned the art of making pottery originally from his
parents.

Early in his life Popovi Da felt the need to let the world know
that he was also an individual. During his early years in school he
used his family surname but later decided to use his tribal name,
which means Red Fox.

Po was born at San Ildefonso Pueblo, April 10, 1923. His mother
was of the Summer Clan, so he was also a member of that group.
The Tewas appear to use their clan membership as moiety membership as well. Other Pueblo tribal members belong to a clan as well
as to a moiety. The Pueblos in Sandoval County belong to one of
two moieties, the Turquoise or the Pumpkin, which are patrilineal.
They also belong to clans, which are bloodlines and are matrilineal.
Whereas the moieties are involved in social, ceremonial, and often
political activities in the dual society system of the Sandoval County
pueblos, the clans are more of a deterrent against inbreeding.

Po started his education at the local government day school at
San Ildefonso. After the sixth grade he went to St. Catherine's in
Santa Fe, where he spent his junior high school years. He was
promoted and skipped a few grades so that he graduated from the
Santa Fe Indian School in May 1939, when he was sixteen years
old; he had transferred to this school from St. Catherine's.

At the Indian School he took art courses to go along with the
pottery work that he had already learned from his parents. Following
high school graduation, he enrolled at the Canyon Art School in
Santa Fe, where he spent the next two years.

At this school he studied the use of a kiln, pottery making as done by non-Indians, oil painting, and drawing. He lived in an apartment with his wife whom he married after their graduation from the Santa Fe Indian School. She was one of his classmates, Anita Montoya from San Juan Pueblo.

By the time Po had finished his two years of special art study, he was drafted by the army in 1944. He was sent to Fort Bliss near El Paso, Texas. For reasons known only to the army, Po was then transferred to Oak Ridge, Tennessee, without benefit of basic training. He spent a few months there before being shipped out. Eventually he was sent to Los Alamos, a few potsherds throw from his native village of San Ildefonso.

At Los Alamos, which was an ultra secret installation with a Santa Fe mailing address, Po was assigned to a special engineering detachment of the army.

Po was discharged from the army in 1946, and he returned to Los Alamos as a civilian, to the same duties and with increased pay. He worked at Los Alamos for three more years.

In 1949, Po applied for a loan for a small business through the GI Bill, which was approved. Heretofore, no Pueblo Indian applicants had been approved for a loan by any bank, since they had no collateral as a guarantee. Po's original loan was for $2,000, and every penny went into the remodeling of an old building in the center of San Ildefonso, which he bought from a tribal member.

Po went to the bank for another $3,000. With this he bought a few pieces of silver jewelry, paintings, and pottery from other Indian artists. He personally went to the Indian artists and craftsmen to make the purchases. He bought the best that he could find among the Navajo, the Hopi, and the Zuni. He also purchased blue-ribbon winning beads from Santo Domingo and drums from Cochiti.

In 1956, Po began to take a special interest in pottery. Again, with his personal training from his parents in the art of firing and decorating, and with the education about kilns he had acquired at the art school in Santa Fe, Po had enough confidence to experiment beyond what his father had taught him. Furthermore, he had several advantages over his father. His mother was now a professional. He could get in his automobile and bring in the fine sand or the firewood in a few hours; whereas his father spent a whole day, traveling by horse and wagon, to do the same.

The result was Maria and Popovi's Studio of Indian Arts, which sold a variety of excellent pottery in traditional black-burnished and matte (dull) ware, terra cotta, polychrome, and sienna. These new products are made through improved firing and dual firing techniques, the result of experiments by Po.

Besides devoting his time to the business of running the studio and decorating and polishing the pottery, Po also made silver jewelry. And as an obligation, as a member of his village, Po was subject to service as an official of the tribe. He also served on the tribal council.

Po was active in the All Indian Pueblo Council, and was chosen by the nineteen pueblo governors as their chairman on November 2, 1950, serving for two years. He was elected as secretary by the same body, and served in this capacity until July 18, 1953.

After that, Po's own tribal leaders chose him three times to serve as governor of San Ildefonso, in 1958, 1959, and 1963.

Maria and Popovi conducted pottery-making workshops at the universities of Northern Colorado at Ft. Collins and Texas Tech in Lubbock, and at the City College of South Pasadena.

Two films, featuring both Maria and Popovi, were produced. One was made by the National Park Service and the other by Coleman Film Enterprises. The latter is titled *Maria of the Pueblos*. The film tells the story of Maria and her pottery renaissance, and the continuation of the art by her son Popovi and her grandson Tony Da, son of Popovi.

Popovi came to believe that pure Indian art can only exist if the artist learns solely traditional art and is influenced by Indian culture. Consequently, his son Tony was not exposed to the kind of art training that Popovi himself had experienced. Tony learned from his family and relied on tribal stories and the characters from these stories. The influence of Tony's Pueblo life and background is very obvious and is expressed in his exquisite style of two-dimensional paintings. His ceramics are generally sienna and polychrome with turquoise eyes for birds and animals, and for special effects.

Before his death, as we sat in a reception room, I asked Po about the evolution of pottery:

"In our pottery we have many distinctive styles within historic periods," he began. "As our society changed throughout the ages, there appeared variations in our art related to the life of people. In time of high prosperity, pottery styles and our artistic talents were directed to forms showing our affluence: detailed lines, fine in form and of many colors and styles. Abundant harvests called for new original creations. The years when our culture was appreciated by those in power resulted in a more adequate life for all of us, and this life was reflected in our art by intricate patterns in design, in basketry, painting, and petroglyphic drawings.

"During droughts and periods of trouble, we created less than at other times. This was not due, as is often believed, to the lack of facilities, but because there were periods of depression and frustration when the mind was controlled by anxiety.

"Fine art within our lives has been balanced and directed in a positive sense by the force about us. If life is unbalanced, as it is now, by the pressure of mechanical things all about us, life seems to lose a man in a cold world of steel where we are frustrated and afraid this frustration will be reflected in our art. Should our civilization terminate today, future anthropologists would be puzzled by finding in our pueblos Japanese artifacts, complex distorted patterns of abstract paintings, and other evidence of the confusion of the world about us."

"What about painting as an art? What can you say about Indian art?" he was asked.

"The best in Pueblo life is reflected by paintings and designs which tend to be four-dimensional. They point to rhythm and the motion in the dance, the action of the horse, the speed of the antelope, the heat of the desert. We have a form of art which is distinctively North American Indian, and we must preserve our way of life in order for our art to continue. From this part of us comes our ability to create, as can be seen from the thousands of designs found on ceremonial and cooking pots from prehistory, dating back to time immemorial. I doubt that the designs improved the cooking, but they were created because they had to be created; it is our role to create," Po said.

"What about Indian values and traditions, how do they affect your art?"

"There is a design in living things; their shapes, forms, the ability to live, all have meaning," Po began. "We must cling to our Indian traditions which exalt beauty. To the white man, religion is a method, a system which he can employ or use at times when necessary. But to us there is no word in our language for an isolated dogma: all we can say is that we have a way of life, and that this is life itself. If we fill our minds with pure materialism and accept a convenient religion, then the backbone of our way of life, of our perception of beauty will be broken, and we will disappear as unseen winds, gone. The white man is not secure. He may be the victim of his own dissolution, undermined by customs, air pollution, in fact by unremovable pollution of all kinds, material and spiritual. They may come to the Indian for the message. So we must not let ourselves get caught up in the onrushing vanishing years or the results of an over-efficient society, highly mechanized, streamlined, rapidly moving at a rate and in a way that to most of the Indians represents a panic.

"Our values are indwelling and dependent on time and space unmeasured. This in itself is beauty. Our first great value is our trusteeship of nature, and this is beauty also. Then there is an order and direction of our lives, a unity, the ability to share the joy of sharing creativeness and minimum competition. This, too, is beauty.

"The Pueblo people all ask you to 'come to our dances' and 'visit our home'; we share our meals. We feel then that we can be part of each other, confluent human forces, sharing, giving. It is not the disease known as obligation, but exists because it exists, and that is enough."

"Indian crafts had their origin in the needs, both practical and aesthetic, of the people themselves," Po said.

Anthony, Joyce Ann, and Janice are the three children of Popovi Da and his wife Anita. Anthony is an artist working out of Santa Fe. Joyce Ann is working in Albuquerque, and Janice graduated from the Haskell Institute in Lawrence, Kansas.

Some of the work of Maria and Po is permanently exhibited at the South Plains Museum in Anadarko, Oklahoma; at the Philbrook Art Museum in Tulsa, Oklahoma; and at the Heard Museum in Phoenix, Arizona.

Popovi Da died at a hospital in Santa Fe on Sunday, October 17, 1971, following a short illness. He was buried in the cemetery at San Ildefonso Pueblo.

Beryl Blue Spruce

Beryl Blue Spruce was the first Pueblo Indian physician. He struggled and fought and suffered his way through the maze of college, medical school, internship, and residency in order to attain this goal.

During our interview, Dr. Blue Spruce recalled the day he received

Dr. Beryl Blue Spruce, M.D., Laguna-San Juan pueblos. (Photograph courtesy of the family.)

his medical degree from the University of Southern California in 1964. "That day," he said, "has got to be *the* day in my life. I remembered my tenuous beginnings, in deciding to become a medical doctor, after spending two years of my early childhood in a hospital with pneumonia and other complications. I thought of the counselor who told me to drop out of college and join the service so that I might enroll in a smaller school with less competition, fewer financial worries, if I could qualify to attend under the GI Bill. And I remember the worst hurt of all thrown at me, the statement that I would never become a medical doctor."

Dr. Blue Spruce did not display any of the usual emotions in talking about the past. "I am very happy in my work," he said, "but I am not proud of the way I had to achieve it. I literally had to crawl under the fence and scratch and fight to stay in."

Beryl Blue Spruce was born in Santa Fe, New Mexico, November 24, 1934. His father, George Blue Spruce, was of the Roadrunner Clan, a Laguna Pueblo Indian from Paguate, New Mexico. His mother was Juanita Cruz Blue Spruce from San Juan Pueblo.

Beryl received his early education at St. Michael's Parochial School in Santa Fe, from the first through the twelfth grades. As we had coffee together, I reminded Beryl of the times he used to come by his father's woodworking classroom looking for small wooden blocks to play with, before the last class swept them up and delivered them to the incinerator. And of the time when he was beginning to learn how to write and was taught the name of the school superintendent, and wrote "Dr. Seymour" on many walls on the school campus. The superintendent had to go to Beryl's parents to get them to make him stop writing on campus walls.

An early bout with pneumonia had weakened his lungs, so that he could not participate in high school athletics. As a result of this illness, he was in a hospital for nine months. It caused him considerable anguish, due to complications, later in his life. Beryl's high school grades made it possible for him to attend the college of his choice, and he chose Stanford University in Palo Alto, California. In the fall of 1953, when grants and scholarships for Indian students were unheard of, Beryl became a freshman at Stanford. He learned at once that this was in no way similar to the high school classes at St. Michael's, where he went home to study and to eat a hearty meal. At Stanford he had to work for his room and board, and study in his spare time. During his first year he was a "hasher" in one of the girls' dormitories, for three meals a day. After classes, he worked in the hospital, where he helped a pathologist with autopsies, and cleaned the room when they were finished. He said, with an expression of satisfaction, that this was where he learned to do the "baseball stitch." After cleaning up at the hospital, he would run to the girls' dormitory, which was at least a mile away, to serve the girls their supper. One day his house mother asked him why he ran every day. Beryl replied that he had to run to his hashing job at the girls' dormitory from the hospital. The house-mother then told him about a French bicycle that had been left by a student about five years earlier. It had been cluttering up the basement of the dormitory where Beryl was living. The young student repaired the bicycle, so that he could ride it daily. Soon afterward, the original owner remembered his bicycle. So Beryl had to give up his transportation and resume his cross-country exercise.

Those were the days when long hair for men was unknown in colleges. However, Beryl often had long hair, mainly, as he said, because he could not afford a haircut. One time the girls to whom he served meals donated money, and Beryl got the best haircut available. That same year he explained that he could not return to New Mexico for the Christmas holidays due to his lack of money. A few days before Christmas, before the girls left for their homes, they presented Blue Spruce with a gift stocking full of candy. At the toe of the stocking was a hundred dollars, with a note that he should use it to go home to spend Christmas with his family.

By the end of the winter quarter, Beryl's grades had suffered, since he had three jobs while also attending classes, and his coun-selor called him in for a talk. The counselor advised Beryl to leave Stanford and join the army so that when he had completed his military tour, he would be eligible for help under the GI Bill, and would not need to work so hard for an education. Furthermore, said the counselor, besides the stiff competition for good grades, medical school was too expensive. Beryl would do better to change his major course of study, he said.

In March 1954, Beryl returned to New Mexico. After some rest, he enrolled at the University of New Mexico, where he spent the next three years. He also took many courses in chemical engineering. This field would be a crutch if the medical degree became an impossibility. However, his grades became respectable again. With renewed confidence, he decided to apply to Stanford for readmission.

He was sure that if he had a bachelor's degree from Stanford, he would find it easier to get into the medical school there. And so he was soon back at Stanford. Once again he worked while attending classes, except this time he had one luxury, a tuition scholarship for $250 as a loan from the Stanford Mothers' Club. He was also the proud possessor of a credit card, which entitled him to purchase real luxuries like milk shakes, ice cream, hamburgers, and so on at the Student Union. His letter of appreciation to Mrs. Eugene Dils, scholarship chairman of the Stanford Mothers' Club, reveals the character of the man, his humbleness, and the times in which he had to strive to the limit of his endurance in order to gain an education. He wrote:

> I am an American Indian, my father and mother being of Queres and Tewa descent. Since my youth, my parents have constantly cultivated ambition in me, and by their example I have grown to appreciate the value of education. Also, because of the serious lack of educated individuals among my people, I am made to realize a desperate exigency for anything which will prepare me for the work I am dedicated by my birth to perform.
>
> At present, among the Pueblo tribes of the Southwest, there is not a single Indian doctor, and medical care of the Indian is a function of a separate branch of the Public Health. Although in some regions the work of this organization is noteworthy, in most Indian hospitals and clinics the lack of dedicated personnel is vividly demonstrated by outmoded facilities and a profound disregard for the Indians themselves. This situation may be readily understood when one considers the small number of skilled medical personnel who are drawn into government services and the even smaller number who consider working among the Indian people an attractive and worthy endeavor. In some hospitals, the situation is so disgusting that many of the Indians in these localities have found it necessary to go elsewhere for their medical needs. Of course, this disregard by the Indian for the facilities offered by the Public Health has been interpreted by some individuals as a reason for abolishing the Indian Health Program altogether.

From this, I believe you can readily see the importance
of my education to me, and the profound desire I have
to become a medical doctor. I have given my life to this
endeavor, and my efforts since grade school have been
directed toward the fulfillment of this goal. While in
high school I led my class scholastically, and so my
decision to study for the medical profession was not
made on the basis of desire alone. I felt then, and I do
now, that I have the ability to become a good and
worthy doctor. For this reason, I have continued in this
direction despite the ridicule and discouragement of
many individuals.

My college career has been the most painful experience
of my life, and because of it the attainment of my ambi-
tion is made almost impossible. To the people who know
me, my college record is a contradiction and not at all
indicative of my ability. . . . I shall never forget your
kindness. As soon as I am able, the full amount of your
loan will be repaid.

After nearly seven years from the time he entered Stanford as a freshman, Beryl Blue Spruce received his bachelor of science degree in June 1960. Another obstacle had been hurdled, but the basic problem was still before him. He had hoped to enter the medical school at Stanford, but Stanford knew of his problems, financial and academic. This university took its choice of students from the cream of its pre-med classes.

He applied to the University of Southern California School of Medicine. He even wrote to a famous Stanford alumnus, Herbert Hoover, who answered: "Unfortunately, we do not know of any person or organization to suggest to you in your search for financial assistance in attending medical school." Finally, he approached Dr. Russell V. Lee, of Palo Alto Medical Clinic, who contacted his son at the School of Medicine at Southern California. Dr. Peter Lee finally was able to help Blue Spruce enter that university, and he wrote: "The committee on admissions has recommended that you be accepted in this fall's entering class. You will need a suitable microscope, and of course the tuition, which will amount to about $620." Now the problem was again money. However, during the past summer he had married a girl he met while attending the

University of New Mexico. As a professional nurse, she would help in funding his continued education. He was also now able to receive aid from such organizations as the Daughters of the American Revolution, United Scholarship Services, California Federation of Women's Clubs, the Bureau of Indian Affairs, and the John Hay Whitney Fellowship Fund. Times were changing.

In his senior year at medical school Beryl had to use an oxygen tank at his home because of his incapacitated lungs. Finally, a part of one lung was removed, and for a time there was doubt if he would be able to receive his medical degree with the rest of his class. In the end, he was able to join his class and receive his degree in person. General jubilation on this occasion was expressed by an old friend from Santa Fe, Charles Minton, who was at that time executive director of the New Mexico Commission on Indian Affairs. He wrote: "I wish I could be there for commencement with you. I am thinking of your talk to the first Regional Indian Youth Council seven years ago, when you said, 'When you've gone through college and you reach up and grab that degree, you're going to have callouses, I don't care what kind of a person you are.' "

That fall Dr. Blue Spruce entered the Albert Einstein Medical Center in Philadelphia as an intern. After two years he took up residency at the Pennsylvania Hospital in Philadelphia, specializing in obstetrics and gynecology for three more years, until 1968. During his residency he also served as a clinical instructor at the University of Pennsylvania. He was now engaged in the work he loved. Soon after completing his residency, Blue Spruce enrolled at the University of Michigan for further graduate work. He received his master's degree in public health here. He then became an instructor at the University of Michigan School of Medicine, Department of Obstetrics and Gynecology, and became a consultant in that area to the University Student Health Service. At Eastern Michigan University Student Health Service, Ypsilanti, he served as a part-time consultant as well.

Now, his medical education and graduate work completed, Beryl turned back to activities in Indian affairs. He was a member of many Indian organizations and also lectured throughout the country on subjects related to contemporary Indian issues. In 1971, he was a participant in the Second Convocation of American Indian Scholars sponsored by the American Indian Historical Society at Aspen Institute for Humanistic Studies, Colorado. There he took a leading part in the seminar on medicine and health care, and his remarks are published in the society's publication on the proceedings of the convocation, titled *Indian Voices.*

At that convocation the ground was laid for Dr. Blue Spruce's fondest dream, the organization of the national Association of American Indian Physicians. Responding to a final question from his interviewer, who asked him to define leadership relative to his field of professional training, Dr. Blue Spruce said:

> *The individual should understand and accept the people he is working with, and the people he is working for. On the surface, it would appear that many public health employees believe what they preach, but under intensive scrutiny it becomes apparent that they merely verbalize these ideas but are not anywhere near nor able to integrate them into their personalities and philosophy. Health workers of the dominant culture view the "specimens of misfortune" through a mirror clouded with bias, prejudice, ridicule, and curiosity. In the final analysis some proof of this lies within the low level of success that public health agencies have achieved in providing health care and in having their services accepted.*
>
> *One of the best methods to alleviate this problem is not so much to try changing the poor directly, or disrobe the minorities of their inherent cultures, imposing upon them the dominant culture, but rather to produce leaders from these groups to work with these people as well as a member of that group. But personnel to work with these people should not be just indigenous helpers, although they serve a distinct and valuable purpose. They should be highly trained and qualified.*

To the question of who provided the greatest influence in his life, Beryl mentioned his family members without hesitation. His father was an instructor in wood carving and woodworking when Beryl was a boy. When Beryl was experiencing difficulty in college, it was his older brother who advised him to compete against *himself* and not against his classmates who had superior academic backgrounds. He was then able to improve his academic standing. It is this brother, George Blue Spruce, himself a doctor, who is now occupying a major position in federal government serving the Indian people.

At the time of the interview in his home at Ann Arbor, Michigan, Dr. Blue Spruce was a successful man. He defined success as the amount of happiness one finds in his work and in relationships with one's family, which for him consists of a wife, the former Ernestine Rodriguez of Espanola, New Mexico, one daughter, Roxanne, and a son, Shawn Beryl. He said that it was only his absolute commitment that brought him to his goal. Twenty-eight years, from 1941 to 1969, is a long time to spend in classrooms, but this Pueblo man did just that. He scratched and clawed to do it. He said he wanted to be a medical doctor so badly that he felt the desire from the tips of the hair on his head to the bottom of the soles on his feet. And because of his sacrifices, hard work, and determination, Beryl Blue Spruce, M.D., M.P.H., was successful in his endeavors.

Unfortunately, the loss of one lung while he was in medical school was too much for him in the Michigan weather. In the winter of 1973, he became ill with pneumonia. He died December 30, 1973. His last request was that he be given a native burial, so his remains were flown to New Mexico and buried at San Juan Pueblo.

Joseph Naranjo

Joseph Lopez Naranjo was a leader of the "Indian auxiliaries," the shock troops and support columns of the Spanish conquistadors. They are significant in the history of the Pueblos, showing a division of opinion and policy, and ultimately a division of allegiance among the Indian people. Naranjo, history reveals, was a traitor to his own people, the staunchest supporter of the Spanish. The auxiliaries he commanded were an important and even a decisive factor in the history of New Mexico.

Fray Angelico Chavez, in an article appearing in the *New Mexico Historical Review* titled "Pohe-yemo's Representatives," traces the genealogical origins of the Naranjo family. The first Naranjo, Chavez writes, was "a very black-complexioned Negro (*negro atezado*), a slave or servant who married an Indian *criada* of Juana de los Reyes, the wife of an original New Mexico settler of the Martinez family." In the second generation, there is mention of one Domingo Naranjo, "son of the *negro atezado* (Mateo Naranjo) and of an Indian housegirl of Mexico." Little is known or reported of this Domingo Naranjo, but he is described as a descendant of Naranjo ancestors who "came as slaves or servants of the first conquerors and settlers." With the third Naranjo generation, Joseph Lopez Naranjo is mentioned as the "son of Domingo Naranjo."

Joseph Naranjo is first encountered by the army of Governor de Vargas at Taos on October 7, 1692. As the Spaniards entered the pueblo, it was found to be abandoned, but after awhile two men came down from the mountains to speak with de Vargas. One was the governor of Taos Pueblo, Francisco Pacheco. The other was a young part-Indian (it is assumed) ladino (one who is proficient in the Spanish language), who called himself Josephillo (little Joe), and was referred to by the Taos as "el Espanol." De Vargas took an immediate liking to the boy. From this time on, Naranjo cast his lot with the Spaniards.

After the so-called peaceful *entrada* of 1692 was accomplished, de Vargas returned to Guadalupe del Paso with his army. It is presumed that Naranjo went along, to return with the army and the colonists in de Vargas's second entry of 1693.

Upon his second and final entry into New Mexico, de Vargas learned that his easy "pacification" of the previous year was a delusion. He found signs of resistance everywhere, but especially in the northern pueblos. He learned that the leaders of the rebellion were the brothers Luis and Lorenzo Tupatu of Picuris, Antonio Bolsas of the Santa Fe Tanos, and Lucas Naranjo of Santa Clara Pueblo, Joseph's brother.

In June 1696, Joseph Naranjo was living in Santa Cruz, where his friend Roque de Madrid was the alcalde. On June 13, an Indian confided in Naranjo that the combined Hopi, Zuni, and Acoma Indians were returning to help the local pueblos destroy the Spaniards. Naranjo notified the alcalde of Santa Cruz. A general alarm was given, and Joseph learned that his brother Lucas was at the head of the new resistance. The revolt lasted until the end of July, with the battle of El Embudo occurring on July 23; Lucas Naranjo, the leader of the rebels, was shot by a Spaniard, Antonio Cisneros, ending the battle.

The following year, 1697, Diego de Vargas was replaced by Pedro Rodriguez Cubero, who served as governor until 1703. Cubero concentrated upon subduing the Rio Grande Keresans from La Cienega de Cochiti, Santo Domingo, and Cochiti. In the latter part of June 1698, after some debate, Cubero, with the help of Joseph

Naranjo, "persuaded" the Keresans to descend from the Enchanted Mesa, north of Acoma where they had taken refuge, and return to the Rio Grande whence they had fled. However, instead of returning to the Rio Grande pueblos, they established themselves in a new pueblo where a church had been built, called San Jose de Laguna. Thus was Laguna Pueblo established on July 2, 1698.

Now we observe Joseph Naranjo in a new role. By 1700, he was alcalde mayor of Zuni. By 1701, Joseph had thoroughly ingratiated himself with the Spanish and had won their trust. He now formulated a petition asking to be given the title of capitan de la guerra over all Indian troops. The petition was addressed to the viceroy himself.

In his petition, written with the help of Fray Antonio Guerra, he said he was a native of the kingdom, and had served the king as alcalde mayor and capitan de la guerra of Acoma and Zuni. When he had received these titles, the petition stated, the Acomas and Rio Grande Keresans were entrenched on the great rock of Acoma, and the Zuni occupied their own fortress mountain. He, all alone, he said, had persuaded these people to come down and return to their pueblos. No Spaniards had helped him, he insisted; it was done by virtue of his own "Christian zeal," he wrote.

Fray Angelico Chavez may be quoted here as stating, in the article mentioned above, that Naranjo said in his petition that "the governor in Santa Fe ordered him to enter the ferocious Hopi Nation, which he did with the custos, Fray Zavaletta, and with Fray Garay Coachea of Zuni and Fray Iranda of Acoma. The party was sorely threatened by the Hopi, but he effectively defended the fathers at the risk of his life. When the Santa Clara Tewa on the rock of Walpi showed signs of surrender, he went up against the prudent advice of the padres, but managed to bring these people back to Santa Fe. Again he returned to Walpi with Fray Garay Coachea to bring back the Tano Indians living there. The father tried to dissuade him from risking his life, but he, after making his confession, bravely went up and argued with the Tanos at Walpi all night at their meeting. He could not persuade them to return to their Rio Grande pueblos, but he got them to make peace with the Spaniards.

"Of the families he himself brought back from the Hopi pueblos, eight were Santa Claras who went to live in San Juan, six were San Ildefonsos, nine were Cochiti, four were Santo Domingos, six were Galisteos, and the rest was the entire Jemez population living in one of their pueblos at that time. All this was done at his own expense without royal aid, as the friars who went with him could testify. This declaration he asked Fray Guerra to certify formally, and with the signature and rubric of Joseph Naranjo." Thus does Chavez describe the petition sent to the viceroy by Joseph Naranjo in his quest for recognition by the Spanish monarchy. In 1704, one Fray Agustin de Colina substantiated Naranjo's statement that he had saved the lives of the padres when they went to the Hopi pueblos.

Naranjo's career continues in the same way it had begun so many years before, when he had cast his lot with the Spanish conquistadors. In March 1701, he and his Pueblo troops were serving under Captain Juan de Ulibarri. Naranjo told the captain that he had information from the Acomas and the newly established Lagunas that the Zunis and Hopis were passing around a "knotted thong." Illegal activities were construed in this information. Resistance was still alive among the Pueblos, it was apparent, and on March 4, 1703, the Zunis killed three Spanish neighbors in their pueblo. At the time, the soldiers and the alcalde were away, but on March 7 Fray Garay Coachea wrote to Governor Cubero that the rebels were lying in wait night and day for Alcalde Mayor Naranjo to return so they could kill him. On March 12, Fray Miranda wrote from Acoma to Governor Cubero that fifty Acoma warriors were ready to leave for Zuni and rescue Fray Coachea, but he was holding them back because the padre had written that he would not leave his post without the permission of his superior. Miranda also reported that Naranjo was especially anxious to go himself, but the Zuni priest had said that the Zunis had laid ambushes for Naranjo all along the way, and so he held back Naranjo also.

In 1704, de Vargas returned to Santa Fe as governor for the second time, replacing Cubero. De Vargas now had the title Marques de la Nova Brazinas. We find Naranjo again, serving as captain of Indian scouts at Bernalillo. On March 27, after livestock raids by Apaches in Cieneguilla and Bernalillo, de Vargas ordered warfare by blood and fire. Joseph Naranjo, captain of Indian scouts, and thirty Indian auxiliaries were sent ahead. This campaign collapsed after April 2, when de Vargas was stricken with a fatal illness. He was taken to Bernalillo, where he died on April 8, 1704.

Joseph Naranjo is next noted in 1706, when he served with Captain Ulibarri again, in an expedition to the *"tierra incognito"*

Segessor I, hide painting, ca. 1720–1729. (Courtesy Museum of New Mexico, Negative No. 149798.)

on the plains, where the Picuris were held captive by Apaches. The area is believed to be somewhere in western Kansas, east of present-day Pueblo, Colorado. The Picuris sought by the expedition were those who had fled from their village in 1696, when de Vargas had led the northern campaign against Picuris and Taos. Their flight had been led by Lorenzo Tupatu, one of the leaders of the Pueblo Revolt of 1680. (How the Picuris Indians had been captured by the Apaches is not known. A scene of this particular encounter at Cuartolejo can be seen at the Museum of New Mexico in Santa Fe and is known as the Segessor Painting No. 1, drawn on a buffalo hide.) Joseph Naranjo was a principal scout, however, utilized by Ulibarri in this expedition. He headed one hundred Pueblo Indians recruited from many of the pueblos, and served as a guide and a contact man with the Apache chieftains. He also discovered a needed water spring, which thereafter bore his name, Ojo de Naranjo. On this trip, the expeditionary force managed to persuade the Apaches to release the Picuris and let them return to their pueblo. Another scout in this group was de l'Archeveque, a French survivor of the La Salle adventure, who had lived in New Mexico since 1691.

On a list of residents at Santa Cruz in 1707, Joseph Naranjo is found to be sixteenth. His friend Roque de Madrid was still alcalde mayor there. Joseph is noted as being married to Catalina, their family consisting of seven persons. He also owned land at this time, across the Rio Grande at La Vega (present-day Espanola). According to Fray Chavez, these were probably the family lands that Joseph inherited after his brother Lucas was killed.

In the early eighteenth century, it was the practice of Pueblo Indian leaders to present themselves to the Spanish governor at Santa Fe. On November 7, 1708, it is noted that Naranjo served as interpreter at such gatherings of Pueblo leaders in that town. The Indians were being endorsed and recognized in their newly elected offices by the Spanish governor, Jose Chacon Medina Salazar y Villasenor, better known as the Marques de la Penuela.

In October 1713, Naranjo led 150 Pueblo auxiliaries in a campaign against the Navajos. He accompanied 50 Spanish soldiers and 20 settlers in this expedition. The group met at San Diego de Jemez Pueblo. Two years later, Naranjo led another auxiliary group against the Navajos. In the same year, 1715, Naranjo was again head scout, commanding 149 Pueblo Indian auxiliaries from the pueblos of

Pecos, San Juan, Nambe, Pojoaque, San Ildefonso, Santa Clara, Tesuque, Taos, and Picuris. Seventy-six of these auxiliaries had guns; the arms of the rest are not indicated. Curiously, there is nothing in the records to indicate any mounts or pack horses for the Indian auxiliaries. It is noted, however, that the soldiers and settlers took with them 36 mules and 239 horses.

In 1719, Antonio Valverde y Cosio became the governor in Santa Fe. His principal concern was the matter of Ute Indians raiding against the northern pueblos. Now there were four raiding tribes—Navajo, Apache, Ute, and Comanche—and there were rumors of French incursions into the Spanish Southwest. The governor, conferring with his captains, and with Naranjo, heard various suggestions as to how to proceed against the Utes, and advised that the garrison proposed by the Spaniards—at Cuartolejo—was not feasible. His advice was taken, and the outpost was not established.

An expeditionary force was assembled to move against the enemy, with forty-two soldiers and three Spanish settlers. Naranjo commanded seventy Indian auxiliaries. Their aim was to find and either placate or defeat the Indian enemy tribes, and to wipe out any French influence or holdings. Head of the campaign was Villasur. In due course, encamped along the banks of the North Platte River, the Spanish force found Pawnee Indians. There was no sign of the French, but it was believed they had been training the Pawnees, and Villasur opened discussion with them using Juan de l'Archeveque as interpreter. The Pawnees did not respond, so negotiations were useless.

Villasur camped his troops by the river for the night. It was a strange night, by all accounts. The Spanish force was awakened by strange noises, and spent the early morning hours apprehensive. They said they heard swimmers in the river during the night. The captain failed to send anyone to check the story out. A dog in the Spanish camp barked in alarm. The captain did not inquire; nor were any extra sentries posted. It was a night filled with secret stirrings. In the dead of the night, from the river, sounding their strange flutelike whistle, the Pawnees attacked. The battle was over before it had really begun. Only thirteen of the Spanish expeditionary force survived the attack. Villasur was killed; so, too, was the priest with the party, Fray Juan Minquez. The survivors later reported that during the battle they came to recognize many of the Pawnees as Frenchmen in disguise.

Joseph Lopez Naranjo ended his career that day of August 14, 1720. He was among those counted dead after the Pawnee attack.

Bartolome de Ojeda

The place of Bartolome de Ojeda in the history of the Southwest is unique. Here I make no judgments, but give the facts as I have learned them. Only an accurate interpretation of history by the Pueblo people can place this man in proper perspective.

Let us briefly review the events preceding the emergence of this man in Pueblo history.

In the Pueblo Indian Revolt of August 10, 1680, the tribal religious leaders united and expelled the Spaniards. Before this revolutionary action, when the Athabascans first arrived in the Southwest, there was peace. The newcomers to the Pueblo lands were the first to experience the sharing tradition of the Pueblo people. Later the Spaniards received a similar welcome. The revolt, with its resulting expulsion of the Spaniards, brought peace once more and freedom from religious interference. It was an uneasy peace. Although the people regained their freedom of religion, there were other forces threatening the Pueblo world.

Intersociety quarrels developed. Hunger caused an increase in plundering by the Navajos and Apaches, who were now on horse-back. After persistent harassment by these tribesmen, some of the Pueblo Indians decided in desperation to seek the help of the Spanish with their devastating firearms. Beset by raids from the Navajos and Apaches on the one hand, but also fearful of reprisals from the Spanish whom they had beaten in combat only a short time before, these Pueblo people decided upon the lesser evil, believing they had chosen survival for their people in attempting to negotiate the return of the conquistadors.

It is believed that a few Pueblo Indians journeyed south to search for the deposed Spaniards. According to Jemez legend, one who joined the group was a man of the Sun Clan from Jemez. This man helped to search for, then aid the Spaniards in their return. Written history does not identify him, but the Indian group and their attempts at negotiation with the Spaniards are mentioned. Prominently described in recorded history is a man from neighboring Zia Pueblo, Bartolome de Ojeda. He is described as a "coyote," which means he was half Indian and half Spanish. He is also mentioned as *muy ladino,* which means that he could read and write, as well as being bilingual in Spanish and the Keresan Indian tongues. He is characterized as a Keresan leader of Indian scouts and troops. Records also indicate that Ojeda had already been to Guadalupe del Paso. In 1689, Governor Cruzate visited the pueblos to determine the situation following the revolt nine years before. Cruzate had received instructions from the Crown in Spain, authorized in 1684 to issue land grants to the pueblos. On this trip Cruzate destroyed a few pueblos, including Zia, the home of Ojeda. This Zia man was one of the prisoners taken by Otermin. Thus Ojeda was present on the day some of the pueblos were given their land grants in September 1689. The Spanish land grant papers read in part: ". . . in the Kingdom of New Mexico and after having fought with all the Indians of all of the other pueblos (villages) an Indian of the Pueblo de Sia named Bartolome de Ojeda was one of those who was most conspicuous in the battle, lending his aid everywhere, being wounded by a ball and an arrow, surrendered who as formerly stated I ordered to declare under oath the condition of the Pueblo de. . . ." So it was Ojeda who testified to the worthiness of each pueblo in receiving their land grant.

From 1692 to 1693, a Pueblo Indian group negotiated a return of the Spaniards to New Mexico. The newly appointed Governor Diego de Vargas led the reoccupation force. A group of Pueblo Indians accompanied him, and the leader of this group of "scouts" was Ojeda.

As the early chroniclers state, Ojeda had come voluntarily to Guadalupe del Paso to join the conquistadors. His role was that of interpreter. He was an informer concerning the state of affairs among the Indians in New Mexico. One of the tasks of the scouts under Ojeda was to deliver letters to the pueblo leaders as the Spanish army approached the Indian villages along the Rio Grande. These letters required them to render obedience to His Catholic Majesty, Charles II. When an Indian village was found to be friendly, de Vargas would advance his "conquerors" up the valley. Written history describes this guarded military action as a "reconquest," a ludicrous way to explain the action of the Spanish, who could proceed safely because they had an Indian informer and "negotiator" who had behind him the armed forces of the Spanish military.

As they reached the vicinity of Bernalillo, after they had delivered the required messages to the Indian leaders in Santa Fe, the auxiliaries under Ojeda were ordered to disband and return to their homes, and to remain there. In return for establishing the foreign Spanish authority over the Pueblos, they were to be provided with beef each Sunday and Wednesday.

Thus was the September 14, 1692, *"entrada"* accomplished. De Vargas returned to Guadalupe del Paso (present-day Ciudad de Juarez, Mexico) with his army. Since Ojeda was again with the force of colonizers that left del Paso on October 4, 1693 (with 900 cattle, 2,000 horses, and 1,000 mules), it is presumed that Ojeda accompanied de Vargas's army.

Following the return of the Spaniards, a fear of punishment turned the Pueblos against the Spaniards. Actions of the Europeans indicated they fully intended to dominate Pueblo life and economy. Only Santa Ana and San Felipe pueblos were willing to aid the conquistadors, while Ojeda's own Zia Pueblo was undecided. The only other Pueblo Indians whom de Vargas found loyal to their promises of the previous year were those of Pecos Pueblo to the east.

Early in 1694, a revolutionary movement was again under way among the Pueblos. Indians from Santo Domingo and Cochiti went to La Cieneguilla de Cochiti, where they fortified themselves against attack. To quell the revolutionary actions of the people, Ojeda commanded one hundred Indian auxiliaries from Santa Ana, Zia, and San Felipe on April 17, 1694, and attacked their fortified positions at La Cieneguilla. On June 4, 1694, the people of Taos, Picuris, Cochiti, Santo Domingo, Jemez, and the Tewas rose in rebellion, killing five missionaries and twenty-one soldiers and settlers. Killed at Jemez was Friar Francisco de Jesus Maria Casanos. During this revolt, Ojeda made an independent foray against the Jemez, took one prisoner, and returned to Zia. He then dispatched a letter to Governor de Vargas on June 8, requesting aid in these words: "As you know, we are on the frontier, and I beg of you to send me firearms, powder, and bullets, for you know well that we are very loyal vassals of His Majesty."

Soon after, Ojeda also advised de Vargas that the rebels at Jemez had made a new agreement, in which they resolved not to lay down their arms until they had killed all the Spaniards, or had expelled them from the province once again. Thus did Ojeda fulfill his role as an informer and alert the Spanish colonialists against his own people. The Pueblo revolutionaries had decided for death rather than submission to the foreign power.

Governor de Vargas opened the campaign against the Pueblos

at Jemez on July 21, 1694. On July 24 he began a surprise assault. Jemez legend says that the animals, the burros, made just as much noise braying as the guns and cannons that were used in devastating fury against the Jemez. Resistance collapsed by mid-afternoon, after a bloody engagement.

The defeat of the Jemez people did not end their revolutionary efforts. Following their battles of the year before, the Keresans from Cieneguilla, Santo Domingo, and Cochiti fled their homes on the Rio Grande in 1695. On August 14 and 15 de Vargas led a force of Spanish soldiers and Indian auxiliaries from Zia, Santa Ana, and San Felipe for an attack on the 357-foot mesa north of Acoma, now called the Enchanted Mesa, where the Keresans had taken refuge at the summit. De Vargas organized his force in two groups. He led one group personally. The other was commanded by Ojeda. But the attackers did not succeed in reaching the summit. After three years of successful opposition, another governor, Pedro Rodriguez Cubero, "convinced" the Keresans to descend.

Bartolome de Ojeda was a capitan mayor de la guerra of the Keres-speaking natives. He did much for the successes of Governor de Vargas. Indirectly he was also responsible for returning Christianity to the Pueblo Indian people, which many accepted as time went on, and most accommodated to their own traditional religion. The social forces and the people making up the population of New Mexico today are many and diverse. It is a strange twist of fate that the very people whom he helped install as the dominant society of this state now do not even speak of him, nor do they recognize his services on their behalf.

Ojeda's later years were spent at Santa Ana Pueblo. Nothing more is known of his last days, his death, or whether he ever went home again to Zia.

The late Querino Romero, then governor of Taos Pueblo, holding the three canes representing Pueblo sovereignty, 1970. (Photograph by Dan Budnik.)

Epilogue

SYMBOLISM LIES AT THE HEART of Pueblo history and society. In today's pragmatic world, the symbolism inherent in the story of the silver-headed canes is unique. In itself, it provides insight into Pueblo history and current relationships with the United States.

The Silver-Crowned Canes

Following the institution of the Spanish form of government among the Pueblos, each governor received a silver-crowned cane of office. Like the American symbol of justice represented by the blindfolded lady holding a balancing scale, the canes given to the pueblo governors are symbols of justice and leadership. A Christian cross is engraved on the head of the cane, indicating that the cane had the blessing of the Catholic church, and its owner had the support of the Spanish Crown. The Franciscan priests apparently originated the giving of canes, taking as their watchword, "The cane and staff to be their comfort and strength, and their token against all enemies," from Exodus 4 and Numbers 17. But several versions exist of the origin of the Spanish canes.

Some historians write that Governor Juan de Oñate issued the canes when he met with the Pueblo leaders at the time of his arrival, accompanied by the original colonists. Another version, according to Chester A. Faris, a former Bureau of Indian Affairs employee, is that the king of Spain, in the 1620s, issued a royal decree for each pueblo, at the close of the calendar year, to choose by popular vote their civil officials. Each elected official was presented with a cane to indicate his authority. When each pueblo had selected its succeeding governor, the cane was handed over to the new governor in appropriate ceremonies.

When Mexico won independence from Spain, sovereignty was established by the new government, and new canes, silver-crowned, were presented to the pueblos. They were again authorized to function in line with previous custom. Today, these Mexican canes (or staffs) are held by the pueblo lieutenant governors.

Another cane is held in the possession of each pueblo governor. It is the Abraham Lincoln cane, which was presented to each pueblo governor in recognition of his authority under the United States Government.

The story of the Lincoln canes is this: In November 1863, Dr. Michael Steck of Pennsylvania, superintendent of the Territorial Indian Service, was called to Washington. While he was there, President Lincoln decided on belated recognition of the Pueblo Indians. Seventeen years had passed since General Kearny had taken control of the Territory of New Mexico for the United States.

Lincoln ordered silver-crowned canes, one for each pueblo. Inscribed on each cane was the name of the pueblo, the year 1863, and the signature of the president, "A. Lincoln." These canes were symbols of the new sovereignty, extending continued authority for the Pueblo form of government.

Dr. Steck returned to the Territory, bringing with him several of the pueblo land patents, and a Lincoln cane for each of the pueblo governors, to be used by them according to their custom and to be passed on to their successors.

A third cane was presented to the governors by New Mexico State Governor Bruce King during his second term in 1980. This cane was presented in order to reaffirm the sovereignty of the pueblo governments. And in September 1987, King Juan Carlos of Spain, while visiting New Mexico, gave a second Spanish cane to the governors. Now each governor has four canes. Thus for more than three centuries there has been continued recognition of Native American government—the most enduring local government in America.

Today, the pueblo governor with his canes is always in evidence at fiestas or special gatherings of the pueblo leaders. In the home of a governor, one can see all the canes prominently displayed. And it is still the tradition to have all the canes of the higher civil officials blessed on January 6, the feast day of the Three Kings.

The pueblo canes are symbols to the people that all power and authority exist in their own form of government; that their government is responsible to the people; and that they owe allegiance to the United States of America. On the other hand, the canes are also symbols of the United States Government's responsibilities for and trusteeship of the pueblos.

Appendixes
A Brief Historical Outline of the Pueblo Indians

10000 B.C.—This is a date generally set, according to evidence found by archaeologists, for a people living in the Southwest, from northern Mexico to the southern halves of Utah and Colorado, the western corners of Oklahoma, Kansas, and Texas, to the southeast corner of Nevada, and most of New Mexico and Arizona, except the southwest part of Arizona as it is today.

3000 B.C.—The remains of corncobs are evidence of food grown at this time by the early southwesterners.

1000 B.C.—There is archaeological evidence of the cultivation of corn, beans, tobacco, and squash, as well as basket weaving at this time.

300 B.C.—Scientific exploration has provided evidence that the southwestern people lived a settled life with permanent habitations by this date.

1 A.D.—Excavated quadrangular and founded pit houses, described as being grouped in clusters, indicate a settled way of life by this time. The entry and smoke hole of the kivas of today are still the same as those of 1,600 years ago.

900 A.D.—By this date the southwestern peoples are known to have traded with people of the south for sea shells, parrot feathers, and other items. The Tiwas along the Rio Grande from Taos to near Socorro and west to Grants traded, as did other Pueblos such as: the Keresans in the Four Corners area, Mesa Verde, Aztec, and Pueblo Bonito; the Tewas along and above New Mexico and the Colorado border area; and the Towas south of the Tewas on the Jicarilla Apache Indian Reservation as it is today. There is evidence of horizontal masonry, the bow and arrow, and a further development of pottery. There is a beginning of a "development" period.

950–1000 A.D.—A beginning of migration to the Rio Grande Valley. The Tiwas migrate to the Rio Grande, splitting the Tiwas into northern and southern Tiwas. Drought is experienced.

1150–1250 A.D.—There is a movement of Keresans from Chaco Canyon. The people of Santa Ana and Zia migrate to the Rio Puerco area. Other Keresans go east from Chaco Canyon and then south to the Rio Grande.

1275–1300 A.D.—The Four Corners area is vacated. The Acoma are found at their present site, as well as north of Grants. Other Keresans move from Rio Puerco to Jemez Creek, present-day Santa Ana and Zia. The Tewas and Towas are centralized.

1150–1350 A.D.—The "classic" or "golden age" of Pueblo development is experienced. Now there evolved a culture, a formalized religion, and a system of government so advanced that the Pueblo Indians could not be referred to as "savages," or *barbaros*. But there is no written language; oral history flourishes.

1350–1700 A.D.—This is a period of maximum expansion of Pueblo Indian culture of New Mexico. There is also the beginning of an alliance with the Spaniards against raiding Indian tribes.

1400 A.D.—Athabascans (Apaches and Navajos) arrive in the Southwest.

The Advent of the Europeans

November 1528—Spaniards are shipwrecked off the Texas coast. Four survivors finally reach northern Mexico in 1536 after traveling across Texas. They hear rumors of the existence of inhabited cities to the north. Rumors of riches help to inspire Viceroy Antonio Mendoza to plan exploration parties.

June 9, 1537—Pope Paul III issues a papal bull, "Sublimus Deus," which proclaims that American Indians are indeed truly men and entitled to liberty and the possession of their property.

March 1539—Friar Marcos de Niza and Estevanico (a black Moroccan) along with an initial exploration party depart from Culiacan. Estevanico and a small band of aides reach Hawikuh in the Zuni country and make contact with the Pueblo Indians. Estevanico is killed by the Zunis for his brazen behavior and threats against the people. Friar Marcos observes Hawikuh from a distance and returns to make a report on the so-called Seven Cities of Cibola. There were only six Zuni villages: Hawikuh, Halona, Kechipawa, Matsaki, Kiakima, and Kwakina.

1539—Francisco de Vitoria lectures at the University of Salamanca, espousing the philosophy that New World natives are free men and exempt from slavery. In time, the principles of de Vitoria lead to a better relationship between the Pueblos and the Spaniards.

1540—Francisco Vasquez de Coronado brings Spanish soldiers and colonizers for purposes of exploring Pueblo country. They arrive at Hawikuh on July 7. Hernando de Alvarado and Fray Juan de Padilla are sent east to explore the Rio Grande. Lopez de Cardenas arrives later, to select permanent headquarters in an area known as Bernalillo today. The Indians are outraged when a Spaniard attempts to attack an Indian's wife. Cardenas leads the Spaniards in battle against the Indians, and many Indians are killed for the invader's crime. Coronado and his soldiers arrive in December. They immediately demand clothing from the Pueblo people. Indians give them the clothes off their backs.

Spring 1542—The Coronado party returns to Mexico, its mission failed, its leader on a litter, and with no gold.

1552—Bishop Bartolome de las Casas returns to Europe, after spending forty years in Mexico and Peru, to write an eyewitness account of Spanish atrocities against the Indian peoples. His writings may have led to a closer scrutiny by the Crown of Spain, and in time a better relationship between the Spaniards and the Pueblo Indians.

1581—A party of thirty-one missionaries returns to Pueblo country. They are led by Lay Brother Agustin Rodriguez and the military man Francisco Sanchez Chamuscado.

1582—A relief party is organized to locate two friars who had remained behind during the year before. A wealthy rancher who is hiding from the law, Antonio de Espejo, volunteers to outfit and lead the party. Reports from the last two expeditions prompt the Spanish Crown to plan permanent settlements in New Mexico.

1590–1591—Gaspar Castano de Sosa undertakes a colonizing expedition independently, without permission from Spain. He plants crosses at all Pueblo villages, and also appoints alcaldes and alguacils (sheriffs). The viceroy appoints Captain Juan Morlete to find and return de Sosas to Mexico under guard.

1593—Francisco Leyba de Bonilla and Antonio Gutierrez de Humana arrive at San Ildefonso Pueblo and settle there, without permission. Bonilla is killed by Humana, and the rest of the party is killed by Indians of the eastern plains while on an exploring trip.

September 1595—Juan de Oñate is awarded a contract to colonize New Mexico, at his own expense.

January 26, 1598—Juan de Oñate and his party leave Santa Barbara for his initial colonizing expedition, with permission from the Spanish Crown.

April 30, 1598—Oñate takes formal "possession" of New Mexico at a point on the Rio Grande below El Paso del Norte. Ownership of the land by the Pueblos is ignored.

July 7, 1598—The first recorded assembly of thirty-eight Pueblo leaders with the Spanish takes place at Santo Domingo Pueblo. Oñate is given permission to settle, and the Pueblo leaders swear allegiance to the king of Spain. The Pueblo country is divided into *alcaldias* (districts), and Franciscan missionaries are assigned to seven pueblos.

July 11, 1598—The Spanish make their settlement at Yungeh Oweenge (Mockingbird Place), and they name the settlement San Gabriel de los Espanoles; it is located on the Rio Grande across from the Tewa village of O'Kang Oweenge, the present pueblo of San Juan.

December 1598—Juan de Zaldiver, nephew of Oñate, is killed by the Acomas. The Indians are dissatisfied with their treatment by the Spaniards, and incidents continue to occur in which antagonisms flare up.

January 1599—The Acomas become militant and engage in a punitive expedition, in which they are defeated by the Spaniards led by Vicente de Zaldivar. Children under the age of twelve are taken by the Spanish, and those over that age are condemned to slavery. Men who are over twenty years old are punished by having one foot and one hand cut off. These bloodthirsty acts further enrage the Indians.

1610—San Gabriel is abandoned as the Spanish capital. La Villa Real de Santa Fe de San Francisco de Assisi is established by the third governor, Pedro de Peralta. A regular mission supply system is started between Mexico City and Santa Fe. During the period 1610 to 1614, the Palace of the Governors is erected at Santa Fe.

1598–1680—This is a period of intensive missionary activities among the Pueblos. In 1617, there were eleven mission churches in New Mexico. Fray Alonzo de Lugo is with the Hemish (Jemez) at

San Jose de Guisewa from 1598 to 1601. Fray Geronimo Zarate de Salmeron is at San Jose de Guisewa from 1618 to 1626. Fray Martin de Arvide is at San Lorenzo de Picuris, and he is at San Diego de la Congregacion at Walatowa (Jemez Pueblo today) from 1628 to 1630. Fray Juan de Salas is at San Antonio de Isleta in 1621, and the church is completed by 1629.

1620—A royal decree of the king of Spain requires each pueblo, with the close of the calendar year, to choose a governor, lieutenant governor, and other officials as needed, by popular vote. They are to carry on the affairs of the pueblo. Silver-crowned canes are given to each pueblo governor as a symbol of his office and authority, with the cross on the silver mount symbolizing the support of the church to his pueblo.

December 1632—Padre Pedro de Miranda, his guard, and two soldiers are killed by natives at Taos. The Pueblo Indians find that the Spanish are requiring them to abandon their ancient religion in favor of Christianity through the Roman Catholic church. They are subjected to taxation, and a veritable feudal system prevails.

1633—Fray Estevan de Perea, agent and custodian of the Inquisition, arrives to conduct an investigation of witchcraft and bigamy among the Pueblos.

1634–1647—Religious persecution of the Pueblos results in conspiracies and sporadic outbreaks against the Spaniards. The Pueblos are organizing to resist the Spanish yoke, but at present there are only isolated incidents of resistance.

1640—The conflict between the Spanish civil and religious authorities becomes so grave that the Franciscans threaten to abandon the missions in New Mexico. The issues are: control over the Indians, the collection of taxes and goods, and mistreatment of the Indians.

1640—The Taos people flee to Cuartolejo, in Apache country, in fear of Governor Luis de Rosas.

1650—The Pueblos of Jemez, Isleta, Alameda (a now extinct Tiwa village), San Felipe, Cochiti, and Taos unite with Apaches to expel the Spanish. Their plans are discovered, and nine leaders are hanged. Others are sold into slavery.

1661–1664—Governor Diego de Penalosa forbids the exploitation of Pueblo Indians by friars in "spinning and weaving cotton mantas." Upon his return to Mexico City, Penalosa is tried by the Inquisition for offenses against the clergy, and a ruinous fine is imposed on him. Later, in France, Penalosa's schemes and the stories of his experiences stimulate the La Salle expedition (1684–1687), which set out to limit the expansion of the Spanish holdings and outposts in the New World.

1670–1675—Saline Pueblos, the people of Abo Quarai, and so forth, move to Isleta.

1675—Four Pueblo Indians are hanged, and forty-three are whipped and enslaved on conviction by a Spanish tribunal of "bewitching" the superior of the Franciscan monastery at San Ildefonso Pueblo.

1676—Raids by the Apache Indians result in the destruction of several pueblos and churches, and the killing of many Spaniards and Christianized Indians. The formerly peaceful and friendly relations between the Apaches and the Pueblos is at an end; the Apaches do not want the Spanish in the Southwest. Some Apaches are captured and are either hanged or sold into slavery.

The Pueblo Revolt

August 9, 1680—Two messengers from Tesuque, Nicolas Catua and Pedro Omtua, are captured by Maestro de Campo and Francisco Gomez Robledo, upon orders from Governor Antonio de Otermin, and brought to Santa Fe. Tension mounts, and the Tesuques kill a Spaniard, Cristobal de Herrera. Indignation increases as the Pueblos sustain demands upon their food stores and services, and endure injustices. Padre Juan Pio goes to Santa Fe for his safety.

August 10, 1680—The commemorative date of the Pueblo Revolt. Padre Juan Pio returns to Tesuque to say mass. He is accompanied by one of the despised soldiers, Pedro Hidalgo. Pio is killed. Twenty-one of thirty-three Franciscans and some four hundred Spaniards are killed in the ensuing revolt.

August 21, 1680—After a hopeless attempt to battle the native warriors and remain in Santa Fe, Otermin gives orders to move out of the area, and begins an exodus to the south when the Indians cut off their water supply. Arriving at Isleta, Tiwas are recruited (history relates they were forced) to assist the fleeing Spaniards. Today, the descendants of these Tiwas reside at Ysleta del Sur.

1680–1692—This is a period during which the Pueblos remain free and independent of the Spanish, having successfully expelled them from their land. Now the Pueblos must take the brunt of raids by marauding tribes, alone.

1681—Governor Otermin returns to the scene of his expulsion to learn the reasons for the revolt and who the leaders were. His troops sack Isleta and burn Sandia Pueblo. The people flee to Hopi country. They remain there until 1742, given sanctuary by their friends the Hopi people. The Pueblo people never divulge the names of leaders of the revolt. That is one reason so little is known about them.

1689—The new governor, Domingo Jironza de Cruzate, also returns to the Pueblos to investigate the revolt. He burns Zia Pueblo, and the people flee to Cerro Colorado, west of Jemez today. Cruzate takes with him a Zia man, Bartolome de Ojeda. Ojeda is present when Cruzate issues land grants to the pueblos—*to their own lands*—on September 20 and 25.

Reconquest: The Spanish Settlement on Pueblo Lands

August 14, 1692—Diego de Vargas and his troops leave for New Mexico. They arrive in Albuquerque September 10; and in Santa Fe September 13 at 4:00 A.M.

December 2, 1692—De Vargas returns to Mexico.

October 4, 1693—De Vargas returns to Pueblo country, with Pueblo leaders under Bartolome de Ojeda of Zia Pueblo. The Indians are sent on a few days ahead of the Spanish, to pave the way for a peaceful return of the Spaniards. Upon arrival at Santa Fe, Luis Tupatu of Picuris is made governor of the region of the northern pueblos.

April 17, 1694—The Keresans under Ojeda attack other Keresans of Santo Domingo, Cochiti, and La Cienega de Cochiti.

July 21, 1694—Ojeda, de Vargas, and Spanish troops attack Jemez Pueblo.

August 1694—Spaniards attack San Ildefonso Pueblo people on Black Mesa.

August 14, 15, 1694—Ojeda, de Vargas, and their troops attack the Enchanted Mesa north of Acoma. The Keresans from the Rio

Grande refuse to surrender, and continue their revolt.

September 11, 1694—Jemez prisoners from the July battle return from Santa Fe.

June 4, 1696—Taos, Picuris, Cochiti, Santo Domingo, and Jemez pueblos, as well as the Tewas, rise in rebellion and kill five missionaries and twenty-one soldiers. Many Rio Grande Pueblos flee to Hopi country, and the Jemez go to the Navajo land in the north.

June 1698—Governor Pedro Rodriguez Cubero, Joseph Naranjo, the Tewa interpreter, and troops persuade Keresans to descend from the Enchanted Mesa.

July 2, 1698—The Rio Grande Keresans from Santo Domingo, Cochiti, and La Cienega de Cochiti refuse to return home and establish themselves in the new pueblo in San Jose de Laguna.

1700–1706—Many present-day pueblos are reestablished following the return of Pueblo people from flights to Hopi and Navajo country.

1702—Alameda is founded by Fray Juan de Sabalita and Cubero for Tiwas from Hopi.

1708—Fray Juan de la Pena moves Tiwas of Alameda to Isleta.

1708—The Isleta mission is reestablished, with a new church in honor of San Agustin.

1716–1718—The Isletas return from Hopi country, where they had fled from 1681 on; this is said to be through the efforts of Fray Carlos Delgado.

1733—A group of Sandias petition Governor Gongora for permission to resettle their abandoned site.

1742—The Sandias return from Hopi country, where they had fled in 1681.

January 23, 1748—Permission for the reestablishment of Sandia Pueblo is granted.

April 5, 1748—The Sandias are granted title to land by Governor Joaquin Codalles y Rabal. This is peculiar, since the land is theirs to begin with.

1767—Great floods engulf the Santa Fe area, and there is much hardship among the Pueblo people in that vicinity.

1776—Fray Francisco Atanacio Dominguez visits the mission churches.

1780–1781—An epidemic of smallpox breaks out among the Indians and kills 5,000. It is particularly virulent among the Hopi people. Consequently, Fray Andres Garcia brings 200 Hopis to the Rio Grande pueblos and distributes them in the various villages.

1780—Galisteo Pueblo is occupied until October, before the people move to Santo Domingo.

July 20, 1818—The Navajo leader Joaquin and his followers come to Jemez Pueblo to tell the Spanish alcalde of their decision to split from the main Navajo tribe to become the Canoncito Navajos.

The Pueblos Ruled by Mexico

February 23, 1821—The Plan of Iguala is adopted by the Mexican revolutionary forces attempting to throw off the yoke of Spain. It includes the following precedent-setting statements: ". . . all inhabitants of New Spain without distinction, whether Europeans, Africans, or Indians, are citizens of this Monarchy, with the right to be employed in any post according to their merit and virtues . . . the person and property of every citizen will be respected and protected by law."

August 24, 1821—The Treaty of Cordoba between Spain and Mexico embodies the above principle.

September 27, 1821—Mexico becomes independent of Spain, and New Mexico becomes a province of Mexico.

October 6, 1821—Mexico issues its Declaration of Independence, which reaffirms that Indians are citizens of Mexico on an equal basis with non-Indians.

1822—With the beginning of the rule of Mexico, trade is opened with the United States, and goods begin to flow along the Santa Fe Trail. William Becknell brings the first wagons from the East across the plains to Santa Fe, thus opening a route for Anglos to penetrate Pueblo country.

March 11, 1824—The Bureau of Indian Affairs is established under the Department of War by the United States Government.

June 30, 1834—The Indian Intercourse Act is passed by Congress, making the unauthorized settlement of tribal lands by non-Indians a federal offense.

1838—Pecos Pueblo is abandoned, and the seventeen survivors move to Jemez Pueblo.

The Territory of New Mexico

May 13, 1846—War is proclaimed between the United States and Mexico.

August 18, 1846—The Territory of New Mexico is annexed to the United States, and General Stephen Watts Kearny makes a peaceful entry into Santa Fe to take possession of the area for the United States.

September 22, 1846—A proclamation of civil government for the Territory is made, with Charles Bent as the appointed territorial governor.

November 22, 1846—Colonel Doniphan negotiates the first United States treaty with the Navajo Indian Nation.

February 2, 1848—The Treaty of Guadalupe Hidalgo is signed, ending the war between the United States and Mexico, and providing that Mexico relinquish all claims to the territory east of the Rio Grande and cede the present New Mexico and upper California areas to the United States. Articles VIII and IX of the treaty provide for recognition and protection by the federal government of the rights to private property established under the Spanish and Mexican regimes.

1849—Responsibility for the Bureau of Indian Affairs is transferred from the Department of War to the Department of the Interior.

April 7, 1849—James S. Calhoun is appointed the first Indian agent in New Mexico.

July 1850—A treaty is drawn up between the United States and the Pueblos with James S. Calhoun acting as agent. However, the treaty was never ratified by the United States Senate. Officials of the following pueblos sign the treaty: Santa Clara, Tesuque, Nambe, Santo Domingo, Jemez, San Felipe, Cochiti, San Ildefonso, Santa Ana, and Zia.

September 9, 1850—Congress passes the Organic Act, which creates the Territory of New Mexico and settles a long-standing controversy with Texas over the region east of the Rio Grande.

March 3, 1851—James S. Calhoun is inaugurated as the first governor of the Territory of New Mexico.

January 10, 1853—A territorial law is passed prohibiting the sale of liquor to Indians, with this proviso: ". . . that the Pueblo Indians that live among us are not included in the word 'Indian.' "

1853—Christopher (Kit) Carson is appointed Indian agent in New Mexico.

July 22, 1854—The office of surveyor general for the Territory of New Mexico is established. Section VIII (10 Stat. 308) provides that the surveyor general, under instructions from the secretary of the interior, should investigate and make recommendations with a view to confirming all bona fide land claims within the newly ceded territory, including the claims of the Indian people. The surveyor general is required to ascertain the nature, origin, character, and extent of all claims to lands under the laws, usages, and customs of Spain and Mexico, and to report on the same. It is not recognized nor stated that the claims of the Indians themselves antedate all other claims, that in effect Spain recognized those claims as rights to occupancy, and that aboriginal ownership would continue to be an issue even until modern times.

August 4, 1854—The territory acquired from Mexico under the Gadsden Purchase is incorporated into the Territory of New Mexico.

December 22, 1858—A congressional act is passed confirming the original Spanish land grants on the basis of reports of the surveyor general for the following pueblos: Acoma, Jemez, Cochiti, Picuris, San Felipe, San Juan, Santo Domingo, Zia, Isleta, Nambe, Pojoaque, Sandia, San Ildefonso, Santa Clara, Taos, and Tesuque. Thus is the complex situation made even more complex, since the question of land grants to Indians is superimposed upon Indian aboriginal rights dating from time immemorial, and now the Indians can claim rights both under the land claims and under their original rights as first owners of the land, whose land was taken without treaty, without payment, without permission, and without knowledge of the Indian people themselves.

January 21, 1861—An act is passed requiring the Pueblos to work on ditches and highways.

1864—Colonel Kit Carson and his troops overwhelm the Navajos fighting for their independence in their Canyon de Chelly stronghold, and move them as captives to the infamous Bosque Redondo.

May 1864—Superintendent Michael Steck returns to Santa Fe from Washington, carrying the "Lincoln canes" for the pueblo governors.

November 1, 1864—Land patents are issued by the United States and signed by President Lincoln for the following pueblos: Nambe, Cochiti, Isleta, Jemez, Picuris, Zia, Sandia, San Felipe, San Ildefonso, Pojoaque, San Juan, Santa Clara, Taos, Tesuque, and Santo Domingo. The governors of each pueblo are invited to come to Washington.

1868—The United States Government returns the Navajo people to their former home, ending their exile.

February 9, 1869—The United States Government confirms the original Spanish land grant to Santa Ana Pueblo.

1871—The decentralization of Laguna Pueblo begins, with the founding of outlying villages. This occurs in part because of a religious dispute between members of the pueblo, as well as because of the pacification of the raiding Navajos.

May 29, 1872—Congress authorizes the extension of federal services to the Pueblo Indians.

1875—The position of interpreter is established for the Pueblos.

1876—The United States Supreme Court sustains the previous decision of the New Mexico Supreme Court, stating that the Intercourse Act of 1834 is not applicable to the Pueblo Indians (*United States v. Joseph,* U.S. 614). This decision deprives the Pueblo Indians of the protection of their lands that other Indian tribes in the country are supposed to enjoy. Consequently, about 3,000 white families, with about 12,000 people, settle on Indian land.

November 19, 1877—A land patent is issued to Acoma Pueblo by the United States Government.

April–July 1878—The Ute Indians are removed from New Mexico to their present reservation in Colorado.

1879—The railroad comes to New Mexico; henceforth life changes for the Pueblo people and all others.

1880—Laguna people migrate to Isleta as a result of American influence leading to differences between "progressives" and the traditional religious people known as "conservatives."

1881—The Albuquerque Indian School in Duranes, one mile northwest of Old Albuquerque, is founded. In 1882, the school moves to its present location on land purchased by the citizens of Albuquerque for this purpose. The school is maintained by the Presbyterian church under contract with the United States, from 1881 to October 1886, when it is taken over and run by the federal government.

April 25, 1883—A land patent is issued to Santa Ana Pueblo by the United States.

1886—Santo Domingo village is nearly destroyed by flood.

March 3, 1891—The Court of Private Land Claims is established by Congress (26 Stat. 854). The court is set up to combine the functions of the surveyor general's office and Congress itself. It conducts investigations and hearings, and renders opinions in the form of decrees. The court, in time, confirms most of the Pueblo tribally owned lands outside the boundaries of the original Spanish grants.

April 20, 1898—The original land grant to Laguna Pueblo is confirmed by the Court of Private Land Claims.

1899—The post of special attorney for the Pueblos is established at a salary of $1,500.

1900—Pojoaque Pueblo is abandoned, and the survivors migrate to Nambe and other areas.

September–October 1904—The most disastrous flood in the history of New Mexico occurs, resulting in the loss of many lives.

November 15, 1909—A land patent is issued to Laguna Pueblo.

June 20, 1910—The Enabling Act is passed by Congress, admitting New Mexico and Arizona into the union. It specifically provides that: ". . . the terms 'Indian' and 'Indian country' shall include the Pueblo Indians of New Mexico and the lands occupied by them." (Challenged for some years, this provision was upheld in 1913 in the case of *United States v. Sandoval*.)

1911—The Southern Pueblos Agency of the Bureau of Indian Affairs is established in Albuquerque. The northern pueblos are administered through offices in Santa Fe.

The Pueblos and the State of New Mexico

1912—New Mexico is admitted to the union as the forty-seventh state.

1913—The Supreme Court, in the case of *United States v. Sandoval*, in effect reverses the decision of the *Joseph* case of 1876. Consequently, some 3,000 families of about 12,000 people find themselves on Indian land unlawfully; they are trespassers.

1922—A reorganization meeting of the All Indian Pueblo Council is held at Santo Domingo, attended by delegates from each pueblo. The precise length of time during which the council has functioned is difficult to determine, but it is considered to be the oldest mutual defense league in the Western Hemisphere. Regular meetings are held by the council to discuss matters of mutual interest, and solutions are sought. The All Indian Pueblo Council is deeply involved with the history and traditions of the Pueblo people.

June 2, 1924—By act of Congress, all Indians are declared to be citizens of the United States, and hence eligible to vote. Some tribes have had this right for many years, and individual Indians who moved to the cities also voted, but the act established the vote for all the rest. Nevertheless, two states did not pass the required legislation: New Mexico and Arizona. Not until 1948, as the result of a lawsuit, was the right to vote given to Indians of these two states.

June 7, 1924—The Pueblo Lands Act is passed by Congress (43 Stat. 636). The Lands Board created by this act is set up primarily to clear the controversy caused by the decision of the Supreme Court in the case of *United States v. Sandoval.* It is to determine the status of Indian land claims with the exterior boundaries of the Spanish land grants, together with other duties designed to clarify claims by and against the Pueblos. The act states:

> *It shall be the further duty of the board to separately report in respect of each such pueblo:*
>
> *(a) The area and character of any tract or tracts of land within the exterior boundaries of any land granted or confirmed to the Pueblo Indians of New Mexico and the extent, source, and character of any water right appurtenant thereto in possession of non-Indian claimants at the time of filing such report, which are not claimed for said Indians by any report of the board.*
>
> *Sec. 2: It shall be the duty of said board to investigate, determine and report, and set forth by metes and bounds, illustrated where necessary by field notes and plats, the lands within the exterior boundaries of any land granted or confirmed to the Pueblo Indians of New Mexico by any*

authority of the United States of America, or any prior
sovereignty, or acquired by said Indians as a community
by purchase or otherwise, title to which the said board
shall find not to have been extinguished in accordance
with the provisions of this Act. . . .

March 3, 1931—The original land grant to Zuni Pueblo is confirmed.

1933—The land of Pojoaque Pueblo is restored to the Pueblos, by order of the Pueblo Lands Board and the federal court. Less than forty descendants of the original families were found living in other pueblos and the neighboring states of Texas and Colorado. Some of these people returned home and are now living on the pueblo land.

February 15, 1933—A land patent is issued to Zuni Pueblo by the United States.

June 18, 1934—The Indian Reorganization Act is passed (48 Stat. 984). This act reaffirms the right of the Indians, including the Pueblo groups, to govern themselves, but under an organizational structure determined by the United States Government. They are allowed to form corporations for the operation of business, and other conditions established by the IRA. The act represents the reversal of the 1887 Dawes Allotment Act, which had as its purpose the breaking up of Indian tribal groups. But the IRA set in motion a Western-type organizational structure destined to become troublesome and controversial, now seen as destructive of traditional Indian government. It also tied the tribal governments and their right to enact laws and govern themselves to the United States because in all matters of importance, the secretary of the interior must approve such actions, including in most cases the election of tribal governing bodies. Jemez Pueblo is the only pueblo to date that has not accepted the provisions of the Indian Reorganization Act by referendum of its members.

December 20, 1935—The United Pueblos Agency is established in Albuquerque by the Bureau of Indian Affairs.

1941–1945—World War II. There are 21,767 Indians in the army in 1945; 1,910 in the navy; 121 in the Coast Guard; and 723 in the Marine Corps, exclusive of officers. The Bureau of Indian Affairs records 71 awards of the Air Medal, 51 of the Silver Star, 47 of the Bronze Star medal, 34 of the Distinguished Flying Cross, and 2 of the Congressional Medal of Honor. More than 40,000 Indians leave their reservations during each of the war years, to take jobs in ordinance depots, aircraft factories, on the railroads, and in other war industries. The Indians invest more than $17,000,000 of their own restricted funds in war bonds, and their individual purchases probably amount to twice that sum.

1943—Los Alamos National Laboratory is founded by the government as an atomic research center. Indians from nearby pueblos were and still are employed there.

March 27, 1947—The Isleta Pueblo constitution is approved by the secretary of the interior, in accordance with the terms of the Indian Reorganization Act.

1948—Indians obtain the right to vote in New Mexico, as the result of a federal court decision.

December 21, 1949—The Laguna Pueblo constitution is approved under the terms of the IRA by the secretary of the interior.

March 1952—The first lease between Laguna Pueblo and the Anaconda Company is signed, providing for the development of uranium deposits discovered on the pueblo grant.

1952—The so-called relocation program is established by the Bureau of Indian Affairs, through an employment opportunities act. Jobs in the cities, adult education, vocational training, and a certain amount of financial aid when Indians move to the cities are provided under the program. Relocation offices are established in principal cities. But the program becomes a dismal failure as Indians complain about inadequate training, lack of available jobs, and failure of the unions to accept as members Indians with such skills as carpentry, bricklaying, or mechanics, thus assuring they will not get employment. Other conditions become the basis for disenchantment with the program and complaints by Indians, such as poverty in the cities, disruption of tribal contracts and family relationships, inadequate supportive services and funds, and abysmally inadequate educational and vocational services.

1954—An industrial development program is inaugurated by the Bureau of Indian Affairs to assist the Pueblos, in cooperation with neighboring communities, in planning and developing programs to attract industry to the areas.

July 1, 1955—The health programs for Indians are transferred from the Bureau of Indian Affairs to the Public Health Service of the Department of Health, Education and Welfare.

1958—An adult vocational training service is established by the BIA, providing on-the-job training not to exceed twenty-four months for Indians living on or adjacent to a reservation.

1962—Overall economic development plans are prepared for five pueblos. Santa Fe Indian School is replaced by a new art school, the Institute of American Indian Arts.

August 1963—The Burnell Company (electronics) of Pelham, New York, completes plans to establish a plant on the Laguna Indian Reservation. Investment over a five-year period is scheduled for $1 million, with the pueblo providing at least ninety percent of the total investment.

1963–1964—The United Pueblos Agency is allocated $2.1 million under the Accelerated Public Works Program. The funds are used to build five community centers for range, irrigation, and forestry improvements, and community parks and play areas.

1964—The pueblos of Tesuque and Nambe create tribal housing authorities to negotiate with the Public Housing Administration in the newly created Mutual Self-Help Housing Project.

1965—The Office of Economic Opportunity appoints a special committee and coordinator to assist Indian groups in preparing community action programs, which work with the tribes within the United Pueblos Agency jurisdiction.

October 19, 1965—The All Indian Pueblo Council adopts a constitution and bylaws. This brings the ancient traditional group into the structure of modern governmental bodies under a Western-type format. The two systems—ancient and modern—now attempt to develop cooperation among both worlds, the Indian and the modern, with the objective of encouraging economic progress, education, and unification of the pueblos on such issues as water rights, land rights, and preservation of Indian cultural values.

December 2, 1970—Congress votes to return Taos Blue Lake to pueblo ownership, and President Nixon signs the bill on December 15 (HR 471). This ends sixty-four years of battle to regain the sacred lake.

1975—Congress passes legislation known as the Indian Self-Determination and Education Assistance Act (Public Law 93-638), signed by President Gerald Ford.

August 1976—The All Indian Pueblo Council takes administrative control of Albuquerque Indian School under the direction of Chairman Delfine Lovato.

1980—The Pueblos observe the three-hundredth anniversary of the 1680 Pueblo Revolt.

April 1980—The Albuquerque Indian School is granted the prestigious North Central Association of Colleges and Schools accreditation.

September 8, 1981—Due to safety hazards at the Albuquerque Indian School, the school moves to Santa Fe and classes begin there on this date.

January 1987—Verna Olguin Williamson is elected the first woman governor of Isleta Pueblo and serves for four years.

January 30, 1990—Zuni Pueblo votes on the Zuni-Cibola National Historical Park and turns it down with 863 against and 125 in favor.

November 24, 1990—The Smithsonian Institution returns 3,500 pictures taken in the nineteenth and twentieth centuries to Zuni Pueblo.

December 4, 1990—Zuni Pueblo celebrates the passage of the Zuni Land Conservation Act of 1990. The act authorizes the appropriation of $25 million to repair Zuni land destroyed by erosion and other forces.

January 1991—Patrick Baca of Sandia Pueblo is appointed by Governor Bruce King as secretary of labor of New Mexico State.

January 15, 1991—Augustine Sando of Jemez Pueblo is inducted posthumously into the distinguished Democratic Party's Hall of Fame.

The All Indian Pueblo Council

According to oral history, a semblance of an All Indian Pueblo Council existed before European contact, mainly to counteract the nomadic raiding tribes following the years A.D. 1400 or A.D. 1525, whichever date one wishes to accept as the arrival of Apaches and Navajos in the Southwest.

In 1598, when Juan de Oñate arrived in Pueblo country with the idea of colonizing, he met with thirty-eight Pueblo leaders at Khe-wa, or Santo Domingo Pueblo. Thus the date of 1598 appears on the logo of the All Indian Pueblo Council to indicate that this date is inscribed in writing by the Spaniards and is considered the date of origin of the council.

Prior to the Pueblo Revolt of 1680 the council met also to plan the uprising. So the All Indian Pueblo Council has been in existence since pre-European contact. The Six-League Iroquois of New York was the only other tribal organization that existed for a time. However, during the Europeans' power struggle, Indian allies were enlisted, and the league members were disrupted.

The All Indian Pueblo Council was still operating prior to 1922, as is evident from the story of Pablo Abeita in this book. But the official modern-day operations of the council began on November 5, 1922, at Santo Domingo Pueblo, when John Collier assembled the Pueblos to explain the Bursum Bill. The story of the reorganization meeting is recorded in the biographies of Sotero Ortiz and Pablo Abeita.

The AIPC logo was developed by me when I served as secretary to Chairman Domingo Montoya in 1970. The finishing touches were done by Jerry Ingram, a Creek Indian from Oklahoma. The mountains represent any mountain near each pueblo. The river down the middle could be the Rio Grande, the Jemez, the Rio San Jose, or the Rio Pueblo at Taos. The fields are self-explanatory, with pictures of the crops that are the lifeblood of the Pueblos: corn, wheat, chile, melons, and squash. The sacred sun symbol is over the mountains, with the date of the first meeting with the Spaniards next to the sun's rays. (See page 18.)

The All Indian Pueblo Council Constitution

Preamble

We, the Pueblo Indians of New Mexico, members of the existing All Indian Pueblo Council, by virtue of our sovereign rights as Pueblo Indians and in accordance with our ancient customs and laws, in order to promote justice and encourage the common welfare, to foster the social and economic advancement of all the Pueblo Indians, to preserve and protect our common interests, our inherent rights of self-government, and our rights as guaranteed to us by treaties, law, and the Federal Constitution of the United States of America, do ordain and adopt this Constitution and By-Laws for the All Indian Pueblo Council for the common benefit of all Pueblo Indians.

ARTICLE I — NAME

This organization shall be recognized by the name of "The All Indian Pueblo Council."

ARTICLE II — MEMBERSHIP

Section 1. Conditions of Membership

(a) The governing body of any duly organized Indian pueblo within New Mexico may become a member of the All Indian Pueblo Council.

(b) To receive recognition, any member-pueblo must satisfy an annual membership fee as described by the All Indian Pueblo Council.

Section 2. Qualifications

(a) Each delegate must be a recognized member of the Indian pueblo he represents, and must be duly authorized by the governing body of that pueblo to appear and represent it.

ARTICLE III — ORGANIZATION OF THE COUNCIL

Section 1. Officers

(a) The executive power of the All Indian Pueblo Council shall be vested in the following officers:

   A. Chairman
   B. Vice-Chairman
   C. Secretary
   D. Treasurer

(b) No person shall be qualified to hold office in the All Indian Pueblo Council who is an employee of the Federal or State governments.

Section 2. Election of Officers

On the last Saturday in January of every odd year, an election shall be held within the All Indian Pueblo Council, at which the officers listed under Section 1 shall be elected by majority vote, through a secret ballot system, to serve for two (2) years from the date of the election.

Section 3. Who May Vote

Every member pueblo of the All Indian Pueblo Council, through its duly authorized delegate, may cast one (1) vote.

Section 4. Candidates

(a) Nominations for the offices of the All Indian Pueblo Council shall be made by the recognized delegates of the member-pueblos, and nominations for the office of chairman shall close at the adjournment of the last regular meeting of every even-numbered year. Nominations for the remaining offices may be made from the floor by the member delegates the day of election.

(b) Each nominee must be a recognized member of one of the member-pueblos, not less than 30 years of age, and must either be present at the time of his nomination or his written consent to serve, if elected, must be filed by the delegate who nominates him.

ARTICLE IV — THE ALL INDIAN PUEBLO COUNCIL AND ITS POWERS

Section 1. The legislative power shall be vested in the All Indian Pueblo Council, and its powers shall be exercised in accordance with and not in conflict with, this Constitution. The All Indian Pueblo Council shall have the following rights and powers:

(a) To employ legal counsel, the choice of counsel and fixing of fees to be subject to the approval of the All Indian Pueblo Council by majority vote of the member-pueblos.

(b) To negotiate with all governments, persons, firms or corporations on matters brought before the All Indian Pueblo Council.

(c) To have the power to contract for and accept loans or grants for the All Indian Pueblo Council.

(c) To have the power to contract for and accept loans or grants for the All Indian Pueblo Council.

(d) To arrange for the maintenance of law and order at the All Indian Pueblo Council functions.

(e) To promote or conduct educational, health, publicity or other campaigns introduced by the member-pueblos.

(f) To promote and foster programs and projects for the protection, benefit, advancement and general welfare of any or all member-pueblos.

(g) To raise revenue for the business of the All Indian Pueblo Council and to regulate the expenditure thereof.

(h) To formulate and adopt by-laws for the proper functioning of the All Indian Pueblo Council.

(i) To formulate the powers and duties of the executive officers.

(j) To do whatever else may be necessary or desirable to promote the general welfare of any or all member-pueblos.

Section 2. In carrying out these powers, the All Indian Pueblo Council and officers will not interfere with the self-government of any member-pueblo.

ARTICLE V — VACANCIES AND IMPEACHMENTS

Section 1. Vacancies

Should any vacancy occur in any of the elective offices of the All Indian Pueblo Council through death, resignation or disqualification through employment with the Federal or State governments, or for any other reason, the Council shall by majority vote have the right to name a successor for the said office for the unexpired term in accordance with the provisions of Article III, provided that in the event the office of the Chairman becomes vacant for any reason, then and in that event, the Vice-Chairman shall thereupon become the Chairman with all duties and powers of the said office.

Section 2. Impeachment

The All Indian Pueblo Council may, by a two-thirds vote of the members, remove any of its officers for neglect of duty, or gross misconduct, provided that the accused shall be given an opportunity to answer any and all charges at the All Indian Pueblo Council meeting called for the purpose. The decision of the All Indian Pueblo Council shall be final.

ARTICLE VI — COMMITTEES

The Chairman, after consultation with the other officers and the consent of the member delegate of the pueblo from which the committee member comes, shall appoint committees from the authorized membership of the member-pueblos. Committees shall consist of at least three (3) members, but not more than six (6). The elected officers of the All Indian Pueblo Council shall be the ex-officio members of all committees.

ARTICLE VII — AMENDMENTS

Section 1. Amendments to Constitution

This Constitution may be amended by a two-thirds affirmative vote of the member delegates at a special meeting of the All Indian Pueblo Council called for that purpose, the said special meeting to be called by the Chairman upon the written request of six (6) member-pueblos. The written request shall include the proposed amendment and shall set forth the reasons and need therefor, and must be transmitted to each member delegate at least 30 days before the special meeting.

Section 2. Amendments to By-Laws

By-Laws to this Constitution may be adopted or amended at any meeting of the All Indian Pueblo Council upon a two-thirds affirmative vote of the member delegates.

ARTICLE VIII — RATIFICATION

This Constitution of the All Indian Pueblo Council shall become effective upon the ratification and approval by two-thirds of the member-pueblos.

ADOPTED: This Sixteenth day of October, in the year of our Lord, One Thousand, Nine Hundred and Sixty-five.

Sam Victorino	Pat Martinez
Acoma Pueblo	Picuris Pueblo
Andy Abeita	John Ray
Isleta Pueblo	San Felipe Pueblo
Joe Mariano	Percy Tapia
Laguna Pueblo	San Juan Pueblo

Tom Romero
  Pojoaque Pueblo
Esquipula Chaves
  Sandia Pueblo
Gilbert Atencio
  San Ildefonso Pueblo
Miguel Armijo
  Santa Ana Pueblo
Fernando Cordero
  Cochiti Pueblo
Abel Sando
  Jemez Pueblo
Amadeo Trujillo
  Nambe Pueblo

Paul Tafoya
  Santa Clara Pueblo
Ralph P. Lovato
  Santo Domingo Pueblo
Joe G. Vigil
  Tesuque Pueblo
Teofilo Romero
  Taos Pueblo
Luciano Pino
  Zia Pueblo
Robert E. Lewis
  Zuni Pueblo

Certified and adopted this 16th day of October 1965, by the officers of the All Indian Pueblo Council:

Domingo Montoya
  Chairman
Benny Atencio
  Treasurer

Paul J. Bernal
  Vice-Chairman
Joe H. Herrera
  Secretary

Officers of the All Indian Pueblo Council
(Since 1922)

From November 5, 1922
1st Chairman:	Sotero Ortiz, San Juan
Secretary:	Pablo Abeita, Isleta
Interpreter:	Jose Alcario Montoya, Cochiti

From May 31, 1940
2nd Chairman:	Joseph Filario Tafoya, Santa Clara
Secretary:	Abel Paisano, Laguna
Interpreter:	Sotero Ortiz, San Juan

From October 12, 1946
3rd Chairman:	Abel Paisano, Laguna
Secretary:	John C. Rainer, Taos

From November 2, 1950
4th Chairman:	Popovi Da, San Ildefonso
1st Vice-Chairman:	Roland Durand, Picuris
Secretary:	Diego Abeita, Isleta (1950–1951)
	Lewis G. Paisano, Laguna (1951–1952)

From November 15, 1952
5th Chairman:	Martin Vigil, Tesuque
Vice-Chairman:	Roland Durand, Picuris
Secretary:	Popovi Da, San Ildefonso
	Joe H. Herrera, Cochiti, from July 18, 1953
1st Treasurer:	Ulysses G. Paisano, Laguna

From February 12, 1955
6th Chairman:	John C. Rainer, Taos
Vice-Chairman:	Teofilo Tafoya, Santa Clara
Secretary:	Joe H. Herrera, Cochiti
Treasurer:	Ulysses G. Paisano, Laguna

From March 1957
7th Chairman:	Martin Vigil, Tesuque
Vice-Chairman:	John C. Rainer, Taos
Secretary:	Joe H. Herrera, Cochiti
Treasurer:	Tom Dailey, Sr., Laguna

From February 7, 1959

Chairman:	Martin Vigil, Tesuque
Vice-Chairman:	Frank Tenorio, San Felipe
Secretary:	Joe H. Herrera, Cochiti
Treasurer:	Tom Dailey, Sr., Laguna

From February 13, 1964

8th Chairman:	Domingo Montoya, Sandia
Vice-Chairman:	Paul Bernal, Taos
Secretary:	Joe H. Herrera, Cochiti
Treasurer:	Benny Atencio, Santo Domingo

From February 18, 1967

Chairman:	Domingo Montoya, Sandia
Vice-Chairman:	Ramos Sanchez, San Ildefonso
Secretary:	Victor Sarracino, Laguna
	Joe S. Sando, Jemez, from February 21, 1970
Treasurer:	Benny Atencio, Santo Domingo

From January 30, 1971

9th Chairman:	Benny Atencio, Santo Domingo
Vice-Chairman:	Delfine Lovato, San Juan-Santo Domingo
Secretary:	Ernest Lovato, Santo Domingo
Treasurer:	Jose Seferino Lente, Isleta

From February 1973

10th Chairman:	Valentino Cordova, Taos-Tesuque, resigned March 1975
Vice-Chairman:	Delfine Lovato, San Juan-Santo Domingo
Secretary:	Ernest Lovato, Santo Domingo
Treasurer:	Ernest Lujan, Taos

From March 1975

11th Chairman:	Delfine Lovato, San Juan-Santo Domingo
Vice-Chairman:	Paul Bernal, Taos
Secretary:	Frank Tenorio, San Felipe
Treasurer:	Gilbert Pacheco, Laguna (Position combined with Secretary)

From 1976

Chairman:	Delfine Lovato, San Juan-Santo Domingo
Vice-Chairman:	Paul Bernal, Taos
Secretary-Treasurer:	Frank Tenorio, San Felipe

From January 1977
    Chairman: Delfine Lovato, San Juan-Santo Domingo
    Vice-Chairman: Paul Bernal, Taos
    Secretary-Treasurer: Frank Tenorio, San Felipe

From January 1979
    to 1982
    Chairman: Delfine Lovato, San Juan-Santo Domingo
    Vice-Chairman: Paul Bernal, Taos
    Secretary-Treasurer: Frank Tenorio, San Felipe

From January 1983
    to 1984
    Chairman: Delfine Lovato, San Juan-Santo Domingo
    Vice-Chairman: Gilbert Pena, Nambe
    Secretary-Treasurer: Seferino Lente, Isleta

From December 1984
    to 1986
    12th Chairman: Gilbert Pena, Nambe
    Vice-Chairman: Stanley Pino, Zia
                             Seferino Tenorio, Santo Domingo, from
                                February 1986
    Secretary-Treasurer: John Gonzales, San Ildefonso

From January 1987
    to 1990
    13th Chairman: Herman Agoyo, San Juan
    Vice-Chairman: Seferino Tenorio, Santo Domingo
    Secretary-Treasurer: John Gonzales, San Ildefonso
                                Daniel Sanchez, Acoma, from December
                                1989

From January 1991
    to 1994
    14th Chairman: James Hena, Tesuque-Zuni
    Vice-Chairman: Benny Atencio, Santo Domingo
    Secretary-Treasurer: Daniel Sanchez, Acoma

Francisco de Vitoria's Principles

1. Since unbelief does not preclude ownership of property, the Indians are not precluded from owning property, and they are therefore the true owners of the New World, as they were before the advent of the Spaniards.

2. The Emperor is not the lord of the whole world, and, even if he were, he would not therefore be entitled to seize the provinces of the Indians, to put down their lords, to raise up new ones, and to levy taxes.

3. Neither is the Pope the civil or temporal lord of the whole world. He has no secular power except in so far as it subserves things spiritual. He can have no power over the dominions of unbelievers and therefore cannot give such dominions to secular princes. A refusal on the part of the aborigines to recognize the power of the Pope cannot therefore be regarded as a reason for making war upon them and seizing their goods. If the Christian religion had been expounded to the Indians with ever so much sufficiency of proof, and they still refused to accept it, this would not render it lawful to make war upon them and despoil them of their possessions.

4. The Spaniards, on the other hand, have the right to go to the lands of the Indians, dwell there and carry on trade, so long as they do no harm, and they may not be prevented by the Indians from so doing. If the Spaniards have diligently informed the Indians that they have not come to interfere in any way with the peace and welfare of the Indians, and if the Indians still show hostility toward them and attempt to destroy them, then, and only then, will it be lawful to make war upon the Indians. In the event of war the Indians may be despoiled of their goods and reduced to slavery, because in the law of nations whatever we take from the enemy becomes ours at once, and so true is this that men may be brought into slavery to us.

5. The Christians have the right to preach the Gospel among the barbarians. The Pope has the right to entrust the conversion of the Indians to the Spaniards alone and to forbid all other nations to preach or trade among them, if the propagation of the Faith would thus be furthered. If the Indians do not hinder the preaching of the Gospel, they may not be subjected by war, whether they accept it or not (Spicer 1969, 172).

Patron Saints of Each Pueblo and Feast Days

JANUARY 23	San Ildefonso
MAY 1	San Felipe
JUNE 13	San Antonio (Sandia)
JUNE 24	San Juan
JULY 14	San Buenaventura (Cochiti)
JULY 26	Santa Ana
JULY 26	Santa Ana at Seama Village on Laguna Reservation
AUGUST 2	Our Lady of Portiuncula, formerly at Pecos Pueblo, now at Jemez (Persingula)
AUGUST 4	Santo Domingo
AUGUST 10	San Lorenzo (Picuris)
AUGUST 12	Santa Clara
AUGUST 15	Our Lady of the Ascension (Zia)
AUGUST 15	Our Lady of the Ascension at Mesita Village on Laguna Reservation
SEPTEMBER 2	San Esteban (Acoma)
SEPTEMBER 4	San Agustin (Isleta) .
SEPTEMBER 8	Nativity of the Blessed Virgin, Encinal Village on Laguna Reservation
SEPTEMBER 19	San Jose (Old Laguna)
SEPTEMBER 25	St. Elisabeth, Paguate Village on Laguna Reservation
SEPTEMBER 30	San Geronimo (Taos)
OCTOBER 4	San Francisco (Nambe)
OCTOBER 17	St. Margaret-Mary, Paraje Village on Laguna Reservation
NOVEMBER 12	San Diego (Jemez)
NOVEMBER 12	San Diego (Tesuque)
DECEMBER 12	Our Lady of Guadalupe (Pojoaque)
DECEMBER 12	Our Lady of Guadalupe de Holona at Zuni, but not observed, as native Shalako festivities are near the same time.

Note: These events are open to the public.

Pueblo Indian Populations

	1980 Census	1990 Census	January 1989 BIA Labor Force Report
Acoma	3,592	2,435	4,350
Cochiti	918	1,199	921
Isleta	3,262	2,784	2,979
Jemez	2,181	1,615	2,378
Laguna	6,233	3,664	7,542
Nambe	438	1,369	435
Picuris	245	1,867	221
Pojoaque	124	2,463	102
Sandia	312	3,940	321
San Felipe	2,145	2,248	2,398
San Ildefonso	520	1,457	632
San Juan	1,806	4,783	1,935
Santa Ana	517	609	549
Santa Clara	1,374	9,640	1,582
Santo Domingo	2,857	2,851	3,446
Taos	1,951	4,486	1,631
Tesuque	312	696	328
Zia	645	613	694
Zuni	6,500	7,057	8,299
Totals	35,932	55,776	40,743

Pueblo Landholdings—1990*

Land in Acres

Northern Pueblos:

1. Nambe	19,124.01
2. Picuris	14,947.18
3. Pojoaque	11,601.44
4. San Ildefonso	26,197.75
5. San Juan	12,236.33
6. Santa Clara	45,827.68
7. Taos	95,341.36
8. Tesuque	16,813.16

Southern Pueblos:

1. Acoma		378,113.69
2. Cochiti		50,681.46
3. Isleta		211,103.00
4. Jemez		89,623.78
5. Sandia		22,870.91
6. San Felipe		48,929.90
7. Santa Ana		61,931.19
8. Santo Domingo		71,092.80
9. Ysleta del Sur (Texas)		97.47
10. Zia		121,599.62
11. Laguna		484,495.08
12. Zuni: New Mexico	(409,344.42)	
Arizona	(10,085.70)	419,430.12

* Bureau of Indian Affairs, Albuquerque Area Office

Bibliography

BOOKS

Archibeck, Ronald P. *Taos Indians and the Blue Lake Controversy.* Master's Thesis. Albuquerque, N.M.: University of New Mexico, 1972.

Bancroft, Hubert Howe. *History of Arizona and New Mexico: 1530–1888.* San Francisco: The History Co., Publishers, 1889. Reprinted, Albuquerque, N.M.: Horn and Wallace Press, 1962.

Bandelier, Adolph F. A. *Final Report of Investigations Among the Indians of the Southwestern United States.* Cambridge, Mass.: J. Wilson and Sons, 1892.

Bandelier, Adolph F. A. *The Southwestern Journals, 1880–1882.* Albuquerque, N.M.: University of New Mexico Press, 1966.

Benedict, Ruth. *Patterns of Culture.* New York: Penguin Books, Inc., 1947.

Bolton, Herbert Eugene. *Coronado, Knight of Pueblos and Plains.* Albuquerque, N.M.: University of New Mexico Press, 1949.

Bolton, Herbert Eugene, ed. *The Oñate Expeditions, Spanish Exploration in the Southwest, 1542–1706.* New York: Charles Scribner's Sons, 1908.

Brayer, Herbert O. *Pueblo Indian Land Grants of the 'Rio Abajo,' New Mexico.* University of New Mexico Bulletin No. 334. Albuquerque, N.M.: University of New Mexico Press, 1939.

Cardinal, Harold. *The Unjust Society, The Tragedy of Canada's Indians.* Edmonton, Alberta, Canada: M. G. Hurtig Ltd., 1969.

Ceram, C. W. *The First American, A Story of North American Archaeology.* New York: Harcourt Brace Jovanovich, Publishers, 1971.

Chavez, Fray Angelico. *Origins of New Mexico Families.* Albuquerque, N.M.: University of Albuquerque, and Calvin Horn Publisher, Inc., 1973.

Cohen, Felix S. *Handbook of Federal Indian Law.* Washington, D.C.: U.S. Department of the Interior, U.S. Government Printing Office, 1942.

Collier, John. *From Every Zenith, A Memoir and Some Essays on Life and Thought.* Denver, Colo.: Sage Books, 1963.

Collier, John. "The Genesis and Philosophy of the Indian Reorganization Act." In: *Indian Affairs and the Indian Reorganization Act,* edited by William H. Kelly. Tucson: University of Arizona Press, 1954.

Crane, Leo. *Desert Drums, The Pueblo Indians of New Mexico.* Boston: Little, Brown and Company, 1928.

Dominguez, Francisco Atanasio. *The Missions of New Mexico, 1776.* Translated and annotated by Eleanor B. Adams and Fray Angelico Chavez. Albuquerque, N.M.: University of New Mexico Press, 1956.

Dozier, Edward P. *The Pueblo Indians of North America.* New York: Holt, Rinehart and Winston, Inc., 1970.

Driver, Harold E. *Indians of North America.* 2d ed. Chicago: University of Chicago Press, 1969.

Eggan, Fred. *Social Organization of the Western Pueblos.* Chicago: University of Chicago Press, 1950.

Erdoes, Richard. *The Pueblo Indians.* New York: Funk and Wagnall, 1967.

Espinosa, Jose Manuel. *Crusaders of the Rio Grande.* Chicago: Institute of Jesuit History, 1942.

Espinosa, Jose Manuel. *The Pueblo Revolt of 1696 and the Franciscan Missionaries in New Mexico.* Letters of the missionaries translated and edited. Norman, Okla.: University of Oklahoma Press, 1988.

Frazier, Kendrick. *People of Chaco.* New York: W.W. Norton and Company, 1986.

Graham, John A., ed. *Ancient Mesoamerica.* 2d ed. Palo Alto, Calif.: The Peek Publications, 1981.

Hackett, Charles, ed. *The Pueblo Revolt, Historical Documents Relating to New Mexico, Nueva Vizcaya and Approaches, to 1773.* Washington, D.C.: Carnegie Institute, 1937.

Hackett, C.W., and C.C. Shelby. *Revolt of the Pueblo Indians of New Mexico and Otermin's Attempted Reconquest, 1680–1682.* Albuquerque, N.M.: University of New Mexico Press, 1942.

Hodge, Frederick W. and Theodore H. Lewis, eds. *The Coronado Narrative, Spanish Explorers in the Southern United States, 1528–1543.* New York: Charles Scribner's Sons, 1970.

Holland, F. Ross, Jr. *Hawikuh and the Seven Cities of Cibola.* Washington, D.C.: U.S. Government Printing Office, 1969.

Horgan, Paul. *Great River, The Rio Grande in North American History.* Vol. 1, *The Indians and Spain.* New York: Holt, Rinehart and Winston, 1961.

Huddleston, Lee Eldridge. *Origins of the American Indians, European Concepts, 1492–1729.* Austin, Texas, and London: University of Texas Press, 1970.

Jones, Oakah L., Jr. *Pueblo Warriors and Spanish Conquest.* Norman, Okla.: University of Oklahoma Press, 1966.

Kelly, William H., ed. *Indian Affairs and the Indian Reorganization Act.* Tucson: University of Arizona Press, 1954.

Kessell, John L. *Kiva, Cross and Crown: The Pecos Indians and New Mexico, 1540–1840.* Washington, D.C.: U.S. Department of the Interior, U.S. Government Printing Office, 1979.

MacNeish, Richard S. "Ancient Mesoamerican Civilization." In: *Ancient Mesoamerica,* edited by John A. Graham, 2d ed. Palo Alto, Calif.: The Peek Publications, 1981.

Marriott, Alice. *Maria: The Potter of San Ildefonso.* Norman, Okla.: University of Oklahoma Press, 1948.

Ortiz, Alfonso, ed. *New Perspectives on the Pueblos.* Albuquerque, N.M.: University of New Mexico Press, 1972.

"The Right to Remain Indian, The Failure of the Federal Government to Protect Indian Land and Water Rights," A Report submitted to the U.S. Commission on Civil Rights by the All Indian Pueblo Council, Albuquerque, N.M., Nov. 8, 1972.

Roosevelt, Theodore. *Winning the West.* New York and London: G. P. Putnam's Sons, 1889–1896.

Salmeron, Fray Geronimo de Zarate y. *Relaciones, 1626.* Translated by Alicia Ronstadt Milich. Albuquerque, N.M.: Horn and Wallace Press, 1966.

Sando, Joe S. *Nee Hemish. A History of Jemez Pueblo.* Albuquerque, N.M.: University of New Mexico Press, 1982.

Schoolcraft, Henry R. *History of the Condition and Prospects of the Indian Tribes of the United States.* Philadelphia: Lippincott, Grambo and Co., 1851. Reprinted, New York: Paladin Press, 1969.

The Southwest Indian Report. Report of the U.S. Commission on Civil Rights, Washington, D.C.: U.S. Government Printing Office, May 1973.

Spicer, Edward H. *Cycles of Conquest.* Tucson: University of Arizona Press, 1967.

Thomas, Alfred B. *After Coronado: Spanish Exploration Northeast of New Mexico, 1696–1727.* Norman, Okla.: University of Oklahoma Press, 1966.

Twenty-Third Annual Report of the Bureau of American Ethnology, 1901–1902. Glorieta, N.M.: The Rio Grande Press, Inc., 1970.

Weigle, Marta and Peter White. *The Lore of New Mexico.* Albuquerque: University of New Mexico Press, 1988.

ARTICLES

Aberle, S.D. "The Pueblo Indians of New Mexico: Their Land, Economy and Civil Organization." *American Anthropologist* 70 (1948).

Anon. "The De Vargas Expedition: The Reconquest of New Mexico." *Old Santa Fe* (April 1914).

Chavez, Fray Angelico. "Pohe-Yemo's Representative." *New Mexico Historical Review* (April 1967).

Dozier, Edward P. "Spanish Catholic Influences on Rio Grande Pueblo Religion." *American Anthropologist* (June 1958).

Ellis, Florence Hawley. "Authoritative Control and the Society System in Jemez Pueblo." *Western Journal of Anthropology* (1953).

"Pueblo Social Organization as a Lead to Pueblo History." *American Anthropologist* (1937).

Flagler, Edward K. "Governor Jose Chacon, Marques de la Penuela: Andalusian Nobleman on the New Mexico Frontier." *New Mexico Historical Review* 65, no. 4 (October 1990).

Spicer, Edward H. "Spanish-Indian Acculturation to the Southwest." *American Anthropologist* (1954).

Underhill, Ruth. "First Penthouse Dwellers of America." *Laboratory of Anthropology* 2 (1845).

INTERVIEWS

Aberle, Dr. Sophie, Albuquerque
Acoya, Clarence, Albuquerque
Aragon, Vidal, Santo Domingo Pueblo
Arquero, Sam, Cochiti Pueblo
Blue Spruce, Dr. Beryl, Ann Arbor, Michigan
Blue Spruce, Mr. and Mrs. George, Sr., Albuquerque
Blue Spruce, Dr. George, Jr., Rockville, Maryland
Calvert, Mr. and Mrs. Delfino, Albuquerque
Cata, Sam, Santa Fe
Da, Popovi, San Ildefonso Pueblo
Hena, James, Tesuque Pueblo
Herrera, Joe H., Cochiti Pueblo
Lewis, Robert E., Zuni Pueblo
Madalena, James R., Jemez Pueblo
Montoya, Domingo, Sandia Pueblo
Montoya, Mrs. Mae P., Isleta Pueblo
Montoya, Porfirio, Santa Ana Pueblo
Ortiz, Dr. Alfonso, Princeton, New Jersey
Paisano, U.G., Albuquerque
Rainer, John C., Sr., Taos Pueblo
Tafoya, Joseph Filario, Santa Clara
Tenorio, Frank, San Felipe Pueblo
Trujillo, Juan Jose, Cochiti Pueblo
Velarde, Pablita, Albuquerque
Vigil, Martin, Tesuque Pueblo
Zuni, Jose Abel, Stewart, Nevada